Crime and Intelligence Analysis

An Integrated Real-Time Approach

Crime and Intelligence Analysis

An Integrated Real-Time Approach

Glenn Grana
Rochester Crime Analysis Center
New York, New York, USA

James Windell
Wayne State University
Detroit, MIchigan, USA

Oakland University
Rochester, Michigan, USA

CRC Press
Taylor & Francis Group
Boca Raton London New York

CRC Press is an imprint of the
Taylor & Francis Group, an **informa** business

CRC Press
Taylor & Francis Group
6000 Broken Sound Parkway NW, Suite 300
Boca Raton, FL 33487-2742

© 2017 by Taylor & Francis Group, LLC
CRC Press is an imprint of Taylor & Francis Group, an Informa business

No claim to original U.S. Government works

Printed on acid-free paper
Version Date: 20160808

International Standard Book Number-13: 978-1-4987-5172-8 (Paperback)

Library of Congress Cataloging-in-Publication Data

Names: Grana, Glenn, author. | Windell, James O., author.
Title: Crime and intelligence analysis : an integrated real-time approach /
Glenn Grana and James Windell.
Description: Boca Raton, FL : CRC Press, 2017. | Includes bibliographical
references and index.
Identifiers: LCCN 2016023230 | ISBN 9781498751728 (alk. paper)
Subjects: LCSH: Crime analysis. | Criminal statistics. | Crime prevention. |
Criminology.
Classification: LCC HV7936.C88 G73 2017 | DDC 363.25--dc23
LC record available at https://lccn.loc.gov/2016023230

**Visit the Taylor & Francis Web site at
http://www.taylorandfrancis.com**

**and the CRC Press Web site at
http://www.crcpress.com**

This book is dedicated to the men and women of law enforcement, the proud members of the U.S. Armed Forces, and the crime and intelligence analysts who support their missions, and to all who have accepted the mantle of integrity as they fight for those who cannot fight for themselves.

Contents

PART II LAW ENFORCEMENT—THEN AND NOW

CHAPTER 4 THE POLICE AND LAW ENFORCEMENT—IT'S
COME A LONG WAY   **79**

CHAPTER 5 POLICE INVESTIGATIONS IN THE TWENTY-FIRST
CENTURY   **99**

PART III INTELLIGENCE AND INTELLIGENCE ANALYSIS

PART IV CRIME ANALYSIS

CHAPTER 10 HISTORY AND TYPES OF CRIME ANALYSIS   195

Acknowledgments

While there are several people who deserve credit and recognition for their encouragement and support during the research and writing phases of this book, this book could not have been written without the years Glenn Grana spent as a Monroe County sheriff's deputy and as an undercover narcotics investigator.

It was during his years working in narcotics that he was taught the craft of gathering, analyzing, and disseminating intelligence. The most important lessons he learned had to do with taking basic information and creating actionable intelligence. For most of his years as a narcotics investigator, intelligence and crime analysis were the greatest weapons he utilized to help dismantle large-scale narcotic organizations.

While working as a police advisor in both Afghanistan and Iraq, Glenn learned the true value of intelligence. It was the intelligence he and his cohorts were supplied with that helped them to survive the rigorous training missions. His work in the field of crime and intelligence analysis continued in earnest when he returned to the United States and became tactical supervisor for the New York State Department of Criminal Justice Services Crime Analysis Center in Rochester, New York. At the Crime Analysis Center, Glenn and his colleagues broke new ground in the emerging field of tactical real-time crime and intelligence investigative work.

Glenn would also like to acknowledge two of the most skilled crime and intelligence analysts he worked with at the Crime Analysis Center, Danielle DiGaspari and Katelyn Anthony. Their highly advanced skill sets in real-time criminal intelligence analysis taught him how to merge the subject matter he had learned throughout his professional years with the emerging field of tactical real-time crime and intelligence investigative work. Out of this learning came the idea to write this book. Glenn thanks them for the patience they had with all of his questions and needs, for which there were many, and for their commitment to the field to which he has dedicated his life's work.

Glenn sends his deepest appreciation to his coauthor, James Windell, for accepting an idea from a novice writer and showing great patience and guidance while teaching him all that goes into writing a book.

Finally, Glenn would like to thank his wife, Marlene, and sons, Michael, Joseph, and Nicholas, for their support and love during all the times he had to work late while being online during a wiretap investigation, for their ultimate sacrifice of allowing him to go over-seas for two years to work a mission he felt so strongly about, and, of course, for their support during the writing of this book.

James would like to acknowledge and thank friends and colleagues who discussed the ideas for this book. They include Kim Byrd, Marvin Zalman, Dave Cutting, Jennifer LaBuda, and Brad Axelrod.

Furthermore, both of us want to thank Mary Jane Peluso for bringing us together and helping us find a publisher for this book, and Jennifer Brady and others at CRC Press for shaping our manuscript into the end product.

Introduction

In the hit CBS crime show *Person of Interest*, which debuted in 2011, the two heroes—one a former Central Intelligence Agency agent and the other a billionaire technology genius—work together using the ubiquitous surveillance system in New York City to try to stop violent crime. It's referred to by some as a science fiction cop show. But the use of advanced technology for crime analysis in almost every major police department in the United States may surpass what's depicted on TV crime dramas such as *Person of Interest*. Real-time crime centers (RTCCs) are a vital aspect of intelligent policing. Crime analysis is no longer the stuff of science fiction. It's real.

In RTCCs, crime analysts analyze data at their disposal and feed essential and critical information to police officers and detectives who are on the street working criminal cases. By drawing on millions of bytes of data and knowing what is critical to pass on to the officers in the field, the analysts in the RTCC play a major role in solving crime, preventing terrorism and other criminal acts, and protecting the safety of both citizens and officers. As a result, crime analysts now play a powerful and essential role in twenty-first-century policing. But analysts need to be trained to do their jobs. Their jobs include

- Reviewing all police reports daily with the goal of identifying patterns.

- Analyzing trends, patterns, and hot spots to let both officers and administrators know about emerging crime in their city or in certain districts.
- Extracting data from records and asking questions that lead to turning data into useful information.
- Creating charts, maps, graphs, tables, and other visual products that communicate and transmit useful information to their police departments and the public.

This up-to-the-minute textbook was written for use in college classrooms and police academies to train students to be crime analysts. More importantly, *Crime and Intelligence Analysis: An Integrated Real-Time Approach*, introduces the hybrid concept of the real-time tactical analyst. Based on Glenn Grana's research and experience, crime analysts need the skills to rapidly data mine during real-time operational situations. That is, officers need immediate information and data that will enable them to respond effectively to various situations, such as

- Routine domestic violence calls
- "Shots fired" calls
- Assault, robbery, and burglary-in-progress calls
- Active shooter, SWAT, and hostage situations

It is not just a matter of analysts transmitting raw data to officers in the field in these kinds of situations. Instead, these common, but often dangerous situations require a workup from a tactical crime analyst.

A tactical analyst can provide a detailed intelligence product, referred to as a workup, focusing on individuals, locations, and many other critical factors that help the responding officer or investigator to be more fully aware of what he or she is likely to encounter. The skilled tactical crime analyst can provide an intelligence-based workup that may include

- Photos
- Social media posts
- Outstanding warrants
- Probation or parole GPS monitoring
- Gang intelligence, which can involve known associates, arrest history, and prior weapons possession

It is one thing to be able to mine data; it's quite another to think like an investigative officer and streamline the massive amount of data available to the tactical analyst in order to feed only relevant, crucial information to the officer. The trained and skilled crime analyst will feed viable information to the investigator so that the investigation moves in the right direction, while avoiding overloading the officer with irrelevant data.

Crime and Intelligence Analysis: An Integrated Real-Time Approach covers all aspects of what crime analysts and tactical analysts need to know to be successful. This book describes the different types of crime analysts, their responsibilities and duties, and how they go about meeting their responsibilities in the best possible ways. In addition, this textbook provides an overview of the criminal justice system, as well as the more fundamental areas of crime analysis, including

- Understanding criminal behavior
- Conducting temporal analysis of crime patterns
- Using spatial analysis to better understand crime
- Applying research methods to crime analysis
- Evaluating data and information to help predict criminal offending and solve criminal cases (including cold cases)
- Understanding criminal investigations
- Using critical thinking

Crime analysts often work in RTCCs, which were first fully functional in New York City and Houston, Texas, just 10 years ago. Today, there are RTCCs in many other cities, including Rochester, New York, where coauthor Glenn Grana works as the tactical supervisor in the Monroe Crime Analysis Center. Previously a crime analyst, Glenn was never a novice at analyzing data or knowing what information officers in the field need. He was a narcotics investigator for more than 20 years and a police advisor in Iraq and Afghanistan, and he has a master's degree in criminal justice administration. Yet, most crime analysts around the country in RTCCs are civilians who are not fortunate enough to have the kind of background and training that Glenn brings to the job.

As RTCCs continue to flourish and come into their own in the twenty-first century, how will civilian crime analysts get training in the investigative process? How will they learn the skill sets that tactical crime analysts working in RTCCs need to do the kind of job that officers on the street require?

The answer is simple: no one really knows yet.

In fact, as Glenn Grana travels around the country speaking at crime analyst conferences, these questions are frequently asked. But another question is also critically important: How will crime analysts in RTCCs achieve creditability if they are untrained before being placed in a position? Officers are depending on them, and being a RTCC analyst is a position that may have life and death consequences.

These questions can be answered through this textbook. This book is designed to be the most comprehensive textbook for criminal justice instructors to teach students who will eventually end up in RTCCs as crime analysts. Heretofore, there have been few textbooks that cover all areas of crime analysis, and it has only been recently that colleges and universities have begun offering classes. Glenn, along with many of his colleagues in the field of crime analysis, is trying to change that as he designs college courses to train civilian analysts. With this textbook, as colleges and police academies begin to realize that they must teach crime analysis courses, there will now be a book they can adopt for their students.

By learning about such things as tactical intelligence, intelligence-based policing, data mining, crime mapping and temporal analysis, evaluating the validity of information, and how to conduct a criminal investigation, students completing courses using this book will be skilled enough to step into a tactical analyst role in a RTCC and deal with the kinds of situations that they are likely to encounter on a daily basis.

The well-trained tactical crime analyst will be able to make critical decisions in a real-time setting, giving officers on the street the kind of information they can use to handle investigations and crime scenes. We designed this book, *Crime and Intelligence Analysis: An Integrated Real-Time Approach*, to help transition the civilian analyst into a tactical crime analyst who is capable of entering the world of the sworn law enforcement officer. Through exceptional training, tactical crime analysts will gain the credibility they need to demonstrate to their sworn law enforcement colleagues that they are a valuable asset who can be counted on to deliver critical information and can be trusted as a vital team member.

Crime and Intelligence Analysis: An Integrated Real-Time Approach is somewhat different from previous books on crime analysis and intelligent policing in the following ways:

- It is coauthored by an experienced crime analyst.
- It is an up-to-date textbook covering areas of crime analysis and real-time crime analysis that are not covered in previous, somewhat older books.
- It is written to fill gaps in crime analysis; specifically, it fills gaps in the area of teaching students to be tactical crime analysts and skilled and credible crime analysts.
- It takes the approach that a crime analysis center operated by a trained crime analyst can play a critical role in the daily operations of law enforcement when seamlessly woven into the investigative and strategic planning process.
- It is designed to teach students to rapidly analyze information obtained from multiple data sources, while applying their understanding of the theories, practices, and basic principles of investigation to aid their law enforcement partners.
- It focuses on the real-time analytical process as it applies to crisis situations (e.g., SWAT, hostage negotiations, and active shooter). Theory is discussed as it relates to both the tactical process and the mindset of the negotiator or crisis team leader and the analytical process and the mindset of the tactical crime analyst.
- It features numerous case studies that will be used to illustrate how the use of data mining and intelligence dissemination by a trained tactical crime analyst aids in the process of actual incidents.
- It uses case studies, scenarios, and questions for discussion to teach students to use their analytical thinking and investigator mindset to help solve real-time situations.

What You'll Find in This Book

This book is divided into five parts. Part I offers background on crime and criminal justice. The first three chapters review various fundamentals about the problems of crime in our society, the measurements of crime, and the theories about what causes people to commit criminal acts.

Part II gives a brief history of law enforcement and helps students to look at the big picture related to the history of policing and how far policing and law enforcement has progressed in the past 200 years. In Chapter 5, an overview of police investigations is provided to help student crime analysts better understand how police officers investigate crimes.

Part III offers four important chapters on intelligence—the lifeblood of both investigators and crime analysts. These chapters explain exactly what intelligence is, how it relates to the work of the crime analyst, how intelligence is collected, and how the crime analyst can analyze intelligence in order to provide the most relevant and important information to detectives and investigators.

Part IV gives an overview of crime analysis, detailing the history and development of crime analysis, while spelling out the different types of crime analysis. There is an emphasis on tactical crime analysis and the duties and responsibilities of the tactical crime analyst.

Finally, Part V sums up what has been learned throughout the book and offers some ideas for the future of policing. While, of course, the authors are not prescient, they do suggest that continued advances in technology in our society will continue to have an impact on policing and investigations. Not only will police departments of the future possess the technology to solve crimes, but also they will be more skilled at preventing crimes.

Pedagogy of This Book

Since this book was written as a textbook for criminal justice instructors and students, each chapter has the needs of both teachers and students in mind. Each chapter starts with an outline of the chapter and a list of objectives for students.

The chapters are written so that students will find the material easy to follow, with headings that clearly show what will follow. But the chapter material is organized so that comprehension is easier. Case studies are included in many chapters to offer real-life examples of how the principles being taught can be applied.

At the end of each chapter are questions for discussion. These questions were selected to help students engage in critical thinking and problem-solving. They are followed by a glossary of important terms, study guide questions for students to test themselves and be better prepared for course exams, and references to show where information and quotes throughout the text can be found.

The authors sincerely hope that this book will be found valuable in teaching and preparing crime analysts of the future to take their places in police departments to aid departments, sworn officers, and the public to better understand and combat crime.

PART I

CRIME AND THE TWENTY-FIRST CENTURY

1

THE CRIME PROBLEM

Chapter Outline

1. The crime problem
2. Who is concerned about crime?
3. Who benefits from the United States having a crime problem?
4. Who really wants to see crime reduced or eliminated?
5. Technology and crime
6. This book and the crime problem

Learning Objectives for Chapter 1

1. Become familiar with the crime problem
2. Understand who is concerned about crime and why
3. Discuss the perceptions and goals of the major players in the criminal justice system
4. Better understand law enforcement approaches to the crime problem
5. Become familiar with concepts and approaches found in this book
6. Learn about intelligence, crime analysis, the crime analysis triangle, and the scanning, analysis, response, and assessment (SARA) analysis model

An elementary school with hundreds of young children is placed on lockdown because a dangerous-sounding man has phoned violent threats to the school office. Immediately, as vague details are posted on social media, parents and other citizens in the school district are suddenly fearful of what could happen. This worst-case scenario recently occurred at an elementary school in Rochester, New York.

With the clock ticking, and the elusive suspect's threatening phone calls increasing, with details of his threats unnerving law enforcement, a profile needed to be established to identify the who, what, where, and why of this potential deadly scenario. But who is responsible to piece together the investigative puzzle?

Clearly, aggressive real-time data mining and rapid dissemination of intelligence is critical to assist the police as the case continues to unfold. The answer, as you will learn in this book, is that it is the tactical crime analyst who is responsible for providing enough information for a disaster to be averted.

In law enforcement, success can be measured in many different ways. Often, and particularly in this elementary school crisis, success may be measured simply in terms of the number of lives saved. Thanks to the tactical crime analyst working this case in the Rochester, New York, real-time crime center, the crisis was successfully resolved—and hundreds of young lives were saved.

But how the tactical crime analyst accomplished this success was entirely dependent on the process that analyst followed.

As a crime analyst, the success you have on your job rests entirely on the process that you follow. The most critical stage in this process is the analytical stage—the stage in which intelligence is gathered. Then, that intelligence is disseminated to law enforcement. But in this case only priority intelligence was relayed to the police, who in turned transmitted that intelligence to officers at the scene.

Analysis has always played a pivotal role in the success of crisis management incidents. Even as critical pieces of information are discovered during the initial collection and verification process, what can be lost, at times, are crucial pieces of information that may lead to a better understanding of the suspect's mindset, his or her motives, and—as happened in Rochester, New York—a peaceful resolution.

The use of a real-time crime analyst, one who can rapidly analyze information and intelligence obtained from multiple data sources while applying his or her understanding of the theories and practices that law enforcement practitioners are trained in, can help to create a unique analytical process. The process that you will learn about in this book will help to establish—and solidify—the credibility and importance of the tactical crime analyst working in a real-time crime environment.

But before tactical crime analysts can contribute to these types of dynamic investigations, they need to be able to draw upon training and experience in order to assist them with their critical need for understanding of the investigative process, the intelligence examination process, and the analytical process, which is required to work effectively and proficiently, in real time, with their law enforcement partners.

This first chapter begins this process by introducing you to the fundamentals of understanding the crime problem and the technological aspects involved with combining the process of criminal investigations, intelligence gathering, and crime analysis. It will also introduce you to how the role of the traditional crime analyst is evolving into a dynamic hybrid role of the real-time tactical analyst—the person who incorporates all of the aforementioned skill sets while working crime in a real-time setting.

Michael Brown, an African American, was 18 when he was shot to death by Ferguson, Missouri, police officer Darren Wilson, a 28-year-old Caucasian, on August 9, 2014. There were disputed circumstances in this shooting incident that resulted in nationwide protests and civil unrest in the small town of Ferguson. The incident sparked vigorous debate about how the police deal with African American suspects. A grand jury failed to indict Officer Wilson, and he was not charged with a crime.

Renisha McBride, a 19-year-old woman, stood on the front porch of a home in suburban Detroit in the early morning hours of November 2, 2013. The homeowner, a 55-year-old airport maintenance worker named Theodore Wafer, opened the inside front door and fired a single shotgun blast that killed Ms. McBride. Several months later, after a trial, a jury convicted Mr. Wafer, a Caucasian, of murder, and he was sentenced to at least 17 years in prison for killing the unarmed woman, who was African American.

At the Boston Marathon on April 15, 2013, two pressure cooker bombs exploded at 2:49 p.m. as runners were racing toward the finish line. Three people were killed and 264 were injured. The suspects were identified within three days as Chechen brothers Dzhokhar Tsarnaev and Tamerlan Tsarnaev. After the suspects killed a Massachusetts Institute of Technology policeman and carjacked an SUV, there was an exchange of gunfire with the police and Tamerlan, shot several times, was killed. Several hours later, Dzhokhar was captured. He went on trial in 2015, was found guilty of using and conspiring to use a weapon of mass destruction resulting in death and the malicious destruction of property resulting in death, and was sentenced to be executed.

On January 27, 2014, Matthew Smith, age 31, of Mohave Valley, Arizona, was sentenced by a U.S. district judge to 35 years in prison for the second-degree murder, child abuse, and assault of two of his stepchildren. The assaults and murder occurred on the Fort Mohave Indian reservation.

Jeremiah Mazoli was charged in Eugene, Oregon, with the theft of two laptop computers and a guitar from a fraternity on the campus of the University of Oregon. He pled guilty to second-degree burglary.

Introduction

All of five of these incidents are real. You may have heard about one or more of them, but probably not all five. Crime happens every day in this country. Some of it is relatively minor, such as the laptop computer and guitar thefts in Eugene, Oregon. Some of it is major, such as the shooting deaths of Renisha McBride and Michael Brown, the Boston Marathon bombing, and the abuse and murder of children in Mohave Valley, Arizona.

Because we see and hear about crimes on televised news shows and read about them in our daily newspapers, we are all very much aware that crime exists. But you may have been the victim of a crime yourself, or you may know someone who has been a crime victim. And while you may be fortunate to simply have heard about what has happened to other people, you may still be very concerned about crime. You may even have voiced your opinion—in a conversation or on your own blog—about the "crime problem" in the United States.

In Chapter 2, we will discuss how much crime actually occurs in this country, but in this chapter, we address this fundamental question: is there a crime problem in this country?

Is There a Crime Problem in the United States?

This is a question that can be viewed from any one of several perspectives.

First, let's start by quoting President Lyndon B. Johnson's opening remarks from his address to a meeting with a group of U.S. governors on the problems of crime and law enforcement:

> The fact of crime and the fear of crime are common across our land. For it has an unrelenting pace. It exacts heavy costs in human suffering and in financial losses to both individuals and communities. It blocks the achievement of a good life for all our people.

Lyndon B. Johnson (1966)

It was President Johnson who appointed the President's Commission on Law Enforcement and Administration of Justice in 1965 to study the American criminal justice system. Johnson assigned the group a task that was viewed then as a staggering challenge of fighting crime and repairing the American criminal justice system. The commission's final report was issued in 1967 and has been described as "the most comprehensive evaluation of crime and crime control in the United States at the time." It laid out reorganization plans for police departments and suggested a range of reforms. In the introduction to this report, the U.S. attorney general, Nicholas Katzenbach, wrote, "The existence of crime, the talk about crime, the reports of crime, and the fear of crime have eroded the basic quality of life of most Americans" (President's Commission on Law Enforcement, 2005).

That was the perspective of the president and the attorney general in the 1960s. It is evident that they were very concerned about the crime problem. President Obama and his first attorney general, Eric Holder, also indicated, about a half-century later, their own concerns about crime and the criminal justice system. In August 2013, the U.S. attorney general introduced the "Smart on Crime" initiative—a package of reforms to the criminal justice system to help ensure that federal laws are enforced more fairly and more efficiently. Among other reforms, the effort promotes diversion courts and other alternatives to incarceration for low-level drug offenders, and urges investment in reentry programs in order to reduce recidivism among formerly incarcerated individuals. President Obama has expressed on several occasions concerns about drug addiction and its relationship to the cycle of crime. Drugs and crime are often linked, President Obama has said, and this is why addressing serious drug-related crime and violence will always be a vital component of the president's and the attorney general's plan to protect public health and safety in America.

Instead of talking about the crime problem, the Obama administration made frequent references to the "drug problem." The Obama administration has made it clear that we cannot arrest our way out of the drug problem, but rather the focus should be on a drug policy that emphasizes the expansion of innovative Smart on Crime strategies proven to help break the cycle of drug use, crime, arrest, and incarceration (National Drug Control Policy, 2014).

However, if you listen to police chiefs and city officials, they have a somewhat different perspective. For instance, in Detroit, the Detroit Police Department reports that violent crimes saw significant drops in 2014, mirroring the decline in homicides, which likely fell to the lowest total in the city since 1967. Robbery had the sharpest decline, dropping from 2836 in 2013 to 1879 in 2014—representing a 34% drop. Carjacking, a subset of robbery, also saw a large drop, from 765 to 525, a 32% decline. However, Detroit police chief James Craig had this to say: "Robberies and carjackings—those are the crimes that strike fear into most citizens" (Hunter, 2015).

In New York City, the crime problem is not seen the same way as it is in Detroit. "The City has made incredible strides in reducing crime in the past few decades," said New York City council member Corey Johnson, chair of the Health Committee. "However, there is much work to be done" (Press Office: City of New York, 2014).

In New Orleans, Louisiana, it's a favorite talking point of Mayor Mitch Landrieu and New Orleans Police Department (NOPD) superintendent Ronal Serpas when they're discussing crime in the Crescent City to say that, yes, New Orleans is the nation's murder capital, but other than that, it's a reasonably safe place.

Landrieu and Serpas say that New Orleans is significantly less dangerous than Orlando, Florida, perhaps America's most popular family destination. Orlando had a 35% higher violent crime rate than New Orleans in 2011, the last year for which national data are available (Crime experts question NOPD stats, 2013). The city's crime problem is murder, Serpas says candidly, and the Landrieu administration has been building a public safety agenda around that fact (Crime experts question NOPD stats, 2013).

But what do ordinary citizens say?

A majority of Americans say there is more crime in the United States than there was a year ago. And it doesn't matter what year you pick. Americans, as Gallup Inc., the national polling company, has found as a long-term trend, believe crime is going up in their community.

For instance, in 2014, 63% of Americans believed crime was increasing (McCarthy, 2015). This percentage is well below the recent high of 74% in 2009. As the percentage of Americans who say crime is up hits one of its lowest points in the past 10 years, just about one in five Americans (21%) say crime is down. Another 9% of Americans say the level of crime has remained the same (McCarthy, 2015).

The Gallup pollsters have consistently found that people in the United States believe crime is up in their area—despite the fact that statistics show that with a handful of exceptions, serious crime has decreased nearly every year from 1994 through 2012. According to the U.S. Department of Justice, Bureau of Justice Statistics, the overall violent crime rate for rape, sexual assault, robbery, aggravated assault, and simple assault fell from 80 victimizations per 1000 persons in 1994 to 19 per 1000 in 2010. In the first decade of that trend, public opinion followed, with the percentage perceiving crime was up falling from 87% in 1993 to 41% in 2001 (McCarthy, 2015). But this shot up to 62% in 2002 and has remained fairly high ever since (McCarthy, 2015).

So, what is the answer to the question? Who is right? Is there a crime problem in the United States?

Maybe the best—and simplest—answer is that it depends on your perspective. Maybe you will be in a better position to answer this question for yourself after you have read Chapter 2, in which you will be able to review the statistics and the most authoritative information available about the extent of crime in the United States. However, perhaps like most decent and rational people in our society would likely contend, you may be of the opinion that as long as there is one murder, one rape, one terrorist bombing, or one burglary, there is still too much crime. Furthermore, you might further argue that our goal should be the elimination of all crime.

Analyzing the Crime Problem

America is not the only country with crime, nor the only one concerned about crime. Every country in the world has crime. They always have and, perhaps, always will. But because of the pervasive problem of crime in all societies, every society has had to develop some kind of system to deal with and manage crime. The history of mankind demonstrates that when people live together in societies and communities, there is a need for rules and laws. And those are needed because inevitably there will be those individuals who will violate the rules, laws, and norms of society. Because there will always be violators of the established norms of a community, there must be a system in place to deal with these offenders.

We know, for instance, that criminal justice systems were in place several thousand years ago. In the time of Hammurabi, the ruler of Mesopotamia, in what is modern-day Iraq, about 2100 BC, Hammurabi enacted a set of laws. This set of laws was called the Code of Hammurabi, and the laws were carved in rock columns and preserved in a temple. Hammurabi's code indicated what behaviors were violations of laws and the corresponding punishment for breaking those laws (Oliver and Hilgenberg, 2006).

A few hundred years later, Athenian law in Athens, Greece, developed the concept that a "private harm" could also be a harm against all society (Gargarin, 2002). In the sixth century BC, the Athenians created a system of "popular courts" in order to ensure that every citizen was granted certain rights and had the ability to appeal decisions (Shelden, 2001). Then, in 452 AD, the Romans codified their laws when the Roman Tribune requested that the laws of Rome be codified and written into 10 tables. Later, two additional tables were added and these became known as the Roman Twelve Tables. These tables spell out various types of crimes, such as murder, bribery, sorcery, and theft. These particular crimes were all punishable by execution, which could be by crucifixion, drowning, beating to death, burning alive, or impaling (Farrington, 2000).

Since these early attempts to codify laws, there have been attempts to inform citizens of the laws and to bring about fair and impartial punishments. Of course, when we look back at the criminal justice systems of European countries from the Middle Ages until the middle of the nineteenth century, we would have to conclude that their systems were rather crude. For example, England did not have any police until watchmen, and later on constables, were employed, beginning around the reign of King Edward I in the twelfth century AD. However, aside from watchmen and constables, who patrolled the streets and watched for fires, England had no police department until Sir Robert Peel organized the London Metropolitan Police in 1829.

Most countries today, including the United States, have an evolved criminal justice system that is multilayered and sophisticated compared with the justice systems in Europe—and other continents— prior to the nineteenth century.

Having laws and criminal justice systems meant that leaders, like Hammurabi, and governments, like the Athenian government, the Roman Tribune, and the English government, thought about the problem and came up with approaches to deal with the crime problem. In effect, each society had to analyze the crime problem and develop a theory that would lead to the implementation of laws or policies that would attempt to contain or decrease the crime problem. For example, by English law, in the early 1700s there were more than 200 crimes that were punishable by hanging (Friedman, 1993). The theory, then, that backed up this approach to trying to stop crime was that if the punishment was severe enough, people would desist from committing crimes.

Cesare Beccaria, who is known as the founder of classical criminology, was an Italian nobleman and jurist who was born in 1738. Dissatisfied with the Italian justice system in the eighteenth century, he developed his own theories about why people committed crimes. He even wrote a book, entitled *On Crimes and Punishment*, in which he explained his theory. Beccaria explained in his book that people are rational and they do things that bring them pleasure and avoid doing things which bring them pain. As a result of this analysis of criminal behavior, Beccaria advanced the idea that certain and swift punishment of appropriate duration and intensity would deter people from committing crime.

In contrast to Beccaria are the more contemporary opinions of Dr. Samuel Yochelson, who, along with clinical psychologist Stanton Samenow, studied more than 250 male criminals and concluded that "the criminal can, and does, choose his way of life freely in his quest for power, control and excitement" (Barger, 1978, p. 1).

Therefore, if you were to subscribe to Yochelson and Samenow's theory, then fear of any form of repercussions would play no part in the decision-making process of why an individual chooses to commit crime. The probability of being caught and punished is a nonfactor, as Mel Barger contends in his article "Crime: The Unsolved Problem" when he writes, "The Criminal, at the time of his lawlessness, is one of the few happy or contented men to be found among us" (Barger, 1978, p. 1).

When comparing the differing opinions of theorists from Beccaria to Yochelson and Samenow, and even more recent crime theorists, it can be argued that when examining what motivates a person to carry out a criminal act, a pattern of behavior can also be identified. Pattern recognition is a critical skill set needed by crime and intelligence analysts in order to be successful when connecting a modus operandi (a method of operation) to crimes of a similar nature.

As we will discuss in upcoming chapters, the critical thinking and the investigative skill sets of the crime analyst compared with those of the typical law enforcement professional may differ somewhat in approach, but both are based on a theory of what causes people to commit crimes. For law enforcement, the investigative mindset often is built upon various criminological theories that focus heavily on examining the motivations of the offender. The crime and intelligence analyst, on the other hand, takes the approach of examining the offenders' behavior. This analytical approach is based partly on the *criminal event perspective*—a nontraditional theory as to why people commit crime, proposed by Vincent Sacco and Leslie Kennedy (2002). These authors contend that the criminal event perspective is "not a theory of criminality, but rather a road map to understanding crime" (Sacco and Kennedy, 2010, p. 799). This perspective will be discussed in more detail in later chapters.

This Book Is an Introduction to Crime Analysis

This book is about crime analysis, which means there must be a theory about crime that will guide the teaching and the approach to the job of analyzing crime and criminal behavior. At this point, we are not ready to put forth that theory. However, we can introduce you to the analysis triangle. This triangle will be referred to throughout this book, and it will serve as one of the main illustrations that suggests a theory for linking crime and criminal behavior to external factors, and the triangle will be important when discussing the significance of data mining and connecting critical pieces of intelligence together (Figure 1.1).

In this analysis triangle, a theory is implicated in the layers of the triangle. The innermost triangle represents the problem facing the crime analyst. To begin to analyze the problem, the crime analyst evaluates and assesses the criminal offender, along with the place (or location) of the criminal offense and the target or victim of that offense. The outer triangle indicates that there is also a handler, a manager, and a guardian in each offense; each plays a role in the criminal event. Also, each has a set of tools with which they facilitate a criminal offense, prevent a criminal offense, or provide a solution or intelligence regarding a criminal offense.

If you don't understand this analysis triangle at this juncture, don't worry about it. As you study this book, its importance in crime analysis will become clearer. However, at this point, it is important to introduce some critical terms and concepts that will be used throughout this book.

Figure 1.1 Analysis triangle as it relates to criminal behavior.

Definitions of Terms and Concepts

The first term is *intelligence*. Intelligence is the data available to, collected by, or disseminated through the tactical crime analyst. The *tactical crime analyst* is the trained analyst whose job it is to analyze crime and criminal events or offenses in order to provide practical intelligence to police officers, the police command, or the public. *Intelligence analysis* refers to what the tactical crime analyst does in his or her position: continually evaluating and analyzing data in order to provide the most useful possible information to police officers. *SARA* is a model that was developed by Professor Herman Goldstein at the University of Wisconsin–Madison to enhance the problem-solving approach to policing. SARA is an acronym that stands for scanning, analysis, response, and assessment. This model will be discussed in detail in later chapters. *Real-time setting* or *real-time crime center* refers to the location where many tactical crime analysts have their "office." A real-time crime center is a room in which the tactical crime analyst has at his or her disposal a bank of computers and extensive websites and data banks that allow access to and analysis of intelligence in order to provide practical and useful on-the-spot information to police officers in the field.

Technology and Crime

This book is about how crime analysts work and what they need to know in order to provide critical and vital information to police officers. Today, technology is advanced enough to allow crime analysts to process and analyze the data at their disposal and feed essential and critical information to police officers and detectives who are on the street working criminal cases. By drawing on millions of bytes of data and knowing what is critical to pass on to the officers in the field, the analyst in the real-time crime center plays a major role in solving crime, preventing terrorism and other criminal acts, and protecting the safety of both citizens and officers.

As a result, crime analysts now play a powerful and essential role in twenty-first-century policing. But in order to do this job, a crime analyst must be properly trained. The job of the crime analyst is not easy. It takes more than a knowledge of computers to do all that crime analysts are expected to do. Some of the tasks of a crime analyst include

- Reviewing all police reports daily with the goal of identifying patterns.
- Analyzing trends, patterns, and hot spots to let both officers and administrators know about emerging crime in their city or in certain districts.
- Extracting data from records and asking questions that lead to turning data into useful information.
- Creating charts, maps, graphs, tables, and other visual products that communicate and transmit useful information to their police departments and the public.

Perhaps most importantly, the crime analyst has to serve the needs of the police officers in the field for immediate information and data that will enable them to respond effectively to various situations, such as

- Routine domestic violence calls
- Shots fired calls
- Assault, robbery, and burglary-in-progress calls
- Active shooter, SWAT, and hostage situations

It is not just a matter of the crime analyst transmitting raw data to officers in the field in these kinds of situations. Instead, these common, but often dangerous situations require a workup from a tactical crime analyst. A *workup* is a detailed intelligence product focusing on individuals, locations, and many other critical factors that help the responding officer or investigator to be more fully aware of what he or she is likely to encounter. The skilled tactical crime analyst can provide an intelligence-based workup that may include

- Photos
- Social media posts
- Outstanding warrants
- Probation or parole GPS monitoring
- Gang intelligence, which can involve known associates, arrest history, and prior weapons possession

It is one thing to be able to mine data; it's quite another to think like an investigative officer and streamline the massive amount of data available to the tactical crime analyst in order to feed only relevant, crucial information to the officer.

The trained and skilled tactical crime analyst will feed viable information to the investigator so that the investigation moves in the right direction, while avoiding overloading the officer with irrelevant data.

And that's what this book will train you to do. In the chapters of this book, you will be introduced to all aspects of what crime analysts need to know to be successful. You will learn more about understanding criminal behavior, understanding statistics and interpreting crime statistics, conducting temporal analysis of crime patterns, using spatial analysis to better understand crime, applying research methods to crime analysis, evaluating data and information to help predict criminal offending and solve criminal cases (including cold cases), understanding criminal investigations, and using critical thinking.

Questions for Discussion

1. What role would a crime analyst likely play in a terrorist situation such as the Boston Marathon bombing? If you were a crime analyst on duty that day in Boston, how would you see your role?
2. Can crime be eliminated completely? Why or why not?

Important Terms

Intelligence: Data available to, collected by, or disseminated through the tactical crime analyst.

Intelligence analysis: Continually evaluating and analyzing data in order to provide the most useful possible information to police officers.

Real-time crime center: Room in which the tactical crime analyst has at his or her disposal a bank of computers and extensive websites and data banks that allow access to and analysis of intelligence in order to provide practical and useful on-the-spot information to police officers in the field.

SARA: Model that was developed by Professor Herman Goldstein at the University of Wisconsin–Madison to enhance the problem-solving approach to policing. SARA is an acronym that stands for scanning, analysis, response, and assessment.

Tactical crime analyst: Trained analyst whose job it is to analyze crime and criminal events or offenses in order to provide practical intelligence to police officers, the police command, or the public.

Study Guide Questions

1. It was President Lyndon B. Johnson who appointed the
   a. President's Commission on Law Enforcement and Administration of Justice
   b. Wickersham Commission
   c. Chicago Crime Commission
   d. Warren Commission
2. According to the Gallup Inc. public opinion polls going back many years, a majority of Americans believe that crime
   a. Is decreasing
   b. Always stays about the same
   c. Is increasing
   d. Is bloodier and more violent than ever
3. The history of humankind demonstrates that when people live together in societies, there is a need for more
   a. Police officers on the street
   b. Drug agencies
   c. Rules and laws
   d. Real-time crime centers
4. Intelligence is the _____ available to, collected by, or disseminated through the tactical crime analyst.
   a. Secrets
   b. Higher IQ
   c. Inside information
   d. Data

5. The tactical crime analyst is the trained analyst whose job it is to
   a. Assign police officers to a beat
   b. Analyze crime and criminal offenses
   c. Assess the reasons why criminals offend
   d. Accurately predict the next bank robbery

References

Barger, M. (1978). Crime: The unsolved problem. Available at http://melbarger.com/Welcome.html.

Crime experts question NOPD stats that paint New Orleans as a safe city with a murder problem. (2013). *The Times-Picayune*, May 18. Available at http://www.nola.com/crime/index.ssf/2013/05/new_orleans_crime_stats_analys.html.

Farrington, K. (2000). *History of Punishment and Torture: A Journey through the Dark Side of Justice*. London: Hamlyn.

Friedman, L. (1993). *Crime and Punishment in American History*. New York: Basic Books.

Gargarin, M. (2002). *Antiphon the Athenian: Oratory, Law and Justice in the Age of the Sophists*. Austin: University of Texas Press.

Hunter, G. (2015). Detroit less violent in 2014, police data show. Detroit News, January 4. Available at http://www.detroit-news.com/story/news/local/metro-detroit/2015/01/03/violent-crimes-decline-detroit/21237927/.

Johnson, L.B. (1966). Statement by the president at a meeting with a group of governors on problems of crime and law enforcement. September 29. Available at http://www.presidency.ucsb.edu/ws/?pid=27894.

McCarthy, J. (2015). Most Americans still see crime up over last year. Gallup Poll. Available at http://www.gallup.com/poll/179546/americans-crime-last-year.aspx.

National Drug Control Policy. (2014). A drug policy for the 21st century. Available at https://www.whitehouse.gov/ondcp/drugpolicyreform.

Oliver, W.M., and Hilgenberg, J.F. (2006). *A History of Crime and Criminal Justice in America*. Boston: Allyn and Bacon.

President's Commission on Law Enforcement. (2005). *The Challenge of Crime in a Free Society*. University Press of Honolulu, HI: University Press of the Pacific.

Press Office: City of New York. (2014). De Blasio administration launches $130 million plan to reduce crime, reduce number of people with behavioral and mental health issues behind bars. Available at http://www1.nyc.gov/office-of-the-mayor/news/537-14/de-blasio-administration-launches-130-million-plan-reduce-crime-reduce-number-people-with.

Sacco, V., and Kennedy, L. (2010). The criminal event perspective. In F.T. Cullen and P. Wilcox (eds.), *Encyclopedia of Criminological Theory*. Thousand Oaks, CA: Sage, pp. 799–801.

Shelden, R.G. (2001). *Controlling the Dangerous Classes: A Critical Introduction to the History of Criminal Justice*. Boston: Allyn and Bacon.

2

WHAT DO WE KNOW
ABOUT CRIME?

Chapter Outline

1. Why we collect crime statistics
2. How we measure crime
3. What we know about crime from these measures
4. Viewing crime based on statistics
5. The crime analyst and crime statistics

Learning Objectives for Chapter 2

1. Understand how crime is measured
2. Gain an objective understanding of crime statistics
3. Be able to discuss the pros and cons of the major measures of crime
4. Understand why crime statistics are important for the crime analyst
5. Understand the CompStat process and its relevance in tactical planning

Almost from the time it was organized in 1893, the International Association of Chiefs of Police (IACP) adopted resolutions to organize or encourage national crime reporting programs. Although originally established to bring about police reform and professionalism in policing, the IACP in 1927 organized the Committee on Uniform Crime Reporting. The basic Uniform Crime Reporting (UCR) Program was developed by this committee, and then adopted and initiated by the IACP in 1929.

It was soon recognized that such a program was too large in scope for the limited budget and staff of the IACP, and help was requested from the federal government. On June 11, 1930, Congress authorized the Bureau of Investigation, which would later be officially renamed the Federal Bureau of Investigation (FBI), to collect uniform crime statistics under Public Law 337, Title 28, §554. Since that time, the FBI has collected crime statistics nationally from police agencies on a voluntary basis, publishing a report—the Uniform Crime Reports—each year.

Almost simultaneously with Public Law 337, President Herbert Hoover created the National Commission on Law Observance and Enforcement in 1929 with George W. Wickersham as its chair. The commission was popularly known as the Wickersham Commission, and this commission conducted the first national study of the U.S. criminal justice system. A voluminous report, the Wickersham Commission report, released in 1931, made many recommendations—some related to the unenforceability of the Volstead Act (which had created Prohibition), some to the shortcomings of the police, but others to improvements needed in the organization of state crime reporting programs.

In 1950, the well-known criminologist Thorsten Sellin published an article in the *Journal of Criminal Law and Criminology*. In this article, Sellin decried the inadequate state of criminal statistics in this country: "Nowhere in the United States today is it possible to find a well integrated and reasonably adequate system of criminal statistics, either on the local, state, federal, or national basis, in spite of the fact that we have long been deeply concerned with the serious character of our crime problem. We should no longer ignore one of the most necessary instruments available to us in our efforts to cope with criminality" (Sellin, 1950, p. 680). He went on to report on the various and sporadic attempts to develop national crime statistics, and he called for the passage of a Uniform Criminal Statistics Act to remedy the problem. Subsequently, the Uniform Criminal Justice Statistics Act was passed in some states, although the American Bar Association was lobbying for its passage in every state (Rosen, 1995).

It was not until 1979, however, that the Bureau of Justice Statistics (BJS) was established under the Justice Systems Improvement Act of 1979, an amendment to the Omnibus Crime Control and Safe Streets Act of 1968. The mission of the BJS is to collect, analyze, publish, and disseminate information on crime, criminal offenders, victims of crime, and the operation of justice systems at all levels of government. The BJS is a component of the Office of Justice Programs within the U.S. Department of Justice.

The National Crime Victimization Survey (NCVS), originally called the National Crime Survey, was started in 1972 in response to a perceived need for more comprehensive information about the extent and nature of crime in the United States. In reaction to rising crime levels in our nation's cities, President Lyndon Johnson in 1965 convened the President's Commission on Law Enforcement and the Administration of Justice (LEAA) to examine the root causes and characteristics of crime in the United States and to recommend policies and programs to address what was seen to be a growing problem. The commission found that the FBI's UCR Program, which was based on crimes reported to law enforcement agencies, although the only program measuring the extent of crime in the nation, did not collect sufficient information to evaluate the extent and nature of the crime that was occurring. The UCR Program obtained (and still does so today) information only on crimes reported to police, and obtained little information about the characteristics of crimes and crime victims or the impact of crime on victims.

To remedy this information void, the LEAA developed pilot studies to explore the viability of using sample surveys to obtain data on crime, including that not reported to police. These initial experiments produced useful results, and LEAA recommended that a national victimization survey be implemented (President's Commission on Law Enforcement, 1967). Ever since, the BJS, in association with the Census Bureau, has conducted a nationwide survey and publishes information on the victims of crime.

Introduction

In this chapter, you will gain a better understanding of the vital role statistics play in criminology, criminal justice, and crime and intelligence analysis. Data analysis has become an increasingly critical component in police administration and crime prevention, as well as in the investigative process. Crime analysts—whether working with data that are stored and evaluated over time or with data based on observation and real-time intelligence collection—rely heavily on examining statistical data. The results of their data analysis are used, in part, to form conclusions that support the justification for tactical recommendations made to address issues related to crime.

Such was the case in the summer of 2014, where along the highways that run through a county located in upstate New York, a "highway shooter" wreaked havoc over a period of several months. Data analysis proved to be a key component in the investigative process as crime analysts studied the data to identify patterns, provide temporal and spatial information, and create strategic maps, such as shown in Figure 2.1.

The map in Figure 2.1 was created using geographic information systems (GIS) technology that extrapolated statistical data from police reports to plot specific points of reference on the map. For the crime analyst, the intelligence learned from the data that populated the map helped to identify similarities between shooting incidents, which in turn helped to identify a pattern that was based on date, time, and location, as well as possible points of entry and egress the suspected shooter may have favored when engaged in shooting at passing automobiles.

Before you are introduced to the analysis process in which an event goes from suspected criminal incident to a documented event and, eventually, to a statistical value analyzed by law enforcement, we will first review the basic concepts of gathering statistics and the analysis of statistics employed in criminal justice. First, let's start with a very basic question: How do we figure out how much crime takes place in America?

How Is Crime Measured?

How much crime is there in America?

That's an interesting—and tricky—question. Crime statistics must be treated with great caution and not a little bit of skepticism. In order

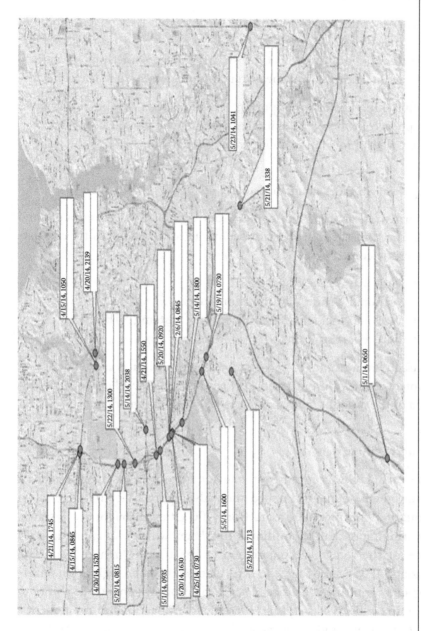

Figure 2.1 Pattern map associated with a highway shooting investigation.

to be both cautious and skeptical, you must ask two questions about crime statistics:

1. Are crime measurements measuring what they purport to be measuring?
2. Does the source of crime statistics have something to gain from the way crime measurements are presented to the public?

By asking these two important questions, you will be less likely to simply accept the crime statistics you are reviewing at face value. But where does information about crime come from?

Reporting on the Amount of Crime

Information about crime comes from agencies, private groups, and scholars. But the four most frequently used data sources for estimating crime come from

- Uniform Crime Reports
- National Crime Victimization Survey
- National Incident-Based Reporting System (NIBRS)
- Self-report studies

Each has advantages and disadvantages, and each can be biased or slanted. But if you put them all together, you are likely to get a fair idea of the amount of crime that takes place in America.

Uniform Crime Reports

The early UCR Program was managed by the IACP, prior to FBI involvement, done through a monthly report. The first report, in January 1930, presented data from 400 cities throughout 43 states, covering more than 20 million individuals, which was approximately 20% of the total U.S. population at the time. On June 11, 1930, through IACP lobbying, the U.S. Congress passed legislation enacting a law granting the office of the U.S. attorney general the ability to "acquire, collect, classify, and preserve identification, criminal identification, crime, and other records" with the ability to appoint officials to oversee this duty, including the subordinate members of the Bureau of Investigation. The attorney general, in turn, designated the FBI to serve as the national clearinghouse for the data collected, and the FBI assumed responsibility for managing the UCR Program in September 1930. The IACP announced this transfer of responsibility in the July 1930 issue of the IACP crime report. While the IACP discontinued oversight of the program, it continued to advise the FBI to better the UCR Program.

Since 1935, the FBI has served as a data clearinghouse, organizing, collecting, and disseminating information voluntarily submitted by local, state, federal, and tribal law enforcement agencies. The UCR Program has remained the primary tool for collection and analysis of data ever since.

During the decade of the 1980s, a series of national UCR conferences were held with members from the IACP, Department of Justice, the FBI, and the newly formed BJS. The purpose of these conferences was to determine necessary revisions to the Uniform Crime Reports, and then to implement those revisions. The result of these conferences was the release in May 1985 of the "Blueprint for the Future of the Uniform Crime Reporting Program." The report proposed splitting reported data into two separate categories; one category would be the 8 serious crimes (which later became known as Part I index crimes) and the other would be 21 less commonly reported crimes (which later became known as Part II index crimes).

Part I index crimes were composed of reported cases in two categories: violent and property crimes. The violent crimes were aggravated assault, forcible rape, murder, and robbery; those classified as property crimes in Part I were arson, burglary, larceny–theft, and motor vehicle theft.

Included in Part II were simple assault, curfew offenses and loitering, embezzlement, forgery and counterfeiting, disorderly conduct, driving under the influence, drug offenses, fraud, gambling, liquor offenses, offenses against the family, prostitution, public drunkenness, runaways, sex offenses, stolen property, vandalism, vagrancy, and weapons offenses.

The Criminal Justice Information Services (CJIS) committees of the IACP and the National Sheriffs' Association (NSA) provide vital links between local law enforcement and the FBI in the oversight of the UCR Program. The IACP, representing the thousands of police departments nationwide, and the NSA, serving sheriffs throughout the country, encourage agencies to participate fully in the program. Both committees fulfill advisory capacities concerning the UCR Program's operation.

In 1988, a Data Providers' Advisory Policy Board was established to provide input for UCR matters. That board operated until 1993, when it combined with the National Crime Information Center Advisory Policy Board to form a single Advisory Policy Board (APB) to address all issues regarding the FBI's CJIS. The current APB ensures a continued emphasis on UCR-related issues. In addition, the Association of State UCR Programs (ASUCRP) focuses on UCR issues within individual state law enforcement associations and promotes interest in the UCR Program. These organizations foster widespread and responsible use of uniform crime statistics and lend assistance to data contributors when needed.

Changes in UCR

In June 2004, the CJIS APB approved discontinuing the use of the crime index in the UCR Program and its publications, and it directed the FBI to publish a violent crime total and a property crime total. The CJIS decided that the crime index and the modified crime index (the number of crime index offenses plus arson) were not true indicators of the degrees of criminality because they were always driven upward by the offense with the highest number, typically larceny–theft. The sheer volume of those offenses overshadowed more serious but less frequently committed offenses, creating a bias against a jurisdiction with a high number of larceny–thefts but a low number of other serious crimes, such as murder and forcible rape.

Other changes over the years in the reporting of crime statistics through the UCR Program included the FBI beginning to record arson rates, as part of the UCR Program, in 1979. This report details arsons of the following property types, such as single-occupancy residential (houses, townhouses, duplexes, etc.), storage (barns, garages, warehouses, etc.), industrial and manufacturing, and motor vehicles (automobiles, trucks, buses, motorcycles, etc.).

The FBI also began collecting data on crimes motivated by gender bias and gender identity bias. This compilation of hate crime statistics came about in response to the Matthew Shepard and James

Byrd, Jr. Hate Crimes Prevention Act of 2009. Also in response to the Shepard–Byrd Act, the FBI modified its data collection so that reporting agencies could indicate whether hate crimes were committed by, or directed against, juveniles. Therefore, in addition to reporting the number of individual victims, law enforcement began reporting the number of victims who were 18 years of age or older and the number of victims under the age of 18 in 2013.

At the fall 2011 CJIS APB meeting, the APB recommended, and FBI director Robert Mueller III approved, changing the definition of *rape*. Since 1929, the FBI had defined *forcible rape* as "the carnal knowledge of a female forcibly and against her will" (U.S. Department of Justice, 2004, p. 19). Beginning with the 2013 data collection, the new definition for the violent crime of rape was modified to "penetration, no matter how slight, of the vagina or anus with any body part or object, or oral penetration by a sex organ of another person, without the consent of the victim" (FBI, 2014, p. 1).

Where Do the Statistics for the UCR Program Come From?

In 2013, FBI UCR data were compiled from more than 18,000 law enforcement agencies, representing more than 98% of the population in the United States. Although reporting by law enforcement is not mandated, many states have instituted laws requiring law enforcement within those states to provide UCR data. The statistics in the UCR Program are based on arrest reports. These arrest reports are broken down by the type of crime for cities, counties, states, and regions of the country. In addition, the FBI collects auxiliary information about these offenses, such as the time of day of burglaries. The expanded offense data include trends in both crime volume and crime rate per 100,000 inhabitants. In regard to homicides, the UCR Program collects expanded homicide data, which includes information about homicide victims and offenders, weapons used, the circumstances surrounding the offenses, and justifiable homicides.

UCR and Violent Crime

Violent crime is composed of four offenses: murder and nonnegligent manslaughter, rape, robbery, and aggravated assault. Violent crimes are defined in the UCR Program as those offenses that involve force or threat of force.

UCR and Property Crime

Property crime includes the offenses of burglary, larceny–theft, and motor vehicle theft. The object of the theft-type offenses is the taking of money or property, but there is no force or threat of force against the victims.

UCR and Clearances

Within the UCR Program, law enforcement agencies can clear, or "close," offenses in one of two ways: by arrest or by exceptional means. Although agencies may administratively close a case, this does not necessarily mean that the agency can clear the offense for UCR purposes. According to the FBI, law enforcement agencies must meet the following four conditions in order to clear an offense by exceptional means. The agency must have

1. Identified the offender
2. Gathered enough evidence to support an arrest, make a charge, and turn over the offender to the court for prosecution
3. Identified the offender's exact location so that the suspect could be taken into custody immediately
4. Encountered a circumstance outside the control of law enforcement that prohibits the agency from arresting, charging, and prosecuting the offender (FBI, 2010b)

Examples of exceptional clearances include the death of the offender (e.g., suicide or justifiably killed by the police), the victim's refusal to cooperate with the prosecution after the offender has been identified, or the denial of extradition because the offender committed a crime in another jurisdiction and is being prosecuted for that offense.

UCR and Crime Rates

The most important information proved by the UCR Program concerns crime rates and arrest rates. A UCR crime rate is like a percentage;

it compares the number of crimes to the size of the population. The UCR Program's crime rates reveal the number of crimes for every 100,000 people in the population. The size of the population depends on the geographical area being examined. For example, if the city of Gotham has 500,000 people and if 5,000 burglaries occurred in this city in a particular year, then the crime rate is determined by this formula: the number of crimes (burglaries, 5,000) divided by the population (500,000). That comes out to 0.01. This result is multiplied by 100,000, which in this example results in 1,000. This means that 5,000 burglaries in Gotham with a population of 500,000 is equivalent to 1,000 burglaries for every 100,000 persons. Consequently, Gotham has a burglary rate of 1,000 per 100,000 persons.

The use of crime rates is important because they allow us to determine whether one city or area has a greater crime problem than another city or area. For instance, in our example in the preceding paragraph, Gotham has a burglary rate of 1,000 per 100,000 persons. However, the city of Metropolis, a larger city in the same state, has a burglary rate of 850 per 100,000 persons. Thus, we could say that when it comes to burglaries, Metropolis is a safer city than Gotham.

UCR and Arrest Rates

UCR data are based on police reports. For this reason, the FBI calls the offenses on which it provides data "crimes known to the police." The crimes known to the police, then, become the "official" number of crimes that the police report to the UCR Program, and that the UCR Program, in turn, reports to the public. How do police departments find out about crimes—the crimes known to the police? These data are based on citizen complaints of crime. For each crime reported, the police tell the FBI whether someone was arrested for that crime or whether the crime was cleared for some other reason—for instance, the death of the main suspect.

For each arrest that occurs, the police report to the FBI the arrestee's age, gender, and race. When someone is arrested for a crime, that crime is counted as being "cleared by arrest." Overall, statistics suggest that the police clear about 20% of all index crimes, although the clearance rate varies by the type of crime (Barkan and Bryjak, 2004).

However, the annual Uniform Crime Reports do provide information about the number of crimes in each category cleared by arrest.

Drawbacks of the UCR Program

The UCR Program provides the official statistics about crime in this country, and those statistics are provided by more than 18,000 police agencies. Thus, the Uniform Crime Reports are the best official compilation of crime in this country. On the other hand, while they are a great resource for researchers, government officials on all levels, and citizens, they fail to provide a completely accurate picture of crime in the United States for the following reasons:

- The UCR Program only counts crime reported to the police; consequently, crime is most certainly underreported.
- The UCR Program counts and classifies crime and some characteristics of arrestees; still, it does not provide complete details about offenses.
- The UCR Program relies on the statistics given the FBI by local and state police departments. This suggests that for various reasons (e.g., manpower shortages and political considerations), crime in a particular location might be misrepresented either intentionally or unintentionally.
- The UCR Program counts only specific violent and property crimes and does not focus on corporate, occupational, or computer crimes.

Results from the UCR Program

What, then, do we know about crime and crime trends from the UCR Program?

The latest statistics from the UCR Program show that

1. In 2013, an estimated 1,163,146 violent crimes occurred nationwide, a decrease of 4.4% from the 2012 estimate.
2. When considering 5- and 10-year trends, the 2013 estimated the violent crime total was 12.3% below the 2009 level and 14.5% below the 2004 level.

3. There were an estimated 367.9 violent crimes per 100,000 inhabitants in 2013, a rate that declined 5.1% when compared with the 2012 estimated rate.
4. Aggravated assaults accounted for 62.3% of violent crimes reported to law enforcement in 2013. Robbery offenses accounted for 29.7% of violent crime offenses, rape accounted for 6.9%, and murder accounted for 1.2%.
5. Information collected regarding types of weapons used in violent crime showed that firearms were used in 69.0% of the nation's murders, 40.0% of robberies, and 21.6% of aggravated assaults.

Furthermore, looking back on the 20-year trends in the UCR statistics, since 1993, both violent crime and property crime have declined in 18 of the past 20 years; the number of arrests were 11,302,000 in 2013—a significant decline from the 14,663,000 arrests in 1994. The number of murders in 2013 was 14,196, whereas in 1994 the number of homicides was 23,326 (FBI, 2015).

National Incident-Based Reporting System

In 1985, a joint task force of the BJS and the FBI was created to study and recommend ways to improve the quality of information contained in the UCR Program (UCR Study Task Force, 1985). This resulted in the NIBRS, and the first collection of data began in 1991. Under NIBRS, participating law enforcement authorities provide offense and arrest data on 22 broad categories of crime covering 46 offenses, while providing only arrest information on 11 other offenses (Bohm and Haley, 2012).

The advantages of the NIBRS compared with the UCR Program is that the NIBRS provides more data on each crime, making it possible to examine crimes in much more detail. It is hoped by the FBI that eventually the NIBRS will replace the UCR Program as the source of official FBI crime information. However, not all police departments have the resources necessary to collect, process, and report the wide array of data. As of 2009, only 44% of the nation's law enforcement agencies were participating in the NIBRS (Masters et al., 2013). According to the FBI, as of 2007, 6,444 law enforcement agencies contributed NIBRS data to the UCR Program. This represents just

25% of the U.S. population and 25% of the crime statistics collected by the FBI. Thus, it seems impractical to make generalizations about crime nationwide (FBI, 2012).

Beyond the UCR Program

The BJS is spearheading the National Crime Statistics Exchange (NCS-X), a program designed to generate nationally representative incident-based data on crimes reported to law enforcement agencies (BJS, 2015). NCS-X will leverage the FBI's existing NIBRS by recruiting a sample of 400 law enforcement agencies to supplement the existing NIBRS data by providing their incident data to their state (or the federal) NIBRS data collection program. When data from these 400 agencies are combined with data from the more than 6000 agencies that currently report NIBRS data to the FBI, NIBRS will be able to produce national estimates of crime that can be disaggregated (separated into its component parts) by victim and offender characteristics, the circumstances of the event, the victim–offender relationship, and other important elements of criminal events. When completed, nationally representative NIBRS data will, it is hoped, increase our nation's ability to monitor, respond to, and prevent crime by allowing NIBRS to produce timely, detailed, and accurate national measures of crime incidents.

NCS-X is a collaborative undertaking supported by the FBI and other Department of Justice agencies. BJS also needs the support of the law enforcement community to ensure its success. NCS-X will be designed to implement efficient and minimally burdensome processes to collect and extract incident-based data from existing records management systems. The NCS-X will be providing technical assistance and funding to the sampled 400 law enforcement agencies and to state UCR and NIBRS programs to enable them to report these additional data to the FBI (BJS, 2015). To encourage participation in the program, the FBI and Bureau of Justice may offer benefits, which may include increased operational and analytic capabilities or resources, training, technical support, and other customized incentives.

A team of partner organizations—including RTI International, the IACP, the Police Executive Research Forum (PERF), the Integrated Justice Information Systems (IJIS) Institute, and the National Consortium for Justice Information and Statistics (SEARCH)—is responsible for developing the implementation plans for NCS-X. This includes coordinating efforts with local law enforcement, state reporting programs, and the software industry. An NCS-X executive steering committee will review possible design and implementation options to ensure the maximum benefit to both participants and key stakeholders (BJS, 2015).

National Crime Victimization Survey

In addition to the Uniform Crime Reports, a second major source of data about crime comes from the NCVS. Once called the National Crime Survey, the NCVS has been conducted annually since 1972 by the Bureau of the Census for the U.S. Department of Justice's BJS.

Although it underwent a redesign in 1992, the basic design of the survey has remained constant through its almost four decades of existence. Essentially, the NCVS is a self-report survey in which interviewed persons are asked about the number and characteristics of victimizations experienced during the prior six months. Survey respondents provide information about themselves (e.g., age, sex, race and Hispanic origin, marital status, education level, and income) and whether they experienced a victimization. Information is collected for each victimization incident, about the offender (e.g., age, race and Hispanic origin, sex, and victim–offender relationship), characteristics of the crime (including time and place of occurrence, use of weapons, nature of injury, and economic consequences), whether the crime was reported to police, reasons the crime was or was not reported, and experiences with the criminal justice system.

The NCVS is administered to persons age 12 or older from a nationally representative sample of households in the United States. The NCVS defines a household as a group of members who all reside at a sampled address. Persons are considered household members when the sampled address is their usual place of residence at the time of the interview and when they have no other usual place of residence. Once selected, households remain in the sample for three years, and eligible persons in these households are interviewed every six months either in person or over the phone, for a total of seven interviews.

Generally, all first interviews are conducted in person. New households rotate into the sample on an ongoing basis to replace outgoing households that have been in sample for the three-year period. The sample includes persons living in group quarters, such as dormitories, rooming houses, and religious group dwellings, and excludes persons living in military barracks and institutional settings, such as correctional or hospital facilities, and the homeless.

To gather data for the annual report entitled "Crime Victimization in the United States," the Bureau of the Census conducts interviews with a national sample of approximately 160,000 people in 90,000 households. The major focus in the set of questions asked adults (i.e., individuals over 12 years of age) is whether they have been victims of crime within the past six months. When it has been determined that an individual in the survey has been victimized, further questions are asked about the victimization.

Although the UCR Program is primarily oriented toward criminals and their crimes, the NCVS focuses mainly on the victims and their victimization. The NCVS includes both reported and unreported crimes. By concentrating on victims and learning more about unreported crimes, the NCVS complements the UCR Program by giving a more complete picture of the extent of crime in the United States.

In the survey, household residents are asked whether they have been a victim in the previous six months of several different kinds of personal crimes. These crimes include robbery, rape, sexual assault, aggravated and simple assault, and personal theft, such as pickpocketing and purse snatching; the NCVS groups these offenses together and calls them "personal crimes" (Barkan and Bryjak, 2004). One household member is also asked whether the family has been victim to a household burglary, other household theft, or motor vehicle theft; the NCVS calls these "property crimes."

If respondents have experienced personal crimes, they are then asked several questions about the offense, including whether and how they were threatened or hurt; the time and place of victimization; whether a weapon was involved and, if so, what type of weapon; how well they knew the offender before the victimization; and whether they reported the offense to the police and, if not, why not. When respondents report a household victimization, they are asked further questions about it, including the value of the item(s) stolen and whether someone was at home at the time the theft occurred.

Since the NCVS is a random sample of the entire nation, its results can be generalized to the rest of the U.S. population. So, for example, if 1% of the sample reports that their automobile was stolen, we can be fairly sure that about 1% of all U.S. families have experienced a motor vehicle theft. This is important because it allows us to estimate the actual number of victimizations in the United States. It also allows us to estimate the rate of victimization per 1000 individuals age 12 and older for personal crimes and per 1000 households for property crimes. For instance, if 1% of households report a stolen car, then we can say that the rate of car thefts is 10 per 1000 households.

Strengths and Drawbacks of the NCVS

The major strength of the NCVS is that it provides a more accurate estimate of the actual number of crimes that take place in the United States than does the UCR Program. In addition, the NCVS lets us know about crimes that go unreported to the police, and also, it is a rich source of information about criminal victimization.

However, there are flaws in the NCVS—just as there are in the UCR Program and all other forms of crime data collection. For instance, it does not include commercial crime and white-collar crime. Furthermore, it does not cover crimes whose victims are under 12 years of age. There could also be inaccuracy if respondents have forgotten about a victimization, or they choose to avoid telling the interviewer about a victimization because of embarrassment in talking about a crime or fear of getting into trouble, or simply because they choose to remain silent about an incident.

Finally, there could be sampling errors, or the question format may not produce valid answers for some people, especially adolescents.

Results of the NCVS

In general, the annual results of the NCVS show that there are many more crimes that are committed than are reported to the police, and subsequently to the FBI, for the UCR Program. It is found by comparing the UCR Program and the NCVS that fewer than half of violent crimes are reported to the police, fewer than one-third of personal theft crimes are reported to law enforcement, and fewer than half of household thefts are reported to the police (Truman, 2010).

Other findings from the 2013 NCVS show that

- The rate of violent crime declined slightly from 26.1 victimizations per 1000 persons in 2012 to 23.2 per 1000 in 2013
- No statistically significant change was detected in the rate of serious violent crime (rape or sexual assault, robbery, and aggravated assault) from 2012 to 2013 (7.3 per 1000).
- From 2012 to 2013, no statistically significant changes occurred in the rates of domestic violence, intimate partner violence, violence resulting in an injury, or violence involving a firearm.
- The rate of property crime decreased from 155.8 victimizations per 1000 households in 2012 to 131.4 per 1000 in 2013.
- In 2013, 1.2% of all persons age 12 or older (3 million persons) experienced at least one violent victimization. About 0.4% (1.1 million persons) experienced at least one serious violent victimization (Langton and Truman, 2014).
- There were an estimated 16,822,000 violent victimizations in 1993; in 2013, there were an estimated 6,126,000 violent victimizations.
- In 1993, there were an estimated 1,922,000 auto thefts in the United States; in 2013, there were an estimated 661,200 car thefts.

One other set of statistics of note from the NCVS has to do with the number of crimes that were unreported to the police. Of the 16,822,000 violent victimizations that were estimated by the BJS based on the NCVS in 1993, it was found that 7,138,000 were reported to the police, but 9,499,000 were not. That means that about 56% (more than half) of violent crimes were not reported to law enforcement in 1993. Comparing that with 2013, it was found that there were 6,126,000 violent victimizations in 2013. Of that number, 2,794,000 were reported, but 3,231,000 (or about 53%) were not reported.

Self-Report Data

Self-reports studies are an important source of information about offenders and their offenses. In that respect, they often provide more information than do the UCR Program and the NCVS about the people who actually commit crimes. Self-report surveys ask people to reveal information about themselves and their own law violations. The basic assumption of self-report studies is that the assurance of anonymity and confidentiality will encourage people to be honest about their illegal activities.

Self-report studies were first used in the 1940s (Thornberry and Krone, 2000). Such surveys are typically given to adolescents, usually students in high school classes, and researchers often use college students as subjects for self-report studies. There are notable self-report surveys, for instance, the Monitoring the Future surveys. Monitoring the Future is an annual survey of 8th, 10th, and 12th graders conducted by researchers at the University of Michigan's Institute for Social Research, under a grant from the National Institute on Drug Abuse, part of the National Institutes of Health. Since 1975, the survey has measured drug, alcohol, and cigarette use and related attitudes in 12th graders nationwide. Eighth and tenth graders were added to the survey in 1991. Overall, 41,675 students from 389 public and private schools participated in the 2013 survey (NIDA, 2014).

Other annual surveys include the Arrestee Drug Abuse Monitoring II (ADAM II) program. Since 2007, the Office of National Drug Control Policy (ONDCP) has sponsored the ADAM II data collection program in nine U.S. counties and the District of Columbia. ADAM II is an annual survey designed to gather information about the drug use of arrested adults. Another annual survey is conducted by the Substance Abuse and Mental Health Services Administration (SAMHSA), whose mission is to reduce the impact of substance abuse and mental illness on America's communities. The National Survey on Drug Use and Health (NSDUH) is the primary source of information on the prevalence, patterns, and consequences of alcohol, tobacco, and illegal drug use and abuse and mental disorders in the U.S. civilian, noninstitutionalized population, age 12 and older.

Results of Self-Report Studies

Self-report surveys are a way to learn more about the "dark figures of crime"—the individuals that don't show up in official statistics. Researchers administering the first self-report survey studies found that there was an enormous amount of hidden crime in the United

States. In fact, those early self-report crime surveys indicated that more than 90% of all Americans had committed crimes for which they could have been arrested and even imprisoned (Bohm and Haley, 2012). Other self-reported crime data indicate that many drug users started using drugs as juveniles, and that heroin addicts are most likely to commit crimes (Fagin, 2007). In addition, it has been found through self-report surveys that there is no difference in the amount of crime committed by lower-class and middle-class youth, even though lower-class youth are much more likely to be arrested, convicted, and incarcerated (Siegel, 2002).

According to Uniform Crime Reports, African Americans make up about 12% of the general population of the United States, yet they account for about 42% of violent crime arrests and 27% of property crime arrests (FBI, 2010a). Whites account for 70% of all arrests, while blacks are arrested for 28% of all crimes. Whites comprise 59% of arrests for violent crimes and 68% of arrests for property crimes (FBI, 2010a). However, nationwide studies using self-report questionnaires find that there are few differences in crime rates between whites and blacks (Huizinga and Elliott, 1987).

Drawbacks of Self-Report Measures

Although self-report surveys have established validity and reliability, they are sometimes criticized because not everyone may be candid about their illegal activities, and some may exaggerate their criminal acts. There is also a "missing cases" phenomenon that is a concern. Since surveys are often given to groups of individuals, such as high school students, some of the people who do not participate or are absent from school when the survey is administered may skew the results.

Comparing the Results of the UCR Program, the NCVS, and Self-Report Measures

There are significant differences between the various crime measures. As just indicated in the previous section, while African Americans are more frequently processed by the criminal justice system, self-report surveys suggest there is no actual difference in the amount of crime engaged in by whites and blacks.

Looking at reported incidents of sexual assault, the UCR Program likely grossly underestimates the number of women who are sexually assaulted. NCVS results suggest that there are perhaps two to three times as many women assaulted than are reported in the UCR Program (Fagin, 2007). Similarly, robbery, aggravated assault, and larceny are all reported by the NCVS at rates two to three times greater than the rates given in UCR data (Fagin, 2007).

Again, according to NCVS findings, an estimated 46% of violent crime was reported to police in 2013, and only 38% of simple assault and 64% of aggravated assault were reported to the police (BJS, 2015).

Reviewing the long-term trends as indicated by both the UCR Program and the NCVS, while there is a great deal of unreported crime, there is congruence between these two important measures of crime when fluctuations in crime are considered. That is, both the UCR Program and NCVS show that crime has declined considerably since 1993, even though NCVS rates of victimization suggest there is much crime that goes unreported. However, both measures indicate the same trends—crime has declined considerably according to both the UCR Program and the NCVS.

Viewing Crime through the Prism of Statistics

While the measures of crime provide us with standardized data on crime, crime rates, and comparative data for states and cities, statistics have their limitations. Perhaps the greatest limitation is that the human factor is missing.

Looking at statistics regarding homicides, burglaries, and sexual assault gives us some idea of the number of these crimes taking place in a location or in the country, but statistics tell us nothing about human suffering. We can learn about the economic costs of crime through statistics and certain kinds of research; on the other hand, we can learn nothing from the annual totals of the UCR Program or NCVS about the emotional toll on families and survivors.

For the crime analyst, there are more immediate concerns: who the offender is, what his or her patterns are, what the offender's motivation is, and how this offender will best be neutralized or apprehended.

Utilizing Statistics as a Form of Accountability: CompStat

CompStat, or complaint statistics, is an accountability process officially adopted by the New York City Police Department in 1994. By and large, CompStat, as used by law enforcement, is an in-house process that holds upper management accountable for crime reduction within their respective areas of patrol.

By utilizing statistical data, with the assistance of GIS technology, police agencies can track crime patterns and view these patterns in a variety of ways. For example, hot spot analysis of specific crime patterns can display spatial clusters relating to hot spot areas of these crimes and then designate the values of these clusters as high and low, with high indicating a greater area of propensity toward the particular crime pattern, for example, robbery, and low indicating a cold spot, or no area of crimes relating to that same pattern.

The basic principles of CompStat are based on the idea of utilizing accurate and timely intelligence about underlying crime conditions. This intelligence would then directly affect tactical decisions that relate to the rapid deployment of personnel and resources needed to relentlessly address, follow up, and reassess the problem.

The Crime Analyst and Statistics

We have indicated that statistics and the various measures used to determine the amount of crime in our society should be viewed with caution, and you should always keep the flaws and drawbacks of each measure in mind. And we think it is not a bad idea to remember the remark that Mark Twain wrote in "Chapters from My Autobiography" in 1906: "There are three kinds of lies: lies, damned lies and statistics." Although this statement probably did not originate with Twain, he made it popular. And since the late nineteenth century, the phrase has been used over and over again—even appearing in the title of several books. However, the caution is still apt today. Depending on the way you arrange numbers and statistics, you can prove just about anything. And often, statistics don't mean much of anything when viewed out of context.

Nevertheless, crime analysts—just like the rest of us—must utilize statistics at times, and sometimes even depend on them in critical situations. Most of the time, though, statistics give us averages and ranges; they do not tell us about the personal side of crime and criminals. Typically, the tactical crime analyst must gather intelligence about individuals, and that's when statistics tend to be useless.

Take, for example, an armed gunman who is holding a child hostage after a bank robbery attempt that has gone wrong. What do the statistics tell us about the risk to children held hostage by a stranger in a failed bank robbery? Does it matter if the analyst can quickly find information that tells him that 78 % of the time, children are released unharmed by gunmen?

Of course, the answer to that is no, it doesn't matter. What is important is what the analyst can quickly learn about this man, his background, his violence history, his motive, and his current state of mind. The statistics don't mean a thing to the worried parents of the child, nor should they mean anything to the hostage negotiator who must find a way to make sure this child is released without injury.

Statistical Data and Law Enforcement: From Incident to Evaluation

Before we talk about the data collection process, we need to take a brief look at the crime analysis process, the mindset if you will, practiced by crime and intelligence analysts. This process defines the why and how related to the analyst's use of data.

Data collection and storage, as important as those processes are, would bear no meaning if the data were left to compile without any forethought as how to utilize the data. Upon collection, data must be examined for any sort of constructive purpose for law enforcement and how law enforcement will address any needs related to the collection and examination of the stored data. This process is referred to as the crime analysis process (Figure 2.2). The crime analysis process follows five steps: (1) data collection, (2) data collation, (3) analysis, (4) dissemination of results, and (5) incorporation of feedback from users of the information (Santos, 2013).

Before we examine the analysis process, however, we first need to review how data are collected and stored before they can be extrapolated for analysis purposes.

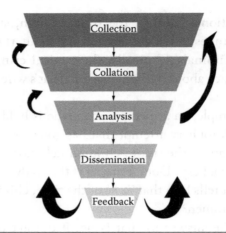

Figure 2.2   Crime analysis process.

Process of Data Collection and Storage

The map relating to the highway shooter in Figure 2.1 at the beginning of this chapter could not be compiled or used by the crime analyst until data had been input into the GIS (geographical data system) as a means to plot the specific points of reference onto the map.

The data were derived from multiple systems that had stored the information once it was input from the various sources that created the data. For example, on a specific day a shooting incident occurred on a stretch of road along the highway. This incident was then called into a 911 operator, who in turn dispatched the call to a police unit by use of the computer-aided dispatch (CAD) system.

The responding officer, upon arrival, then created a report noting all of the particulars of the incident: date, time, location, vehicle description, and any other relevant information associated with that specific incident.

This police incident report was then uploaded into the police department's record management system (RMS). Once the report was in the RMS, it could then be searchable in multiple ways, by crime report number, location, victim name, and so forth.

The information could also be put into the GIS. (You will learn more about this in Chapter 12.)

At this point, all the crime analyst would need to do is open the GIS and create a map using all of the information that was available from the data sources just mentioned. The following is a list of the various systems, along with the strengths and limitations each has in terms of data collection and storage:

- Computer-aided dispatch
- Records management system
- Geographic data system

Computer-Aided Dispatch

Usually, CAD is maintained by the agency responsible for 911 dispatching. CAD captures and stores several vital pieces of information for future use:

1. Calls received to 911
2. Calls dispatched
3. Which police car was dispatched
4. When the call to the police patrol was made, when it was dispatched, when an officer was on scene, and when the call was cleared
5. Calls initiated by police officers
6. Notes from the responding officers
7. Location of the call
8. Action taken by the officer
9. Situation found by the officer

This information is stored in CAD, but CAD, in and of itself, has no analysis capabilities. The simple purpose of CAD is to track the status of every call to its completion. In addition, an important aspect of CAD is to efficiently manage the resources of the police department relative to the volume of calls. Most police departments receive a high volume of calls—most of which have little or nothing to do with crime or violence. However, it is important for the department's supervisory staff and administration to know two things:

1. What cops do you currently have available to respond to a call for service?
2. Which officer(s) is closest to the location?

In many police departments, the GIS is often integrated into CAD. When GIS and CAD are integrated, police dispatchers have various features available to them. This includes full address information, such as alerts and past incidents; a map of the area, including street names, major buildings, and fire or emergency medical services zones; and the ability to link web cams, traffic cameras, building floor plans, and other documents or images to a map.

Records Management System

Many, if not most, police departments have an RMS. This is a system that allows the collection and storage of relevant police data. For instance, the RMS of a typical police department will collect and store

- Crime reports
- Arrest reports
- Field interview forms
- Accident reports
- Investigative case tracking
- Evidence (property management)
- Citations
- Warrants

Usually, an RMS is limited to records directly related to law enforcement operations.

It does not deal with the general business functions (budget, payroll, human resources functions, etc.) of a department. However, because of operational needs, an RMS may include the maintenance of duty rosters, law enforcement personnel records, and vehicle fleet maintenance records.

Furthermore, information may be entered into the RMS through automated field reporting, where there is real-time live access to all crime reports, and manual data entry, where there is less chance for technical failure, although it is a slower process.

ArcGIS

ArcGIS is a GIS software program developed by ESRI, a California-based company that has been specializing in GIS since 1969. Now used by more police departments than any other GIS software, ArcGIS gives a police agency the ability to take data from CAD or RMS, give the data a geographic location, and put them on a map.

This result does not happen automatically, and an intelligence analyst will need to be trained in the geocoding process—the process of assigning an actual location on a map based on the address given—before the information appears on a map in a usable format. Once that happens, though, the crime analyst can conduct a spatial analysis of crimes (often referred to as hot spot identification) and find other valuable information.

Working the Collected Data Using Data Sets

Most often, in order to properly use data, the crime analyst or intelligence analyst will need to access data from a variety of sources. Too often, data stored in RMS or CAD were not created to suit the needs of crime analysis. Therefore, data sets must be used to begin an analysis. The primary data sources for the crime analysis will come from RMS, CAD, and ArcGIS. And the most commonly sought data include incident reports, arrest records, calls for service, and accident reports. The intelligence analyst must be able to connect to the database when he or she needs the information.

This chapter has addressed the basic question related to what we know about crime. In the chapter, we discussed the processes of crime collection, how crime is measured, and the utilization of statistics in order to learn more about crime and examine crime patterns. The highway shooter investigation mentioned at the beginning of the chapter is an excellent example of how the processes that involve the organizing, collecting, and disseminating of information proved to be relevant—as all of these processes played a critical role in the investigation.

The intelligence and statistical information used during the GIS process also played a predominant role in the CompStat meetings that were held during the span in which the crimes were being committed and investigated.

The highway shooter case also involved a complex procedure of crime analysis that relied heavily on the aid of technology. As a result, the analysis supplied to the investigators included the total understanding of a wide range of computer systems and programs, combined with the criminal investigative thought process—a process that will be discussed in detail in later chapters. The overall process of analysis was crucial in order to effectively disseminate the raw data that were extrapolated from the various systems in order to come up with a theory that could be used to create a workable, strategic, tactical plan.

Investigations that deal with immediate public safety concerns, such as the highway shooter case, usually involve a large volume of intelligence having to be analyzed at a rapid pace. Although the highway shooter was not identified in that investigation, the investigative team, which was composed of several police agencies, utilized crime and tactical analysis as a means to stay on pace with the investigation while keeping the flow of information fluid between agencies.

Questions for Discussion

1. Since both the UCR Program and the NCVS demonstrate that crime has been steadily declining since 1993, what is the reason for this great crime decline?
2. Are we as a society becoming less violent? Why or why not?
3. What is the future of statistics in law enforcement?

Important Terms

ArcGIS: Geographical information systems software program developed by ESRI, a California-based company that has been specializing in GIS since 1969. ArcGIS gives the crime analyst the ability to take data from CAD or RMS, give it a geographic location, and put it on a map.

Bureau of Justice Statistics: The BJS was established in 1979 under the Justice Systems Improvement Act of 1979, an amendment to the Omnibus Crime Control and Safe Streets Act of 1968. The mission of the BJS is to collect, analyze, publish, and disseminate information on crime, criminal offenders, victims of crime, and the operation of justice systems at all levels of government.

CAD: Computer-aided dispatch; system maintained by the agency responsible for 911 dispatching. CAD captures and stores several vital pieces of information for future police use.

CompStat: Accountability and management system used by many police departments to determine the hot spots of crime and to better deploy personnel and develop effective crime control strategies.

Crime rate: The UCR Program's crime rate reports the number of crimes for every 100,000 people in the population.

Dark figures of crime: Self-report surveys are a way to learn more about the dark figures of crime—the individuals that don't show up in official statistics.

National Crime Statistics Exchange: Program designed to generate nationally representative incident-based data on crimes reported to law enforcement agencies. It involves the FBI recruiting a sample of 400 law enforcement agencies to supplement the existing NIBRS data by providing their incident data to their state (or the federal) NIBRS data collection program.

National Crime Victimization Survey: Conducted annually since 1972 by the Bureau of the Census and the Department of Justice, this random survey focuses on the victims of crime.

National Incident-Based Reporting System: Under NIBRS, participating law enforcement authorities provide offense and arrest data to the FBI on 22 broad categories of crime covering 46 offenses, while providing only arrest information on 11 other offenses. This reporting system may replace the UCR Program in the future.

RMS: Records Management System; system that allows the collection and storage of relevant police data for future use.

Self-report data: Data collected from individuals who are asked to reveal information about themselves and their offenses.

Uniform Crime Reports: Collection of crime statistics from more than 18,000 state and federal law enforcement agencies and complied by the FBI into an annual report.

Study Guide Questions

1. Most Americans seem to have little or no accurate knowledge about whether crime is
   a. Going up or down in their community

   b. Something to be concerned about
   c. A rational behavior
   d. A good or bad thing
2. According to the NCVS, criminal victimization has been steadily declining for more than
   a. 5 years
   b. 10 years
   c. 20 years
   d. 30 years
3. Comparing the UCR Program to the NCVS, it is found that
   a. Most crimes are reported to the police
   b. More than half of all crimes are not reported
   c. Most murders are never reported
   d. More than two-thirds of all crimes are solved
4. According to the UCR Program, African Americans make up about 12% of the general population, but account for about
   a. 98% of all violent crime arrests
   b. 75% of all violent crime arrests
   c. 42% of violent crime arrests
   d. 12% of all violent crime arrests
5. Crimes in the FBI's Uniform Crime Reports are grouped into two broad categories, which are
   a. Murder and rape
   b. Assault and battery
   c. Serious crimes and nonserious crimes
   d. Violent crimes and property crimes
6. The NCVS focuses on
   a. Criminals and their disordered minds
   b. Victims and their victimization
   c. The motives of criminal offenders
   d. The reasons why criminals hurt others
7. CAD, ArcGIS, and RMS all give crime and intelligence analysts the ability to
   a. Access and analyze data
   b. Solve crimes on the spot
   c. Work shorter hours
   d. Find private information about people

References

Barkan, S.E., and Bryjak, G.J. (2004). *Fundamentals of Criminal Justice*. Boston: Pearson Education.

BJS (Bureau of Justice Statistics). (2015). National Criminal Statistics Exchange. Washington, DC: BJS. Available at http://www.bjs.gov/content/ncsx.cfm.

Bohm, R.H., and Haley, K.N. (2012). *Introduction to Criminal Justice*. 7th ed. New York: McGraw-Hill.

Fagin, J.A. (2007). *Criminal Justice* (2nd ed.). Boston: Allyn and Bacon.

FBI (Federal Bureau of Investigation). (2010a). Uniform crime reports. Washington, DC: FBI. Available at http://www.fbi.gov/about-us/cjis/ucr/crime-in-the-u.s/2010/crime-in-the-u.s.-2010/tables/table-43/10tbl43a.xls.

FBI (Federal Bureau of Investigation). (2010b). Offenses cleared. Uniform crime reports. Washington, DC: FBI. Available at https://www.fbi.gov/about-us/cjis/ucr/crime-in-the-u.s/2010/crime-in-the-u.s.-2010/clearances.

FBI (Federal Bureau of Investigation). (2012). NIBRS general FAQs. Washington, DC: FBI. Available at https://www.fbi.gov/about-us/cjis/ucr/nibrs/2012/resources/frequently-asked-questions-about-nibrs-individual-agency-data/.

FBI (Federal Bureau of Investigation). (2013). *Summary Reporting System User Manual*. Washington, DC: FBI.

FBI (Federal Bureau of Investigation). (2014). Frequently asked questions about the change in the UCR definition of rape. FBI. Available at https://www.fbi.gov/about-us/cjis/ucr/recent-program-updates/new-rape-definition-frequently-asked-questions.

FBI (Federal Bureau of Investigation). (2015). Uniform crime reports. Washington, DC: FBI. Available at https://www.fbi.gov/about-us/cjis/ucr/ucr.

Huizinga, D., and Elliott, D. (1987). Juvenile offenders: Prevalence, offender incidence, and arrest rates by race. *Crime and Delinquency*, 33, 206–223.

Langton, L., and Truman, J.L. (2014). Criminal victimization. NCJ 247648. Washington, DC: Bureau of Justice Statistics. Available at http://www.bjs.gov/index.cfm?ty=pbdetail&iid=5111.

Masters, R.E., Way, L.B., Gerstenfeld, P.B., Muscat, B.T., Hooper, M., Dussich, J.P.J., Pincu, L., and Skrapec, C.A. (2013). CJ: *Realities and Challenges*. 2nd ed. New York: McGraw-Hill.

NIDA (National Institute on Drug Abuse). (2014). Monitoring the future. Rockville, MD: NIDA. Available at http://www.drugabuse.gov/related-topics/trends-statistics/infographics/monitoring-future-2013-survey-results.

President's Commission on Law Enforcement and the Administration of Justice. (1967). The challenge of crime in a free society. N. Katzenback, Chairman. Washington, DC: U.S. Government Printing Office (NCJ #000042).

Rosen, L. (1995). The creation of the Uniform Crime Report: The role of social science. *Social Science History* 19(2): 215–238. Available at http://www. jstor.org/stable/1171511.

Santos, R.B. (2013). *Crime Analysis and Crime Mapping* (3rd ed.). Thousand Oaks, CA: Sage.

Sellin, T. (1950). The Uniform Criminal Statistics Act. *Journal of Criminal Law and Criminology* 679: 679–700.

Siegel, L.J. (2002). *Criminology: The Core*. Belmont, CA: Wadsworth.

Thornberry, T.P., and Krone, M.D. (2000). The self-report method for measuring delinquency and crime. In D. Duffee, R.D. Crutchfield, S. Mastrofski, L. Mazerolle, D. McDowell, and B. Ostrom (eds.), *CJ 2000: Innovations in Measurement and Analysis*. Washington, DC: National Institute of Justice, pp. 33–83.

Truman, J. (2010). Criminal victimization, 2010. NCJ 235508. Washington, DC: Bureau of Justice Statistics. Available at http://www.bjs.gov/index. cfm?ty=pbdetail&iid=2224.

UCR Study Task Force. (1985). Blueprint for the future of the Uniform Crime Reporting Program. Washington, DC: U.S. Department of Justice. Available at www.ncjrs.gov/pdffiles1/bjs/98348.pdf.

U.S. Department of Justice. (2004). *Uniform Crime Report Handbook 2004*. FBI. Washington, DC: U.S. Government Printing Office. Available at https:// www2.fbi.gov/ucr/handbook/ucrhandbook04.pdf.

3

WHAT CAUSES PEOPLE TO COMMIT CRIMES?

Chapter Outline

1. Theories about crime causation
2. Classical theories
3. Biological theories
4. Psychological theories
5. Sociological theories
6. Is it nature or nurture?
7. Criminological theories and the crime analyst
8. Models and methods to address crime
9. Why do we still have crime?

Learning Objectives for Chapter 3

1. Better understand the major theories of crime causation
2. Gain an understanding of what criminological theories are relevant to the crime analyst
3. Learn more about the models and methods used by law enforcement to address the problem of crime
4. Address the questions related to why crime has not been eliminated

It is better to prevent crimes than to punish them. This is the fundamental principle of good legislation, which is the art of conducting men to the maximum of happiness, and to the minimum of misery, if we may apply this mathematical expression to the good and evil of life. But the means hitherto employed for that purpose are generally inadequate, or contrary to the end proposed. It is impossible to reduce the tumultuous activity of mankind to absolute regularity; for, amidst the various and opposite attractions of pleasure and pain, human laws are not sufficient entirely to prevent disorders in society.... To what a situation should we be reduced if everything were to be forbidden that might possibly lead to, a crime? We must be deprived of the use of our senses: for one motive that induces a man to commit a real crime, there are a thousand which excite him to those indifferent actions which are called crimes by bad laws. If then the probability that a crime will be committed be in proportion to the number of motives, to extend the sphere of crimes will be to increase that probability. The generality of laws are only exclusive privileges, the tribute of all to the advantages of a few.

Cesare Beccaria (1764)

The following statement refers to the process by which a particular person comes to engage in criminal behavior.

1. *Criminal behavior is learned.* Negatively, this means that criminal[ity] is not inherited, as such; also, the person who is not already trained in crime does not invent criminal behavior, just as a person does not make mechanical inventions unless he has had training in mechanics.
2. *Criminal behavior is learned in interaction with other person in a process of communication.* This communication is verbal in many respects but includes also "the communication of gestures."
3. *The principal part of the learning of criminal behavior occurs within intimate personal groups.* Negatively, this means that the interpersonal agencies of communication, such as movies and newspapers, play a relatively unimportant part in the genesis of criminal behavior.
4. When criminal behavior is learned, the learning includes (a) techniques of committing the crime, which are sometimes very complicated, sometimes very simple;

(b) the specific direction of motives, drives, rationalizations, and attitudes.

Edwin Sutherland (1960)

Control theories assume that delinquent acts result when an individual's bond to society is weak or broken. Since these theories embrace two highly complex concepts, the *bond* of the individual to *society,* it is not surprising that they have at one time or another formed the basis of explanations of most forms of aberrant or unusual behavior. It is also not surprising that control theories have described the elements of the bond to society in many ways, and that they have focused on a variety of units as the point of control.... I begin with a classification and description of the elements of the bond to conventional society. I try to show how each of these elements is related to delinquent behavior and how they are related to each other. I then turn to the question of specifying the unit to which the person is presumably more or less tied, and to the question of the adequacy of the motivational force built into the explanation of delinquent behavior.

Travis Hirschi (1969)

Theories about the Origins of Crime

If you are like most people, when you hear of a particularly horrific or brutal crime, you may ask, "How could someone do something like that?"

It's that kind of question that motivates criminologists to study the reasons why people commit crimes. But beyond that, criminal justice researchers and theorists have been trying to explain the reasons criminal violators offend in order to combat crime and develop programs to reduce or prevent crime.

Early Theories

Hundreds of years ago, philosophers and criminologists developed theories of deviant behavior based on social and religious morals.

Scientific observations were not employed, nor was there empirical research to determine why some people were deviant. When people behaved in deviant or immoral ways, it led those who were in positions of authority to theorize about the nature of good and evil.

In the Middle Ages, there seemed little differentiation between sin and crime (Fagin, 2007). If an individual was deviant, it was because he or she was evil, morally weak, or had the devil inside him or her. Given these kinds of explanations, the religiously based criminal justice system of the time took what was seen as appropriate action to deal with the morally deficient—which is why lawbreakers were frequently tortured, burned at the stake, or subjected to trial by ordeal. Trial by ordeal referred to various methods of torture that usually featured magical or superstitious ways of determining moral guilt (Siegel, 2006).

Classical Theories

Cesare Beccaria is known as the founder of classical criminology. Beccaria was an Italian nobleman and jurist who was dissatisfied with the justice system of his time. Born in 1738, Beccaria viewed the Italian justice system as using extreme punishment in a legal system in which laws were arbitrary and unfair. In his efforts to make changes, Beccaria wrote a book entitled *On Crimes and Punishment* in 1764. In this book, Beccaria explained his belief that people are rational and do things that bring them pleasure and avoid doing things that bring them pain. Furthermore, he was of the opinion that people are responsible for their actions. He advocated certain and swift punishment of appropriate intensity and duration for the offense committed. If this kind of response was used consistently, he theorized, then it would deter people from committing crimes.

The English philosopher Jeremy Bentham lived at about the same time as Beccaria. Bentham is credited with the formation of the neoclassical school of criminology. The neoclassical school of criminology is very similar to the classical school of thought in that both believe criminal offending is a matter of free will choice.

The difference between them, though, is that Bentham's view is that sometimes there are mitigating circumstances. For instance, children, according to Bentham, shouldn't be held to the same degree of accountability as an adult. Furthermore, Bentham argued that someone suffering from mental illness should be exempt from criminal liability.

In short, both the classical and neoclassical schools of criminology believed people are rational and that they make free will choices about committing crimes.

Biological Theories

Dissatisfaction with the classical approach to explain crime first appeared toward the end of the nineteenth century. At that time, crime was viewed by many as a growing problem, and it was observed by many that the harsh punishments of the time seemed to have little effect on criminal offending.

At about the same time, the emerging use of the scientific method, along with the development of social science, began to change how people viewed social problems and how problems might be solved. Charles Darwin described his theory of evolution through natural selection in his book *The Origin of Species*. Emile Durkheim noted differences in rates of suicide in different regions of France. Durkheim employed observations to develop a social theory of suicide in his book *Suicide*. Both Darwin and Durkheim were pioneers in the scientific method, which was based on observation. Rather than just thinking about problems, both believed that scientific questions were best answered when scientists first gathered facts and data.

This scientific approach gave rise to the positivist school of criminology. The positivist school saw human behavior as based on a combination of internal and external influences, such as biology, psychology, and social factors. While the classical school still saw crime as emanating from free will and choice, positivism believed it was a combination of internal and external forces that shaped behavior.

The Positivists

The early positivists, such as Cesare Lombroso, who lived from 1836 to 1909, considered biological attributes to be the real roots of crime. Lombroso took body measurements of offenders in Italian prisons and concluded that there were "born criminals." These born criminals had distinctive body measurements and skull sizes.

Positivism, following Lombroso and others, continued to be influential as it played a major role in explaining criminal behavior. But with the development of psychoanalysis in the late nineteenth century and the growth of psychology in the late nineteenth and twentieth centuries, the theories of the mind became much more prominent in offering explanations for the causes of crime.

Psychoanalysis and Psychology

While Sigmund Freud's psychoanalytic theory was used to offer explanations as to why some people might commit crimes, biological theories became much more refined as increasing and more sophisticated research in the areas of genetics, chromosomal abnormalities, glandular dysfunction, chemical imbalances, and nutritional deficiencies helped offer other biological theories.

In general, all psychological explanations look inside the human mind for the causes of criminal offending. The oldest and perhaps one of the most influential theories was Freud's psychoanalytic theory. Although Freud did not set out to explain criminal behavior, some of his followers offered explanations based on psychoanalytic theories.

Basically, psychoanalytic theory views behavior as resulting from the interactions of the three components of personality: the id, the ego, and the superego. Freud saw the id as the instinctual, primitive part of the personality. The ego was that part that mediated between the self-centered desires of the id and the learned values of the superego. The superego acts as a person's conscience, but develops from the values an individual learns early in life. When there is a faulty ego or superego, then these two parts of the personality fail to control the id. This results in personality imbalances, and the result is likely to be deviant behavior.

Although psychoanalysis was influential in the early part of the twentieth century, it gave way to other psychologically based theories.

Other Psychological Theories

Psychological theories about the causes of crime go back to the nineteenth century. In addition to Freud's psychoanalytic theory, Charles Goring studied the mental characteristics of English convicts. By studying more than 3000 convicts, he found that there was a relationship between crime and a condition he called defective intelligence, which included such traits as feeblemindedness, epilepsy, and insanity.

Other psychoanalysts who followed Freud or studied with him were seemingly more interested in criminal behavior than was Freud. August Aichhorn, for instance, examined many delinquent youth and concluded that social stress alone could not account for delinquent or criminal behavior. Aichhorn said there had to be a predisposition for antisocial acts (Siegel, 2006). Such predisposition, according to Aichhorn, included impulsivity, a tendency to consider one's own needs more important than others' needs, and a lack of guilt.

More recently, psychologists have linked criminal behavior to a psychological condition called disruptive behavior disorder (Siegel, 2006). Children and teens can experience either of two forms of disruptive behavior disorder. One is oppositional defiant disorder, in which young people show an ongoing pattern of uncooperative, defiant, and hostile behavior toward authority figures. Adolescents with oppositional defiant disorder may frequently lose their temper, argue with adults, be easily frustrated and moody, and abuse drugs as a form of self-medication (Siegel, 2006).

The other form of disruptive behavior disorder is conduct disorder, which is a much more serious behavioral and emotional disorder. Young people who are diagnosed as having a conduct disorder have difficulty following rules and are usually viewed as being antisocial. They may be involved in such behaviors as fighting, bullying others, committing sexual assaults, robbery, and cruelty to animals. Although it is not precisely known what causes conduct disorders, research has implicated brain dysfunction, neurotransmitter (the chemicals that send messages in the brain) irregularities, and genetics (Siegel and Welsh, 2009).

There has been growing research in recent years to show that there is a link between mental illness and criminal behavior. That is, when people have such serious mental illness as schizophrenia, bipolar disorder, and severe depression, there appears to be an increased risk for serious, violent crimes. Studies in recent years have found a positive relationship between psychotic disorders and criminal violence (Siegel, 2006).

Other psychologists developed a cognitive theory of crime hypothesized that criminal offending results from habits of thought and interpretations of reality. More recent refinements of cognitive theory suggest that criminals interpret situations differently than noncriminals. For example, criminal offenders might tend to view situations in more hostile ways and then are most likely to respond with aggressive behavior.

Reacting against psychoanalytic and dynamic psychological explanations were psychologists and psychiatrists such as Samuel Yochelson and Stanton Samenow, who rejected the idea that criminal behavior was a symptom of buried conflicts. Yochelson and Samenow theorized that criminals choose to commit crimes and that the cause is the way they think. All criminals are alike, Yochelson and Samenow concluded, in how they think; they think in distorted and twisted ways. Punishment, however, will not cure distorted and criminal thinking. They must be taught to think differently (Samenow, 1984).

Sociological Explanations

Sociological explanations of crime look at criminal behaviors as emanating from environmental influences. Early and influential sociological theories were proposed beginning in the 1930s. For example, Edwin Sutherland suggested that delinquent behavior is learned in much the same way that people learn other things—by observation, role modeling, and reinforcement.

Sutherland called his learning process theory differential association, and he proposed that an individual becomes a criminal by associating with people who condone violation of the law. In effect, criminal attitudes are learned from others (Cole and Smith, 2007).

While Sutherland's differential association was an early sociological explanation of crime, there are several others, including the following:

- Blocked opportunity: Criminal behavior results from lack of access to legitimate means for achieving goals.
- Labeling theory: When society reacts negatively toward an individual or labels him or her, the person acquires a negative self-image and acts accordingly.

- Social bonding: If an individual has weak bonds to society, then that person is less likely to respect the customary social rules or laws.
- Social strain: These theories focus on social disorganization, anomie (a state of normlessness in society), and subcultures that focus on negative social structure and relationships. Developed most completely by Robert Agnew, it is believed that in some individuals, crime may provide an effective short-term solution to strain (Siegel, 2006).
- Subculture theories: These theories focus on an identifiable segment or group characterized by specific patterns of behavior. These identifiable segments could include gangs and some lower social class neighborhoods.
- Conflict theories: These views of the causation of crime look at how powerful groups in society make the laws that confer criminal status on the least powerful members of society.
- Critical or radical criminology: The emphasis in these theories is on social class inequality and economic conditions, rather than on the characteristics of the individual criminal.
- Gender based: These theories focus on why women are not represented in crime statistics—or even in theories about crime causation. The gender-based theories support the idea that it is how the justice system responds to women's criminal offending that explains why there are fewer arrests and less incarceration of women.
- There are also social process theories within the broad category of sociological theories. These theories concern themselves with the process by which people become criminals. The social process theories include the following:
- Learning theory: While learning theory can be viewed as a psychological theory in which people learn by using other people as models, it is also a social process theory. As a social process theory, criminologists look at how individuals might become criminal by learning from the media, including—and perhaps most importantly—television. Whether the process is learning or imitation, the end result is the same: what people see on TV, in the movies, or in video games may influence how they behave (Reid, 2009).

- Control theories: In these approaches, the focus is on explaining why people obey the law. People who follow the law are said, by these theories, to do so because they respond to appropriate social controls. For instance, Travis Hirschi's control theory emphasizes social bonds. The basic concept of control theory is the individual's bonds to the family and other social institutions.

Finally, there are a number of so-called integrated theories. These theories of the causation of crime attempt to explain delinquent and criminal behavior from several points of view. The integrated approaches try to combine various schools of thought regarding crime causation to explain criminal offending. The major integrated theories are the following:

- Developmental and life course theories: These approaches take the position that age-related variables explain the changes in delinquent and criminal behavior best. The life course approach is based on the premise that development is an ongoing process that unfolds over the entire life span.
- Age-graded theory: Sampson and Laub developed a theory that contends that people are inhibited from offending by their social bonds to the age-graded institutions (such as school, work, and marriage) at various stages of their lives (Siegel and Welsh, 2009).
- General theory: Robert Agnew contributed a general theory (in addition to his strain theory) that argues that such factors as personality traits, types of social support, and peer relationships must all be taken into account to determine why people offend. In addition, Gottfredson and Hirschi proposed a general theory of crime that suggests that it is a lack of self-control caused by inadequate child-rearing practices by parents, along with various in-born traits, that leads to impulsiveness and risk-taking behavior (Siegel and Welsh, 2009).

Is It Nature or Nurture?

The survey of the leading explanations of criminal offending does not really address the central question related to nature versus nurture: Are criminals born or made?

Some biological explanations—especially those that show that genetics seem to play a critical role in some criminal offending—make a strong argument for a *nature* explanation of crime. Some research, for instance, shows that a strong indicator of a person's tendency to commit crimes is related to the criminal behavior of fathers, thus suggesting that criminals are born (Siegel and Welsh, 2009).

On the other hand, various sociological explanations showing that poverty, social organization, and social environment are related to criminal behavior make an equally strong case for a *nurture* explanation of crime (Masters et al., 2013).

Although it may be fun to debate the nature versus nurture question, the bottom line is that there is as of yet no clear and convincing research for either side. The best answer that can be proposed at this time is that both biological and inherited traits and psychological traits and social influences play important roles in explaining criminal offending. It is still too early to say that we can predict with any great certainty which young children will and which young children will not grow up to be future criminals.

Which Theory or Theories Work Best for the Crime Analyst?

When comparing the number of different criminological theories, it is clear that no one theory is a perfect explanation of the causes of crime. However, from the point of view of the crime analyst, a more important question needs to be asked: Which theory or theories help to understand the criminal offender's motivation? And a follow-up question that needs to be asked is this: Can an offender's pattern of behavior be identified?

In crime analysis, pattern recognition is a critical skill set needed for the crime and intelligence analyst to be able to deduce the distinct pattern or method of operation. There are, perhaps, three theories that provide the greatest utility for the crime analyst.

1. *Rational choice theory*: In the latter half of the twentieth century, there were criminologists busily constructing alternative theories to the classical theory or the neoclassical theory of crime. The major problem with the classical theory was

that this theory held all people equally responsible for their criminal behavior. People—the classical school of thought contended—were all rational, intelligent beings who exercised free will. Yet, this rigid theory failed to take into account what we all know for a fact: people are different. Some people are less intelligent, less rational, and sometimes even severely mentally ill.

This, of course, is why the neoclassical school had an alternative theory. That was that while they agreed that people were rational and made their free will decisions, there were some individuals who committed crimes because of factors beyond their control. Age, mental illness, and other factors could influence the choices people make and affect a person's ability to form criminal intent, or *mens rea*.

One alternative was Ronald Clarke and Derek Cornish's rational choice theory. They argued that delinquents and adult criminal offenders are rational people who make calculated choices about what they are going to do before they act. Clarke and Cornish contend that offenders collect, process, and evaluate information about the crime and make a decision whether to commit it after they weigh the costs and benefits of doing so. Offenders, for instance, will decide where to commit their crime, who or what to target, and how to carry it out. This theory, in fact, has been confirmed through research with criminal offenders. Many offenders do study the potential targets and pick their crime target after considering the alternative targets. Gang violence and drug world violence is not necessarily random, but is often based on choices made to further some goal, such as to enhance prestige, make a big score, or reduce direct competition.

2. *Routine activities theory*: Lawrence Cohen and Marcus Felson advanced a theory that is somewhat similar to that put forward by Clarke and Cornish. The routine activities theory examines the crime target, but they argue that three elements must converge before a crime will be committed:
   a. Motivated offenders
   b. Suitable targets

c. An absence of people—referred to as guardians by Cohen and Felson—who might deter the would-be offender

This theory suggests that a motivated offender is a person who is inclined or easily tempted to commit a crime. However, there must be a suitable target (e.g., a window to a house left unlocked or a car without locked doors or an alarm system), and there must be an absence of guardians (e.g., police in the area, a security guard, a security camera, or citizens paying attention). In other words, the importance and relevance of this theory is that it says that situational factors and free will are relevant—and maybe crucial—to the commission of a crime.

3. *Criminal personality theory*: One theory that has been controversial is that proposed by psychologists Stanton Samenow and Samuel Yochelson. They have advanced the theory that criminals, not the environment, cause crime, and that there are patterns of thinking common to all hard-core criminals regardless of their background (Reid, 2009).

According to Samenow and Yochelson, the family has no particular effect on criminals. Instead, people who grow up to be criminals begin at an early age to engage in self-destructive patterns of antisocial behavior. Furthermore, these individuals engage in thinking errors, which are typical for most people at some times, but in the offender are taken to extremes. For example, offenders may make assumptions like the rest of us, but they act on their assumptions and may even assault or kill someone based on their assumptions. Samenow contends that criminals build themselves up at the expense of others, and that they view human relationships as avenues for conquest and triumph. They employ any possible means to achieve their own ends, including deception, intimidation, and brute force. Furthermore, they do not consider the impact of their behavior on others.

What Use Does the Tactical Crime Analyst Have for Criminological Theories?

Obviously, if the tactical crime analyst is working in a real-time crime center and a crisis arises, say with the example we used in

Chapter 2 of the gunman who is shooting at passing cars on a freeway or, in another scenario, a bank robbery gone wrong in which a would-be bank robber is trapped in a bank with one or more hostages, it perhaps doesn't really matter what criminological theory the crime analyst in the real-time crime center subscribes to. His or her job is not to come up with the motivation behind why a gunman is shooting at cars or why a man tried to rob a bank. The task he is presented with is to get facts and intelligence to the officers on the scene so that the gunman can be apprehended without any passing motorists being victimized, or so that the hostage crisis is resolved with no harm to the hostages in the bank or the officers surrounding the bank.

However, it would behoove crime and intelligence analysts to gain a thorough understanding of how and why crime and disorder occur if they are to be involved in the process of intervention and prevention. In fulfilling their role in assisting law enforcement through the analysis of crime and disorder problems, there will be times when a familiarity with criminological theories will be important in addressing a particular crime problem. We suggest that analyzing the reasons why a particular criminal is engaging in a series of offenses may be vital in contributing to law enforcement efforts to solve a crime problem or apprehend an offender.

In the next sections, we review several police strategies created as intervention and prevention efforts to directly address the crime problem. These models and methods can be part of the general knowledge of crime analysts in carrying out their various functions.

The predominant models and methods to address crime problem issues are

- The standard model
- Community policing
- Broken windows
- Problem-oriented policing
- Intelligence-led policing

Crime and intelligence analysis, including real-time tactical analysis, plays a crucial role in several methods of policing that are intended to address the issues of crime and why it continues to occur. A more detailed discussion of these five models and methods follow.

The Standard Model

In terms of the general public's perception of how law enforcement goes about their business within a community, the standard model offers the closest description of that perception. As is painted on the sides of most marked police cars in America, "To serve and to protect" is the general mission statement that all—or nearly all—of American law enforcement agencies have adopted.

The ideology best associated with this mantra can be found within the "reactive, incident-driven standard model of policing" (National Research Council, 2004; Weisburd and Eck, 2004). In the standard model, law enforcement provides services, primarily based on 911 calls, and then investigates those calls for service as they are dispatched. Therefore, the standard model is a reactive form of policing.

From the analysts' perspective, success is measured through a variety of statistical conclusions, such as analyzing the response times of the calls for service and tallying the number of arrests made during the total number of incidents dispatched and investigated. These conclusions are then used to justify managerial decisions, for instance, determining when to increase the uniform presence to areas prone to a higher volume of crime or determining strategy to identify factors needed to aid in crime solvability. More importantly, these statistical conclusions help in identifying the underlying motivations involved in why individuals continue to commit crime.

Community Policing

When law enforcement includes the input of the community when creating strategies to combat crime problems and related social issues, they are acting within the framework that supports community policing. The ideology central to the success of community policing is based on the notion that "reinvigorating communities is essential if we are to deter crime and create more vital neighborhoods" (Bureau of Justice Assistance, 1994, p. 1).

In order to proactively work to prevent crime and the problems associated with social discord, community policing relies heavily on a symbiotic relationship between law enforcement and its community partners. For this relationship to thrive, it is imperative to have a steady flow of information, combined with regular meetings and personal interactions, between the two parties in order to properly address issues related to crime and disorder.

From the analysts' perspective, specific issues identified and raised by community leaders can help in the analytical exploration of why these issues are occurring and help to assist law enforcement with analysis and conclusions that can be used to better understand the crime-related issues that have affected the community as a whole.

Broken Windows Policing

One school of thought among those who study crime as a behavioral science is that if the area in which one lives is left to deteriorate, then the inhabitants of that area will thrive on criminal behavior as a means of survival and control. This generalization can be used to support the theory of broken windows. The concept of broken windows was first explained by James Q. Wilson and George Kelling (1982). In their original article, they wrote that the police should focus their efforts on targeting specific criminal behavior that leads to the deterioration of the geographical area in question. The intent of the police removing or covering up graffiti, fixing (or making sure they are fixed) broken windows in buildings, and discouraging panhandlers and prostitutes from freely loitering on streets is to prevent more serious crime from happening (Wilson and Kelling, 1982).

From an analytical perspective, mapping hot spot areas of specific types of crimes, such as prostitution, street corner vices, and narcotics activity, can help to identify significant temporal and spatial factors. Once these factors are identified and analyzed and the data are disseminated to law enforcement, they can be used to support tactical planning that is intended to target those specific areas while addressing those specific crimes.

Problem-Oriented Policing

While the factors surrounding the basis of the three forms of policing just discussed focused primarily on attention to a wide range of issues associated with crime and criminal behavior, problem-oriented policing shifts its focus to the identification of a specific issue that directly leads to crime. The idea is that the police take a proactive role in identifying, understanding, and responding to problems, not just incidents (Goldstein, 2001).

Problem-oriented policing relies on the scanning, analysis, response, and assessment (SARA) model approach, as discussed in Chapter 1, to derive strategies for best responding to the problem behavior.

From the analysts' perspective, by using SARA as a means of a long-term analytical assessment to a specific problem, the cause of the problem can be identified, examined, and addressed over a period of time. Problem-oriented policing methods lead to discovering new and more effective strategies for dealing with crime problems. It places a high value on new responses that are preventive in nature, that are not dependent on the use of the criminal justice system, and that engage other public agencies, the community, and the private sector when their involvement has the potential for significantly contributing to the reduction of the problem. The main idea is to support building a body of knowledge that supports the further professionalization of the police while directing attention to the central issue(s) that created the problem. Analysis can aid in the development of a strategic plan that may be used to address, and eventually resolve, the main issue and aid in preemptive enforcement intended to reduce further incidents stemming from the original problem.

Intelligence-Led Policing

As we go into more detail later in this book, you will see that while crime analysis is a valuable tool in the day-to-day "statistical" mindset of law enforcement, intelligence supplies the data from which analysis is drawn. From the perspective of real-time tactical analysts, data mining from multiple intelligence sources is the main task in obtaining data and intelligence. As you may have already gathered, throughout this book the words *data* and *intelligence* will carry the same meaning and be virtually interchangeable. Technically, the word *intelligence*, when used as a noun in military or government work, has traditionally referred to information gained from the enemy. However, in this book and writing from the perspective of the crime analyst, the word *intelligence* will refer to information (data) that is gathered to advance the work of the analyst.

With this out of the way, intelligence-led policing relies heavily on the gathering, sharing, assessment, and dissemination of information (intelligence) used to aid in strategic planning and proactive enforcement measures.

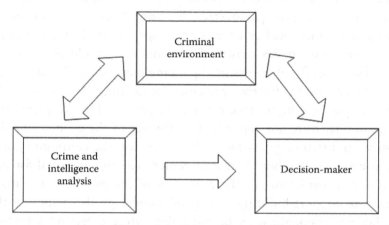

Intelligence-led policing analytical process

While intelligence-led policing incorporates many of the ideologies found with other methods of policing, such as community policing and problem-oriented policing, it walks a fine constitutional line with how it collects and disseminates intelligence (Guidetti and Martinelli, 2009). The implementation of intelligence-led policing is meant to anticipate crime trends and proactively create prevention strategies while at the same time respecting citizens' privacy rights. According to Guidetti and Martinelli (2009, p. 1), intelligence-led policing is a conceptual framework of conducting policing as "a business model and an information-organizing process that allows police agencies to better understand their crime problems and take measure of the resources available to be able to decide on an enforcement tactic or prevention strategy best designed to control crime."

From the crime analyst's perspective, the intelligence gathered should be deemed sound and reliable, and it should be used to develop strategies intended to address specific problems.

Modus Operandi of the Criminal Offender

You learned above that the standard model of policing is a reactive type of policing based on criminal incidents reported to law enforcement. That means that the police investigate crimes when they are reported. Often, the investigation may center on the victim and how that person became a victim.

The victim precipitation theory is based on the premise that "the person who gets hurt significantly contributes to the outbreak of violence" (Karmen, 2001, p. 104). Therefore, it is assumed that victims, either directly or indirectly, contribute to their own victimization by placing themselves at some level of risk. "Different types of offenders target different types of victims; therefore, determining the level of risk the victim engaged in helps us gain an understanding of the unidentified offender" (Schlesinger, 2009, p. 76).

Identifying the circumstances of how the victim came to be involved in a crime helps to better understand the modus operandi (MO) of the perpetrator of the crime. The MO of a criminal offender refers to that person's method of operation, his or her style or patterns. From the crime analyst's perspective, it is important in many crimes to identify the MO of *both* the offender and the victim. The MO of some criminals is to gain a knowledge of the daily routines of their victims.

Victims who place themselves in vulnerable or precarious situations may be more susceptible to becoming victimized. A young woman, for example, who chooses to walk to her car alone in the early morning hours, after the bar closes, may easily fall prey to a criminal whose MO is to stalk the bar district in hopes of finding such a victim.

MOs can range from a burglar always choosing to break into their target locations from a rooftop to a robber choosing a knife as his favorite weapon during an armed robbery. The MO can represent a comfort zone that helps the offender feel safe when committing his or her criminal act.

To the crime analyst, an MO is an investigative indicator that can be identified, mapped, analyzed, and assessed when there is a crime pattern, or crime spree. But identifying the MOs of both the criminal and his or her victims may be used in determining what type of tactical preparations need to be implemented in order to identify or predict the crime pattern—if not the actual individual.

Why Do We Still Have Crime?

After several hundred years of the development of different crime theories and various models of policing, we may well ask this question: Why does crime continue?

We learned in Chapter 2 that crime has been steadily decreasing for more than 20 years and continues to set records for lows in both violent and property crime. But, of course, we haven't eliminated either violent crime or property crime. And we may even speculate as to whether it is, indeed, possible to rid our society (or any society) of crime altogether. This may be as much a philosophical or religious question as it is a criminal justice question. Nonetheless, it should be related to questions that we are constantly asking: Can we reduce crime to negligible levels? What role should law enforcement play in attempts to continue to reduce crime? Can the technology used in intelligence analysis and tactical crime analysis produce even greater reductions in crime?

It is tempting to resign ourselves to saying that crime is part of human nature, and as long as we produce rational, thinking, often-flawed human beings, we will always need law enforcement and ongoing efforts to keep crime at a minimum. None of the theories we discussed promised that crime could be completely eliminated. Perhaps it should be the goal of our criminal justice system to strive to do away with criminal offending.

In covering the many theories of the causes of crime in this chapter, we have run the risk of confusing students even more about the reasons why people violate the law. But that is the nature of both criminal justice's and humankind's attempt to better understand both normal and deviant behavior. It would be wonderful if there was one theory that explained criminal offending so that we knew who would commit a crime beforehand. At this stage in the ever-evolving state of criminal justice, that is just not possible. However, we did suggest three criminological theories in this chapter as being most relevant for intelligence and tactical crime analysts: (1) rational choice theory, (2) routine activities theory, and (3) criminal personality theory. Learning more about these theories and keeping them in mind whenever you are trying to understand criminal offending—in either general or specific instances—should serve you well.

Also, in this chapter we covered five methods or models of policing that seem most prominent among police departments. They may also help to explain how and why crime has been decreasing. We are not saying that any one or all five of these police methods are responsible for crime reductions, but they could be related. Again, we strongly encourage you to get to know these policing models in detail so that they can contribute to your analysis of intelligence, statistics, and criminal problems.

In Chapter 4, we will step away for a few chapters from statistics and analysis to give you some history of the development of policing. We will then be able to put the pieces of our puzzle together in future chapters as we connect crime statistics, criminological theories, policing, models of policing, and intelligence and tactical crime analysis. Ultimately, we will describe how everything comes to together to help you see the big picture of how analysis and policing intersect to help prevent crime as well as solve crime problems.

Questions for Discussion

1. Since 1994, crime in the United States has been steadily decreasing. What are some of the likely reasons for this great crime decline?
2. What criminological theories make the most sense to you?

Important Terms

Classical theory: Basic theory of criminology that believes that people have free will and make rational decisions about committing crime.

Criminal personality: This theory suggests that criminal offenders perceive the world in a way that leads them to criminal behavior.

Criminological theory: Theory that attempts to explain why people commit crimes.

Intelligence: Data or information gathered related to criminal activities or problems.

Modus operandi: Criminal offender's method of operation, style, or patterns.

The positivists: The early positivists, such as Cesare Lombroso, considered biological attributes to be the real roots of crime.

Psychoanalysis: Set of psychological and psychotherapeutic theories that believe that an individual's behavior is in part determined by early childhood experiences.

Routine activities theory: Theory of crime causation that explains that crime is dependent on the situation and circumstances.

Trait theories: Trait theories subscribe to the belief that certain inborn or enduring traits influence behavior.

Study Guide Questions

For questions 1–5, indicate whether the statement is true or false.

1. _____ Cesare Beccaria is known as the founder of classical criminology.
2. _____ The early positivists, such as Cesare Lombroso, who lived from 1836 to 1909, considered biological attributes to be the real roots of crime.
3. _____ In general, all psychological explanations look inside the human mind for the causes of criminal offending.
4. _____ More recently, psychologists have linked criminal behavior to a psychological condition called disruptive behavior disorder
5. _____ Sociological explanations of crime look at criminal behaviors as emanating from environmental influences.
6. There has been growing research in recent years to show that there is a link between
   a. Mental illness and criminal behavior
   b. Poor hygiene and criminal behavior
   c. Lack of motivation and criminal offending
   d. Sloth and criminal behavior
7. Edwin Sutherland suggested that delinquent behavior is
   a. Inborn and not learned later in life
   b. Learned in much the same way that people learn other things
   c. All about exposure to the media
   d. Related to inadequate parenting

8. Travis Hirschi's control theory emphasizes
   a. Learning and reinforcement
   b. That parents are the reason for all delinquency and crime
   c. Social bonds
   d. Children's relationships to friends
9. In the theory proposed by Ronald Clarke and Derek Cornish, delinquents and adult criminal offenders are
   a. Impulsive people who don't think
   b. Irrational individuals who never make conscious decisions
   c. People who never evaluate information
   d. Rational people who make calculated choices about what they are going to do
10. The standard model of law enforcement is a
    a. Reactive form of policing
    b. Form of policing that emphasizes fixing broken windows
    c. Style of policing related to the SARA approach
    d. Proactive form of policing

References

Bureau of Justice Assistance. (1994). *Understanding Community Policing. A Framework for Action.* Washington, DC: Bureau of Justice Response Center.

Cole, G.F., and Smith, C.E. (2007). *Criminal Justice in America* 5th ed. Belmont, CA: Wadsworth.

Fagin, J.A. (2007). *Criminal Justice: A Brief Introduction.* Boston: Allyn and Bacon.

Goldstein, H. (2001). Problem-oriented policing in a nutshell. Presented at the 2001 International Problem-Oriented Policing Conference, San Diego, December 7.

Guidetti, R., and Martinelli, T. (2009). Intelligence led policing—A strategic framework. *Police Chief Magazine.* Available at http://www.policechiefmagazine.org/magazine/index.cfm?fuseaction=display&article_id=1918&issue_id=102009.

Karmen, A. (2001). *Crime Victims: An Introduction to Victimology* 4th ed. Belmont, CA: Wadsworth.

Masters, R.E., Way, L.B., Gerstenfeld, P.B., Muscat, B.T., Hooper, M., Dussich, J.P.J., Pincu, L., and Skrapec, C.A. (2013). *CJ: Realities and Challenges.* 2nd ed. New York: McGraw-Hill.

National Research Council. (2004). Effectiveness of police activity in reducing crime, disorder and fear. In W. Skogan and K. Frydl (eds.), *Fairness and Effectiveness in Policing: The Evidence.* Washington, DC: National Academies Press, pp. 217–251.

Reid, S. T. (2009). *Crime and Criminology.* 12th ed. New York: Oxford University Press.

Samenow, S.E. (1984). *Inside the Criminal Mind.* New York: Times Books.

Schlesinger, L. (2009). Psychological profiling: Investigative implications from crime scene analysis. *Journal of Psychiatry & Law* 37(1), 73–84.

Siegel, L.J. (2006). *Criminology.* 9th ed. Belmont, CA: Thomson Wadsworth.

Siegel, L.J., and Walsh, B.C. (2009). *Juvenile Delinquency: Theory, Practice, and Law.* 10th ed. Belmont, CA: Wadsworth.

Weisburd, D., and Eck, J.E. (2004). What can the police do to reduce crime, disorder, and fear? *Annals of the American Academy of Social and Political Sciences* 593: 42–65.

Wilson, J.Q., and Kelling, G. (1982). Broken windows: The police and neighborhood safety. *Atlantic Monthly,* March. Available at http://www.theatlantic.com/magazine/archive/1982/03/broken-windows/304465/.

PART II
LAW ENFORCEMENT—
THEN AND NOW

4

THE POLICE AND LAW ENFORCEMENT—IT'S COME A LONG WAY

Chapter Outline

1. The police—the beginnings
2. Development of law enforcement in the United States
3. State and federal law enforcement
4. Role of police officers
5. Patrol function
6. Eras of police reform and change
7. New developments in policing
8. CompStat
9. Policing in the 2000s

Learning Objectives for Chapter 4

1. Become familiar with the history of policing in America
2. Understand the development of the dual policing system in the United States
3. Gain a better understanding of the functions of patrol officers
4. Develop insight into the transitions in policing during the latter half of the twentieth century
5. Become more familiar with CompStat and the first computer innovations in policing

American policing is a product of its English heritage. The British colonialists brought with them the criminal justice system of their country. This included English common law, the high value placed on individual rights, the court system, forms of punishment, and law enforcement institutions…. The English heritage contributed three enduring features to American policing. The first is a tradition of *limited police authority*. The American legal tradition seeks to protect individual liberty by limiting government authority. Continental European countries, by contrast, give their law enforcement agencies much broader powers…. The second feature inherited from England is a tradition of *local control* of law enforcement agencies. European countries, by contrast, have centralized, national police forces. Local control contributes to the third feature, a *highly decentralized* and fragmented system of law enforcement. The United States is unique in having an estimated 20,000 separate law enforcement agencies, subject only to minimal coordination and very little national control or regulation.

Samuel Walker (1992)

We want to illustrate how unbelievably basic, how absolutely fundamental, how inextricably intertwined with human development that the origin of crime analysis is. Civilization exists to promote the general welfare of its citizens, starting with ensuring their safety from each other. A society's police must carry out this most basic function, and its crime analysts are the cerebrum of this effort.

A History of Crime Analysis (2015)

Introduction

The thin blue line, as used in the colloquial sense by those in law enforcement, represents the fragile boundary that rests between those who serve in law enforcement and those who do not. It also can be viewed, by some, as a shaded veil intended to protect the world of those who are sworn to uphold the law from their many detractors.

What is significant here is that terms such as these, and the inferences that go along with their meanings, illustrate the simple fact that there is much to be learned from the law enforcement profession and, more importantly, the individuals who swear an oath to serve and protect the constitution of the United States.

From the long-ago days of 1285, when the Statute of Winchester was proposed by King Edward I of England and passed into law by royal assent, formally establishing the constable watch system of protection that provided for one man from each parish to be selected peacekeeper, to the present-day police officer, the evolution of the structure of law enforcement continues to define, and redefine, what we know about this noble, and dangerous, profession.

When most people think of the criminal justice system, they think first of the police. Law enforcement is—at least to many citizens—the face of the criminal justice system. It is the one part of the justice system most people have contact with, and it's the agency most people expect will deal with crime. In fact, very few people have dealings with prosecuting attorneys, judges, or any aspect of the correctional system. But everyone has had an encounter with a police officer—either through a request for help or by being stopped for a traffic violation.

But it is the police that Americans expect will respond to crime, and it is anticipated that the police will do their job by investigating a crime and ultimately solving that crime.

Law Enforcement Response to Crimes

In the simplest form of explanation, a crime occurs, a person is victimized, and the police are called to investigate. While it is not quite that simple, particularly as it relates to the investigative process, what is accepted in a matter-of-fact manner these days is that the police respond to reported crime.

Think of recent well-known criminal events. For instance, there was the shooting of movie theater patrons by James Holmes in Aurora, Colorado, on July 20, 2012. Twelve people were killed and 70 people injured in the shooting. Although the shooting occurred around midnight in the crowded movie theater, police officers responded to the scene within a few short minutes, and began sending victims to the hospital before emergency medical services arrived. Other officers arrested James Holmes, who was standing next to his car near the theater, within minutes of the incident.

Then, there are the financial crimes of Bernard Madoff. When a government agency—the Securities and Exchange Commission (SEC)—was alerted to possible irregularities related to Bernard Madoff's investment company, it began an investigation. When the SEC found evidence of possible criminal wrongdoing, it notified the FBI. The FBI then conducted its own investigation into Madoff and his company's financial transactions.

When the Federal Bureau of Investigation's (FBI) investigation was concluded, charges were brought before the Department of Justice, federal prosecutors levied charges, and Bernard Madoff was arrested in December 2008 and later indicted. Plea bargaining then began between the federal government and Madoff and his attorneys. Eventually, a plea deal was reached and Madoff accepted a guilty plea in 2009.

Then, there is the case of New York assembly speaker Sheldon Silver, who for more than 20 years was one of New York's most powerful and canny politicians. He was arrested in January 2015 on charges of taking nearly $4 million in payoffs and kickbacks. The 70-year-old Democratic assemblyman was taken into custody by the FBI on federal conspiracy and bribery charges that carry up to 100 years in prison and could cost him his political seat. He was released on $200,000 bail. In February 2015, he was indicted on corruption charges, but two months later he was indicted on other corruption charges that surfaced during the continuing investigation into his financial affairs. Although indicted, it may be months or years before he goes to trial.

As we can see in all three cases, when a crime has been committed, or at least alleged to have been committed, law enforcement responds. The law enforcement response will depend on the crime— whether it is a federal crime or a state crime—and where the crime occurred.

Do State or Federal Law Enforcement Officers Respond?

If the crime represents a violation of a state law, then the local police respond. We saw this in the James Holmes theater shooting case. The shootings took place in Aurora, Colorado, and local police officers from the Aurora Police Department responded and took jurisdiction of the case. However, the FBI later took charge of the investigation and the Aurora Police Department and the FBI worked together to gather evidence.

On the other hand, if the crime is a violation of a federal law, then—as we saw in the Madoff crime and in the Sheldon Silver case—the federal government responds to the crime.

Joint state and federal investigations can eventually lead to task forces being formed with the purpose of combining the investigative resources of both agencies as they work to solve pattern-related crimes. A case in point is the upstate New York retail store service desk armed robberies of 2013. As a result of more than 10 daytime armed robberies from the service desk areas of a national retail store chain, the Hobbs Act Task Force was formed in New York that year.

Investigators from local police agencies teamed with members of the FBI for the purpose of working as a task force responding to—and investigating—armed robberies that were identified to be pattern crimes. Pattern crime refers to a series of crimes that follows a certain pattern. The task force collectively worked on "solvability factors" (key elements necessary for the successful completion of a criminal investigation; usually include such factors as eye witnesses, identification of a suspect, and address of the primary suspect) and investigative leads that were developed by the task force members and the crime analyst assigned to the team.

The Hobbs Act Task Force worked to enforce a U.S. federal law named after Congressman Sam Hobbs. The Hobbs Act was enacted by the U.S. Congress in 1946 to "prohibit actual or attempted robbery or extortion affecting interstate or foreign commerce" (Office of the United States Attorneys, 2015, p. 1). The Hobbs Act specifies that when a robbery occurs at a location that deals with interstate commerce, then the charges levied against the perpetrator, once apprehended, increases the mandatory minimum federal sentence if he or she is found guilty.

In this case investigation, the crime analyst participated in task force briefings and was involved in data collection and storage, suspect and pattern identification and research, and crime mapping, as well as the issuing of all bulletins associated with the pattern crimes.

How Did Our Dual System of Policing Evolve?

When the first U.S. Congress met in 1789, it adopted a law called the U.S. Judiciary Act of 1789. This act established the U.S. federal judiciary. Along with the federal judiciary, the U.S. Marshals Service was also created by this act. This first law enforcement agency was formed to be the enforcement arm of the federal courts. However, since no other mention was made in the Constitution about law enforcement or the police, it was up to the new country to develop a system of policing.

Since America was colonized by the English, it is no surprise that early citizens of the fledgling country were people who were familiar with the systems previously developed in England. The major system developed in the new country was the constable watch system. The watch system employed in the cities and urban areas developed in the middle years of the nineteenth century.

The watch system as it developed in England's towns and villages generally meant that men—usually ordinary citizens—would be responsible for patrolling the streets watching for any kind of criminal activity. Constables, again, based on the system that had been used in England prior to the nineteenth century, were mostly supervisors of watchmen.

In America, Boston developed a watch system as early as 1634 (Bohm and Haley, 2002). Essentially, that was the predominant policing system in America for the succeeding 200 years. Citizens were expected to serve as the watch, but some of the citizens could afford to pay a watch replacement, and as a consequence, often the worst kind of men ended up protecting the community (Bohm and Haley, 2002).

Much later, particularly in rural and southern areas of the United States, the office of sheriff was established and the power of the posse was used to maintain order and apprehend offenders (Bohm and Haley, 2002). That meant that two forms of law enforcement (in addition to the U.S. Marshals, who helped bring law and order to the western frontier) began to evolve. There was the watch in villages, towns, and cities, and the sheriff in rural areas and counties. Some areas in the northern parts of the United States often had both systems.

Although England organized its London Metropolitan Police in 1829, America didn't imitate the English model for several years. The first American police department in the north was created in Boston in 1838 (Dempsey and Forst, 2010). It was in the 1840s that New York City combined its day watch and night watch to form the first paid, unified police force (Bohm and Haley, 2002). Then, in 1853, the New York state legislature created the Municipal Police Department. However, it was found to be so corrupt that it was abolished by the legislature four years later (Bohm and Haley, 2002). The legislature replaced it with the Metropolitan Police. Other big-city police departments were created later on in the 1850s and 1860s. For instance, Philadelphia combined its day and night watches in 1854 to bring about its own police department.

The First Police Departments

The duties of the first police officers in those early years were very similar to what the watchmen were doing. But after the Civil War, city police departments began to establish a unique identity as they began to wear uniforms, carry nightsticks, and arm themselves with firearms. However, it can be said that police work was primitive in the early years. Early police officers, in the nineteenth century, performed many duties they do not have today, including cleaning streets, inspecting boilers, caring for the poor and homeless, operating emergency ambulances, and performing other social services (Dempsey and Forst, 2010). Following the English tradition, police officers in the north were not issued firearms, although this changed by the 1860s.

Another form of early policing was established in what were becoming the key slave states of the south. These states were Virginia, North Carolina, and South Carolina. And the form of policing evolving in these states was the slave patrols (Oliver and Hilgenberg, 2006). Although the slave patrols actually began in the seventeenth century, they were organized to prevent slaves from escaping from their owners. As time went on, the slave patrols would develop into more formal, government-sanctioned entities as they were legislated into existence (Oliver and Hilgenberg, 2006). For example, the code of 1705 in Virginia allowed the patrols to check blacks who were not on plantation property to ensure they had appropriate documentation and were not escaped slaves.

The slave patrols were often made up of hired hands from plantations, and frequently they treated blacks with suspicion and hostility. Sometimes, blacks were mistreated, tortured, or even murdered (Oliver and Hilgenberg, 2006).

Transitional Policing

There was little change in policing from the time of the early formation of police departments in the 1850s until the 1930s. It was apparent to many that changes were needed because, according to Oliver and Hilgenberg in *A History of Crime and Criminal Justice in America* (2006), the reality of American policing was that the police were corrupt, tied into politics, and very brutal in their approach to dealing with citizens.

As the country headed into the 1920s and the grand social experiment known as Prohibition created a new series of crimes and law enforcement challenges, police departments were unable to cope with the demands brought about by the attempt to ban the manufacture, distribution, transportation, sale, or consumption of alcohol. However, the status of police officers did not make their jobs any easier. Police officers in the 1930s were generally underpaid, poorly trained, and ill equipped (Oliver and Hilgenberg, 2006). It was a low-status job often given to political cronies or brutish men without an education (Walker, 1992). In addition, corruption was rampant. Often, police officers worked with politicians who themselves worked with gangsters, and the whole system ensured that gangsters could make sure that thirsty Americans could get booze—no matter what the federal law said.

Many cities, as well as the federal government, were concerned about the rise in crime and the flourishing bootlegging business. More than 100 surveys and studies were conducted during the 1920s to study the police problem, crime, and the criminal justice system (Oliver and Hilgenberg, 2006).

The most significant of these studies was the one initiated by President Herbert Hoover in 1929. Named the National Commission on Law Observance and Enforcement, this commission was under the direction of George W. Wickersham, the U.S. attorney general. In 1931, the National Commission on Law Observance and

Enforcement, most commonly known simply as the Wickersham Commission, gave its report and recommendations. The Wickersham Commission's report concluded that Prohibition was unenforceable, but the report condemned the police and said that the police by and large were corrupt, that brutality by the police was widespread, and that police officers at all levels were ill equipped, ill trained, and ill prepared to perform the duties of law enforcement (Oliver and Hilgenberg, 2006).

Following the Wickersham Commission's report and the number of recommendations given in it (e.g., one recommendation was for more extensive training for new police recruits, as well as for officers already on the job), it might be expected that changes would be forthcoming. That was not the case, however. There was no immediate response, but over the next few decades, gradual changes would come about.

Police chiefs and police organizations, with such forward-thinking men as August Vollmer and O.W. Wilson leading the way, brought about improved standards for hiring police officers, improved education and training, and better equipment for the police (Dempsey, 1999).

Research on Policing and the Prevention of Crime

The assumption is that putting more officers on the street will lead to reduced crime. This strategy is referred to as preventive patrol. However, this assumption has been tested to see if it works. The first such research project was conducted in 1974 and was called the Kansas City Preventive Patrol Project. Conducted to test the degree to which preventive patrol affected such things as offense rates and the level of public fear, the experiment was relatively simple (Walker, 1992).

The southern part of Kansas City, Missouri, was divided into 15 areas. Five of these areas were patrolled in the usual fashion, five others featured doubled patrols, and the last five saw patrols eliminated altogether (no officers were assigned to these five areas and officers only went into those areas when they were called).

The results? Surprisingly, in the three sections of the city there were no significant differences in the rate of offending in terms of burglaries, robberies, auto thefts, larcenies, and vandalisms. Furthermore, citizens didn't seem to realize any changes in the patrol patterns, and there seemed to be no difference in citizen's fear of crime during the study (Schmalleger, 2012). This study called into question the wisdom of random preventive patrol. However, the Kansas City experiment did usher in an era of more evidence-based policing in which police practices have been put to the test to see which are effective and which are not.

Role of Police Officers Today

In the typical police department today, the job of police officers involves a wide variety of functions. But the major roles played by the police are patrol, traffic enforcement, peacekeeping and order maintenance, and investigating crimes.

In the second half of the nineteenth century, policing in big cities took on the role of providing public health services, as well as other social welfare functions. For example, in Boston, police officers often served soup to the indigent, and the homeless were housed at night in police stations (Oliver and Hilgenberg, 2006). These welfare services tended to disappear in the twentieth century, and policing began to focus more on maintaining order and enforcing the laws (Walker, 1992). As the twentieth century proceeded, certain police roles emerged. For instance, patrol officers took on a readily identifiable role in terms of their traffic functions and responding to crime scenes. However, detective divisions, established to investigate past crimes, were first formed by the second half of the nineteenth century.

In the following, Glenn Grana explains what police officers do:

> During the course of my 21-year career, when people learned that I was a police officer, they routinely asked me what it was exactly that I did. This question always seemed puzzling to me given that law enforcement was constantly being portrayed in the movies and on television. From uniform cops racing from call to call, lights and sirens ablaze, to undercover detectives infiltrating the seedy criminal underworld, the world of law enforcement never seemed to shy away from the theatrical stage. What continued to

surprise me, however, was how little the general public actually knew about law enforcement and the role of the police officer.

In the early stages of my career, I had the opportunity to serve as a field training officer (FTO), training new recruits as they just finished the classroom portion of their police academy training. During the initial meeting with the newly assigned recruit, I would hand him or her an organizational chart of our agency. An organizational chart illustrates the entire organizational structure of a police department by breaking down each tier, from top-level management to the precinct patrol level. It also highlights each specialized unit—including the detective bureau, the mounted patrol, and narcotics, to name a few.

I would explain to the recruits that they needed to gain a full understanding of the organizational structure of the agency they worked for to help them better understand the different aspects of policing that exist in order to successfully address the needs of the department and, more importantly, the community that the department served. For example, an organization as large as the New York City Police Department (NYPD) serves a population of more than 8 million people and, as such, needs to ensure it has the manpower, resources, and equipment needed to properly police a populace that large. The NYPD is in sharp contrast to a department such as the Brockport (New York) Police Department, which serves a community of approximately 8000 people with 13 full- and part-time police officers (Brockport Police Department, 2015).

With a larger demographic, such as the metropolitan New York area, specialized units are needed to address a large number of issues that result in police action, including such issues as drugs, violence, and domestic violence. That's why the NYPD has many more specialized units (narcotics squad, gang enforcement unit, SWAT, etc.) that are needed to handle special community concerns.

I always tried to emphasize, both to new recruits and to people who were simply curious about what exactly I did as a police officer, that to understand the various roles that a police officer performs, you need to understand the needs, and societal issues, emanating from the community that is being policed.

Patrol Function

Uniformed police officers do a number of very different jobs on a daily basis. Whether they are providing patrol services in a car, on horseback, or on a bicycle, the primary goals of police patrol are to deter crime, enhance feelings of public safety, and be available for public service.

In regard to making officers available for service, the response of uniformed patrol officers, who are typically the first responders when a call is received at a police station, can be important in making an arrest or helping to secure a crime scene. However, in many instances, response time has no effect on clearing a crime. But this has little to do with patrol officers themselves. Many times a crime is not detected immediately after it occurs, so response by the police may not be critical. In addition, people often delay calling the police. And, although patrol officers may be available to respond to a call, there may be administrative details that result in delays in information given to the officers on the street (Dempsey, 1999).

But, it is the police dispatcher who notifies patrol officers in the vicinity to go to the scene. When uniformed officers arrive at the crime scene, they have an important set of tasks to carry out. They must

- Secure and preserve the crime scene
- Determine if a crime, indeed, has been committed
- Identify witnesses and potential suspects
- Ask for emergency medical assistance if there is an injury
- Report back to their supervisor as to whether a crime has occurred and indicate whether detectives or crime scene technicians should be dispatched to the scene

Given this set of responsibilities, their effective and efficient handling of the crime scene can be essential, and it can even be said that is the most crucial aspect among the steps that will be taken leading to the gathering of evidence and the eventual solution of the crime (Walker, 1992).

Patrol officers play other roles in addition to being first on the scene of a crime. They have an important role in providing what Bayley (1994) calls a symbolic presence. In Bailey's view, the police—especially uniformed officers—are a symbol of police presence and validate for citizens that law enforcement is doing their job and making citizens feel safe. Whether uniformed officers are directing traffic when a traffic light has malfunctioned or when sports fans are leaving the parking areas after a football game, their mere presence helps to reassure citizens that law and order exists (Bayley, 1994).

Additionally, patrol officers serve the public in many other ways by, for instance, answering questions or coming out to a neighborhood to deal with domestic violence incidents, responding to a security alarm that has signaled a possible break-in, or dealing with a complaint of noise from a neighbor's party.

Peacekeeping and Order Maintenance

Although patrol officers and traffic patrol officers make up the bulk of policing (Fuller, 2010), the police do a great variety of other things, all of which may fall under the heading of peacekeeping and order maintenance. For example, duties in this category include

- Responding to domestic dispute situations
- Controlling crowds at various public events, such as concerts, baseball games, and parades
- Working vice as an undercover officer
- Dealing with the mentally ill
- Working with juveniles
- Responding to emergencies, such as natural disasters, terrorist attacks, and blackouts

Traffic Enforcement Functions

Local police agencies and state highway patrols are responsible for ensuring safety on the streets and highways. In some states, state police officers patrol freeways, expressways, and interstate highways, while local police patrol provide traffic enforcement services on lesser streets and roadways. The major responsibilities of highway patrol officers are to respond to traffic accidents, set up roadblocks to detect drunken drivers, and generally enforce traffic laws.

Criminal Investigations

According to the Worldwide Law Enforcement Consulting Group, a training and law enforcement consulting organization, an investigation is "an examination, a study, a survey and a research of facts and/or circumstances, situations, incidents and scenarios, either related or not, for the purpose of rendering a conclusion of proof" (Fundamentals of criminal investigation, 2015). When a police officer investigates, he or she makes a systematic inquiry, closely analyzes, and inspects while dissecting and scrutinizing information.

Later in this book, we will look at how important it is for both civilian intelligence analysts and tactical analysts to have a basic understanding of the process of criminal investigations. This can help the analyst develop an investigative mindset that can lead to better and more relevant intelligence provided to criminal investigators. For now, however, let us look at the investigative process as it relates to the police and how they investigate crimes and suspicious events.

Investigative Process

Regardless if the crime involves the theft of a bicycle from a garage or the violent murder of a woman alone in her house, the process of investigation follows the same format:

- Identification of the crime scene, victims, and witnesses
- Gathering evidence and clues as to who perpetrated the crime and what may be the possible motive
- Interviewing persons with knowledge relevant to the crime to enhance (or eliminate) solvability factors (factors related to the event that may lead to solving the case)
- Following up on any forensic leads
- Identification, apprehension, interview, and arrest of suspect(s)

The Investigator

A well-trained investigator should be able to follow up, and expand upon, this process regardless of the complexities of the investigation in question. And while the skill set needed to effectively investigate crime can be learned through training, and repetition, an investigator must also be able to objectively consider all scenarios that present themselves during the course of the investigation.

Remaining objective during the investigative process can aid an investigator when assessing the facts presented to him or her, thus enabling the consideration of all possible scenarios. Understanding the reasoning for why the criminal may have committed the crime can help the investigator to better understand the suspect's thought process. Gaining a better understand of the suspect's thought process can help when evaluating the facts relevant to the investigation.

These same traits hold true for skilled intelligence and tactical analysts as they research and reason their way through the intelligence analysis process while assisting in the investigative work.

Eras of Police Reform Leading to Change

During the first 15 to 20 years of the twentieth century, there were attempts to reform the police, although these attempts were not very successful. But at the same time, the use of technology by police departments—the use of bicycles, cars, and radios, for instance—enabled the police to respond more quickly to emergencies.

Throughout the 1930s, 1940s, and 1950s, there was increasing professionalism of the police. However, the 1960s and 1970s were times of great tension and change, creating a very turbulent time for police departments in the United States. Civil rights disturbances, antiwar demonstrations, campus disorders, and urban riots all taxed police departments across America. But by the 1980s and 1990s, the turbulence of those two decades gave way to a more peaceful era. Although the police were grappling with new issues, such as terrorism, school shootings, and bombings, it was a time that ushered in several positive developments.

Among the new developments of the 1990s was the introduction of the computer revolution in policing, involving new ways of looking at and dealing with communications, record keeping, fingerprinting, and criminal investigations. Other positive developments that began during the 1990s were a sudden reduction in crime and the birth of two new major concepts in police work: community policing and problem-oriented policing. Although no one can say for sure, it may be that all of these new developments had an impact on what Franklin Zimring called the "great American crime decline" (Zimring, 2008).

New York City has shown some of the most dramatic reductions in crime of all major cities in the United States. One explanation for the crime decline in New York City that is often cited by city officials and police administrators there is aggressive police tactics like those introduced by the city's former commissioner William J. Bratton (Dempsey and Forst, 2010). Bratton completely reengineered the NYPD to make reducing crime its primary objective (Silverman, 1996). The primary idea behind Bratton's reengineering was a process known as CompStat.

CompStat

CompStat is the name of a specific program implemented by the NYPD in 1994 (Silverman, 2006). Silverman (2006, p. 267) has described it "as perhaps the most important organizational innovation in policing during the latter half of the 20th century."

The name *CompStat* comes from a computer file called comparative statistics. Central to the program are weekly crime strategy sessions conducted at police headquarters. At these weekly meetings, computer-generated maps are used to provide a wide variety of crime details. Precinct commanders are held responsible for any increases in crime and must present innovative solutions to manage their precincts' crime problems (Dempsey and Forst, 2010). In discussions about what the computer maps indicate about crime problems, crime fighting techniques are developed for implementation.

There is a four-step process that is the essence of CompStat:

1. Timely and accurate intelligence
2. Use of effective tactics in response to that intelligence
3. Rapid deployment of personnel and resources
4. Relentless follow-up and assessment (Dempsey and Forst, 2010)

What CompStat allows the NYPD and other police departments who have also adopted the use of CompStat to do is to pinpoint and analyze crime patterns almost instantly, respond in the most appropriate manner, quickly shift personnel and other resources as needed, assess the impact and viability of anticrime strategies, identify bright, up-and-coming individuals from within the ranks of the police department, and transform the organization more fluidly and more effectively (Dodenhoff, 1996).

Policing in the 2000s

As America and the rest of the world entered the new millennium, further advances in technology helped police departments go beyond CompStat and develop new and unique ways to analyze crime and use information and intelligence in smarter ways. Although police agencies are still plagued by some of the same old problems—such as brutality, racism, and corruption—new approaches to fighting crime have changed how some police departments are managing crime problems.

Those technological changes in criminal investigations are discussed Chapter 5.

Questions for Discussion

1. Would the United States be better off if it had a less fragmented and more centralized system of policing?
2. In what ways are patrol officers more important than detectives?

Important Terms

CompStat: Program and a process that involves analyzing information and intelligence to better combat crime problems.

Kansas City Preventive Patrol Project: Research project conducted in Kansas City in 1974 to determine if police presence in the form of patrol officers had an effect on crime rates. It was found that the presence—or absence—of patrol officers had almost no effect on crime rates.

National Commission on Law Observance and Enforcement: Commission, also known as the Wickersham Commission, appointed by President Herbert Hoover in 1929 to study crime in the United States.

Patrol officers: Uniformed police officers who perform a variety of functions, including responding first to calls to the police department and handling traffic duties.

Slave patrols: Organized groups of men who captured escaped slaves from Southern states.

Watch system: Ordinary citizens responsible for patrolling the streets to watch out for fires or crime.

Study Guide Questions

For questions 1–5, indicate whether the statement is true or false.

1. _____ The oldest law enforcement agency in the United States is the FBI.
2. _____ Federal law enforcement officers are involved when a federal law is violated.
3. _____ The London Metropolitan Police was established in 1829.
4. _____ The conclusion of the National Commission on Law Observance and Enforcement was that Prohibition was enforceable.
5. _____ Patrol officers are typically first responders when a call comes into the police station.
6. Slave patrols were organized in the south in the United States to
   a. Defeat the Ku Klux Klan
   b. Protect slaves from abuse
   c. Prevent slaves from escaping from their owners
   d. Investigate crimes on plantations
7. The Wickersham Commission was the more informal name for
   a. The International Association of Chiefs of Police
   b. The National Commission on Law Observance and Enforcement
   c. The Knapp Commission
   d. None of the above
8. The outcome of the Kansas City Preventive Patrol Project was that
   a. Crime went up in areas with decreased patrol officers
   b. Citizens realized that there were fewer officers in some areas

    c. There were no differences in the role officers in most crime categories

    d. Citizens' fear of crime went up

9. Patrol officers do various tasks, including

    a. Solving crimes

    b. Investigating police corruption

    c. Performing forensic work and detecting crime

    d. Responding to domestic disputes and emergencies, and controlling crowds

10. CompStat was an important development in the 1990s because it

    a. Created stress for precinct commanders

    b. Allowed police departments to pinpoint and analyze crime patterns

    c. Led to an increase in crime

    d. Slowed down the use of police personnel

References

Bayley, D.H. (1994). *Police for the Future.* New York: Oxford University Press.

Bohm, R.H., and Haley, K.N. (2002). *Introduction to Criminal Justice.* 3rd ed. New York: Glencoe/McGraw-Hill.

Brockport Police Department. (2015). Brockport Police Department. Available at http://brockportpolice.org/.

Dempsey, J.S. (1999). *An Introduction to Policing.* 2nd ed. Belmont, CA: Wadsworth Publishing.

Dempsey, J.S., and Forst, L.S. (2010). *An Introduction to Policing.* 5th ed. Clifton Park, NY: Delmar.

Dodenhoff, P.C. (1996). LEN salutes its 1996 People of the Year, the NYPD and its Compstat process: A total re-engineering and strategy-making that has transformed the nation's largest police force – as it will law enforcement in general. *Law Enforcement News*, December 31, 1–4. Available at https://www.lib.jjay.cuny.edu/len/96/31dec/html/feature.html.

Fuller, J.R. (2010). *Criminal Justice: Mainstream and Crosscurrents.* 2nd ed. Upper Saddle River, NJ: Prentice Hall.

Fundamentals of criminal investigations. (2015). Clifton Park, NY: Worldwide Law Enforcement Consulting Group. Available at www.worldwidelawenforcement.com.

A history of crime analysis. (2015). Lowell: University of Massachusetts Lowell. Available at http://faculty.uml.edu/jbyrne/44.203/MACA-historyofcrimeanalysis.pdf.

Office of the United States Attorneys. (2015). Hobbs Act—Under color of official right. Washington, DC: Office of the United States Attorneys. Available at http://www.justice.gov/usam/criminal-resource-manual-2404-hobbs-act-under-color-official-right (accessed September 30, 2015).

Oliver, W.M., and Hilgenberg, J.F. (2006). *A History of Crime and Criminal Justice in America*. Boston: Allyn and Bacon.

Schmalleger, F. (2012). *Criminal Justice: A Brief Introduction*. 9th ed. Upper Saddle River, NJ: Prentice Hall.

Silverman, E.B. (1996). Mapping change: How the New York City Police department reengineered itself to drive down crime. *Law Enforcement News*, December 15, 1–6. Available at https://www.lib.jjay.cuny.edu/len/96/15dec/html/12.html.

Walker, S. (1992). *The Police in America: An Introduction*. 2nd ed. New York: McGraw-Hill.

Zimring, F. (2008). *The Great American Crime Decline*. New York: Oxford University Press.

5

POLICE INVESTIGATIONS IN THE TWENTY-FIRST CENTURY

Chapter Outline

1. Criminal investigations
2. Development of the detective in America
3. Collecting evidence for use in court
4. Procedural law
5. Rule of law in collecting evidence
6. Search and seizure
7. Search warrants
8. Warrantless searches
9. Interrogation and the Fifth Amendment
10. The crime analyst and the criminal investigator

Learning Objectives for Chapter 5

1. Understand the primary role of the police investigator
2. Become familiar with the rule of law in collecting evidence of a crime
3. Be conversant with the rules regarding search and seizure
4. Gain a better understanding of when a warrantless search may be conducted
5. Know the rules of interrogation of suspects
6. Begin to appreciate the association between investigation and intelligence

Police patrols may be the primary crime control tactic of law enforcement. However, the second major tactic is investigation of reported crimes by detectives. While police patrols have been around since the beginning of police departments in America, the detective specialist in policing is of more recent vintage. Not until around the beginning of the twentieth century did municipal police departments create the position of detective (Kuykendall and Roberg, 1982).

A number of factors converged near the end of the nineteenth century to bring about a demand for public police investigations of crime and criminals. Prior to that, citizens could hire private detectives—like those that worked for the Pinkerton detective agency. As the nineteenth century morphed into the twentieth century, fewer private citizens were able or willing to hire private detectives to find and recover stolen property (Langworthy and Travis, 1999). In addition, there was the public perception of a rising crime rate and the ineffectiveness of patrol officers in identifying and apprehending offenders. It might be said that the Keystone Kops—bumbling and incompetent police officers of the silent film era—of the early part of the twentieth century reflected one popular perception of the police in general. But it may have been the competency of the Pinkerton detectives, too, that provided the model of a police detective that led to the public's acceptance of the police department detective (Langworthy and Travis, 1999).

Introduction

Detectives are responsible for criminal investigations. A criminal investigation is a lawful search for people and items useful in reconstructing an illegal act or omission and analyzing of the mental state of the person or persons committing that act or omission (Weston and Lushbaugh, 2006).

The objective of criminal investigation is to determine truth as far as it can be discovered in any inquiry; it is a probing from the unknown to the known (Weston and Lushbaugh, 2006). Successful investigations are based not only on fidelity, accuracy, and sincerity in lawfully searching for the facts, but also on an equal faithfulness, exactness, and probity in reporting the results (Weston and Lushbaugh, 2006).

Criminal investigation means collecting evidence. Evidence is the only means by which the judge or the jury can be convinced of the truth or untruth of allegations and accusations made by defendants in a court of law. It is the job of detectives to collect all of the evidence and present it first to prosecutors and then to the court, but given this, the first item of concern is whether the evidence collected will be admissible in court. Admissibility depends on whether the evidence is relevant, material, and competent.

In our criminal justice system, the defendant is presumed to be innocent and it is the task of the prosecution to prove the case against the defendant beyond a reasonable doubt. The reality of this system is this: accusations of crime must be supported in court by legally significant evidence. It is incumbent on the criminal investigator—the detective—to have a knowledge of evidence and its legal significance in order to be successful. In the final analysis, the success of an investigation depends on the evidence collected and its legal significance (Weston and Lushbaugh, 2006).

Rules of Procedure in Collecting Evidence

In a perfect scenario within the field of criminal justice, a crime is committed and the suspect is immediately caught, smoking gun in hand, and shortly thereafter offers a legal, signed confession of his guilt. However, this is not the way these scenarios get played out in reality. Rarely is the suspect even remotely in the vicinity of the crime, and the smoking gun? No smoking gun with his fingerprints on it. Instead, the "smoking gun" is usually a piece of physical evidence left behind at the scene.

Regardless of the evidence left behind at the scene, there are very well-defined rules of procedure that must be followed so that any evidence collected by the police can be later used in court. The Fourth Amendment to the U.S. Constitution is a brief amendment, but it has an important function in preserving the rights of citizens. The Fourth Amendment reads:

> The right of the people to be secure in their persons, houses, papers, and effects, against unreasonable searches and seizures, shall not be violated, and no Warrants shall issue, but upon probable cause, supported

by Oath or affirmation, and particularly describing the place to be searched, and the persons or things to be seized. (Hall and Ely, 2009, p. 413)

Once a criminal investigation has commenced, and a crime scene has been identified, the need to properly collect and maintain evidence related to that investigation is crucial to the achievement of a successful arrest and prosecution in the case. As Hess and Orthman (2010) put it, "a primary purpose of an investigation is to locate, identify, and preserve evidence—data on which a judgment or conclusion may be based" (p. 122). The proper collection of evidence will help strengthen the case for the prosecution while eliminating any room for suggestion of a false arrest by the defense. However, the collection of evidence cannot begin without the actual crime scene being located. The preliminary search of a location thought to be related to the commission of a crime aids in establishing proof that the scene was in fact linked to the crime itself. Once the scene is determined to be that of the actual crime scene, then the act of evidence collection begins.

Photographing the crime scene as it appeared, prior to the disruption caused as a result of a search for evidence, helps to maintain the integrity of its original condition as it appeared just after the crime was committed and before the suspect had fled. The image of an undisturbed crime scene is a powerful piece of evidence that a jury can use when evaluating the mindset of the criminal as to why and how they committed the crime. Also, pre-search photographs of a crime scene can aid in establishing the condition and placement of evidence prior to the evidence being collected and secured.

Once the scene is secured and photographed, the placement of markings next to items of evidence being seized helps to establish, by number, which item was found first and the location of each item as it pertains to its collection. An evidence log is also needed to chronologically log the collection of each piece of evidence by date, time, number of item, and location. Photographing the item once it is marked—and prior to its collection—helps to aid the prosecution when they attempt to piece the scene together for a jury.

Upon marking, logging, and photographing evidence, the next step is to physically collect the evidence for examination and testing.

Following established protocol when collecting evidence helps to eliminate any suggestion that the item seized was contaminated or collected improperly. In addition, abiding by the proper method of collection helps to maintain the integrity of any laboratory tests that are meant to establish a connection between the suspect and the item seized.

The final step in the process of crime scene investigation has to do with after-search photographs. These photographs are intended to document the crime scene as it appeared once the search and seizure of evidence was completed. It aids in defending against any accusation that property left behind was intentionally damaged or that any important piece of evidence was left behind either negligently or intentionally. The before, during, and after photographs of a crime scene help to complete a necessary visual aid, not only for investigators to refer to as they continue on in their investigations, but also for any judge or jury to ponder as a point of reference when connecting an item to the location at which it was found.

Search and Seizure

The Fourth Amendment governs the search and seizure of evidence in a criminal case. There are three important elements of this amendment that control the activities of law enforcement when it comes to searching for and collecting evidence. These critical elements have to do with

- When suspects and their property can be searched
- When a search warrant is needed
- How a search warrant is obtained

Stop and Frisk

A police officer can search a suspect if the officer has a search warrant or if the search is incident to a lawful arrest. But what if the officer wants to stop and frisk a suspect?

Although it has been common practice over the decades—virtually since police departments were established—for officers to stop and frisk suspicious people, it hasn't always been exactly clear whether the police actually had the right to stop a suspicious individual and whether they could conduct a frisk looking for weapons or contraband. However, in the court case of *Terry v. Ohio* (1968), the U.S. Supreme Court defined this right and the parameters of what constitutes a stop and frisk.

The *Terry v. Ohio* case involved an officer who observed three men walking slowly back and forth in front of a store. The officer thought the men were acting in a suspicious manner, and he concluded they might be casing the store for a robbery. The officer confronted the three men and, after asking some questions, patted them down. In the process of patting them down, he discovered that two of the men were carrying revolvers. He arrested the men, and they were subsequently charged with carrying concealed weapons.

Later, in court, the men claimed that the officer did not have probable cause to search them. Therefore, they argued that the search was illegal and the guns should not be admitted into evidence. The case was appealed up to the U.S. Supreme Court. The Supreme Court agreed the officer did not have probable cause, but the court made a distinction between a search without a warrant (which would require probable cause) and a stop and frisk. The court held that a frisk (or a pat-down of the outer clothing of an individual) is essential to the proper performance of a police officer's investigative duties (Albanese, 2013).

Procedural Law

Law enforcement—and indeed the entire criminal justice system—is governed by procedural law. Procedural law is a body of laws for how things should be done at each step of the criminal justice process. Procedural law includes court procedures, such as rules of evidence, and police procedures, which involve such things as search and seizure, arrest, and interrogation (Fagin, 2007).

Rules of Evidence

Rules of evidence stipulate the requirements for introducing evidence and define the qualifications of an expert witness and the nature of the testimony he or she may give (Fagin, 2012). Rules of evidence affect police officers' conduct because collecting evidence is part of their job. The rules state that evidence gathered through immoral, illegal, or unconstitutional means should not be used as evidence in a trial.

Exclusionary Rule

Evidence is declared inadmissible under the exclusionary rule, and the rule prohibits the use of evidence or testimony obtained in violation of the Constitution. The origins of the exclusionary rule can be traced back to a 1914 case heard by the U.S. Supreme Court. The case was *Weeks v. United States* (1914), and the court ruled that evidence against Freemont Weeks, who was accused of transporting lottery tickets through the mail, was obtained without a search warrant. Weeks took action against the police and petitioned for the return of his private possessions. The conclusion of the Supreme Court was unanimous. The court held that the seizure of items from Weeks's residence directly violated his constitutional rights. The court also held that the government's refusal to return Weeks's possessions violated the Fourth Amendment. To allow private documents to be seized and then held as evidence against citizens would have meant that the protection of the Fourth Amendment, declaring the right to be secure against such searches and seizures, would be of no value whatsoever. This was the first application of what eventually became known as the exclusionary rule (Bohm and Haley, 2012).

In 1961, in *Mapp v. Ohio*, the Supreme Court extended the exclusionary rule by requiring that state courts use the rule—just as it was used in federal court proceedings. *Mapp v. Ohio* (1961) was a case involving a woman by the name of Dolree Mapp. The police received a tip from an informant that there was evidence at her home related to a bombing suspect. The police arrived at Ms. Mapp's house and asked for permission to search her house. Ms. Mapp refused them permission and they left. Later, they returned, and this time they said they had a search warrant and they waived a blank piece of paper at her.

The police proceeded to search her home. They did not find any evidence of a bombing suspect, but they did find some obscene material. Ms. Mapp was arrested and was convicted in state court of possession of obscene materials (Fagin, 2007). Ms. Mapp appealed her conviction on the basis that her Fourth Amendment rights had been violated. The Supreme Court ruled that the same standards as in *Weeks v. United States* applied to defendants in state courts. That is, illegally obtained evidence would be inadmissible. As a result, Ms. Mapp's conviction was reversed.

Fruit of the Poisonous Tree Doctrine

The exclusionary rule, as established in 1914 by *Weeks v. United States*, applied to primary evidence. That means that direct evidence (e.g., a photo album containing photos of missing and presumed dead individuals) obtained by illegal means would be excluded, but that any other evidence (perhaps the burial sites of some of those bodies, which were discovered based on those photos) would still be permitted. However, this was further clarified a few years after the *Weeks v. United States* decision.

In *Silverthorne Lumber Co. v. United States* (1920), the U.S. Supreme Court added another rule of evidence—the fruit of the poisonous tree doctrine. In this decision, the court declared that the rules of evidence applied not only to evidence directly obtained by illegal means, but also to any other evidence garnered indirectly. For instance, if the police obtained the financial records from the residence of a suspect, but gathered this evidence without a search warrant, they could not use those records to determine what bank accounts the suspect had and then get a judge to sign a legal search warrant in order to seize those bank accounts.

Although the *Silverthorne Lumber Co. v. United States* case only applied to federal courts, this doctrine was expanded to state courts in the 1949 case of *Wolf v. Colorado*. In effect, the Supreme Court in *Wolf v. Colorado* (1949) held that state courts had to enact procedures to protect the rights of citizens against police abuses of search and seizure.

Exceptions to the Search Warrant Rule

The Fourth Amendment's intent is that search warrants be secured by the police in order for a search and seizure to take place. In order for the police to obtain a search warrant, there must be probable cause. Probable cause means that there is a likelihood of a direct link between a suspect and a crime (Fagin, 2007).

However, over the years, the U.S. Supreme Court has authorized a number of circumstances in which the police can conduct a search or seizure without a search warrant. The most important of these search warrant exceptions are

- Search incident to a lawful arrest
- Plain-view searches
- Consent to search
- Exigent circumstances
- Search of automobiles
- Search of persons: stop and frisk
- Public safety exceptions
- Good faith exceptions

Search Incident to a Lawful Arrest

When the police are making a lawful arrest, they are entitled to a search of the person arrested without a search warrant. This right was articulated by the Supreme Court in the case of *Chimel v. United States* (1969). In this case, the court ruled that the police can not only search the person, but also search the area within the immediate control of the individual. They cannot extend this search beyond the person's reach or to other rooms (Fagin, 2007).

Plain-View Searches

Evidence that is within plain view of a police officer is subject to confiscation. The court declared in *Harris v. United States* in 1968 that if a police officer has the legal right to be somewhere, any contraband that is in his or her view can be seized.

If, for instance, a police officer has been invited into a suspect's house, and the officer sees stacks of money, along with weapons and plastic bags that could contain heroin, on a nearby table, such evidence can be seized. However, the police cannot look in closets, in covered containers, or under a table cloth, for example. On the other hand, the court has ruled that the police do not have to act blind or stupid. What this means is that the police do not have to be careless or inattentive. If an officer sees a stack of wooden boxes with the words

"Rifles—Property of the U.S. Army" stenciled on the sides, the officer has probable cause to believe that there are guns in the boxes and that they very likely are not the legal property of the individual.

Consent to Search

A warrantless search can also be conducted if a person gives consent to search. For example, according to the Supreme Court, if an individual allows an officer to come into her home and then consents to the request "Do you mind if I look around?" she has given consent to a search and any evidence located can be seized by the officer. That includes looking in closed containers in a car (*Florida v. Jimeno*, 1991).

Exigent Circumstances

Officers can make an arrest or conduct a search without a warrant under exigent circumstances. An exigent circumstance refers to a situation in which a police officer must act swiftly and the officer determines that he or she does not have time to go to a court to seek a warrant (Cole and Smith, 2007). For example, if officers are in hot pursuit of a fleeing suspected felon or if there are sounds of a struggle coming from within a house and it is possible someone might be in danger, officers need not stop to obtain a warrant and thereby risk losing evidence or allowing a suspect to get away.

To justify a warrantless search, officers do not need to prove that there was a potential threat to public safety (Cole and Smith, 2007). Officers often have to make on-the-spot decisions to apprehend a suspect or seek evidence when it is thought that delay might result in evidence being lost or destroyed. Practically speaking, judges are often reluctant to second-guess a police officer who has had to make a split-second decision when the urgency of a situation required—in the officer's judgment—a warrantless search (Cole and Smith, 2007).

Search of an Automobile

If the police have probable cause, they can search an automobile without first obtaining a search warrant. The courts have taken note of the special circumstances of cars and motorized vehicles as long ago as 1925 and established the Carroll Doctrine.

The Carroll Doctrine came out of the case of *Carroll v. United States* (1925). The special circumstances of a car or automobile, of course, are that cars and other motorized means of transportation are readily mobile and they can be moved if there is a delay while an officer is attempting to get a search warrant. In the Carroll Doctrine, the Supreme Court stated that evidence obtained in the search of an automobile without a warrant is permissible if the police have probable cause to believe a crime has occurred.

The exclusionary rule applies to automobile searches if the officer does not have the right to stop a car and driver in the first place. Lacking a reason to make a traffic stop makes any evidence confiscated inadmissible.

One other aspect of an auto search is the searching of a vehicle that has been impounded. If, for instance, a car has been illegally parked in a street's no parking zone and is towed to an impound lot, a search and inventory of the belongings of the car can be conducted. Any contraband found in an inventory search can be used as evidence (Cole and Smith, 2007).

Search of a Person: The Pat-Down Search

We have already discussed the pat-down search or the stop and frisk. This is essentially a warrantless search because, as indicated previously, it is a limited search, as only the outer clothing of the individual can be patted down. And the primary purpose of a stop and frisk is to ensure the safety of the police officer.

Public Safety Exceptions

There are many circumstances encountered by law enforcement when the public good is paramount. For example, the police can pursue a fleeing felon into an apartment building and search for the individual. Likewise, if an armed suspect who just robbed a bank and shot a bank employee flees into a nearby neighborhood, the police could search houses and other places where the suspect or his weapon could be found.

Furthermore, public safety concerns allow for the search of airline passengers, and travelers (and their vehicles) who are crossing a border into another country. Evidence seized in these types of searches could legally justify an arrest and could be used as evidence in court (*Florida v. Bostick*, 1991).

Good Faith Exception

Another search that has been authorized by the court as not requiring a search warrant is when the initial warrant has an error, thus rendering it invalid. For example, if during the filling out of a search warrant the wrong address is entered on the warrant and the police carry out a search at that incorrect address, evidence found at the wrong address can be seized. In effect, the court has said that there is no misconduct by the police and it was a good faith mistake on the part of law enforcement.

Interrogation of Suspects

After an arrest has been made and a search has been carried out, the police have the authority to question the individual. There is no place in the Constitution where the word *interrogation* is mentioned. However, it is implied in the Fifth Amendment:

> No person shall be held to answer for a capital, or otherwise infamous crime, unless on a presentment or indictment of a Grand Jury, except in cases arising in the land or naval forces, or in the Militia, when in actual service in time of War or public danger; Nor shall any person be subject for the same offense to be twice put in jeopardy of life or limb; nor shall be compelled in any criminal case to be a witness against himself, nor be deprived of life, liberty, or property, without due process of law; nor shall private property be taken for public use, without just compensation. (Hall and Ely, 2009, p. 413)

The implication of an interrogation occurs in the section of the Fifth Amendment "nor shall be compelled in any criminal case to be a witness against himself." The writers of the Bill of Rights were well aware of historical precedence in England, as well as other countries, where individuals were forced to testify against themselves because they were subjected to torture in order to exact a confession from them.

The U.S. Supreme Court, in the landmark 1966 case of *Miranda v. Arizona*, established that the Fifth Amendment pertained to police interrogations and confessions obtained by law enforcement.

This important case involved Ernesto Miranda, who was arrested at his home in Phoenix, Arizona, for suspicion of rape, and was taken to the Phoenix Police Station. He was identified by a rape victim as her assailant. He was placed in a police interrogation room and questioned by two police officers. After two hours, the officers left the room and had a written confession signed by Miranda. A typed paragraph at the top of the confession indicated that it had been made voluntarily "with the full knowledge of my legal rights, understanding any statement I made may be used against me" (Albanese, 2013, p. 174).

Ernesto Miranda subsequently went to trial and was convicted of kidnapping and rape. He was sentenced to 20–30 years in prison. But he appealed his conviction on the grounds that he did not have legal representation during interrogation.

When this appeal reached the U.S. Supreme Court, the court noted that Ernesto Miranda was uneducated, indigent, and "a seriously disturbed individual with pronounced sexual fantasies" (Albanese, 2013, p. 174). Since only the police were present during interrogation and since the police officers admitted that they did not inform him that he had the right to an attorney during interrogation, the court had reason to doubt whether the confession was truly voluntary.

The Supreme Court overturned Miranda's confession, stating that his confession was inadmissible as evidence. To safeguard the rights of individuals in future cases, in the opinion throwing out Miranda's confession, they provided a five-point warning, which is now well known as the Miranda warning. We all can recite the Miranda warning because it has been used so frequently in movies, cop shows on TV, and police procedural novels:

You have the right to remain silent. You have the right to an attorney. If you cannot afford an attorney, one will be provided for you. Any statements made by you can and will be used against you in a court of law.

In addition, the Supreme Court's decision stated that

- The suspect must be warned prior to any questioning that he or she has the right to remain silent.
- Any statements made by the person can be used in a court of law.
- The suspect has the right to the presence of an attorney.
- If the person cannot afford an attorney, one will be appointed prior to any questioning.
- Opportunity to exercise these rights must be afforded to the suspect throughout the interrogation.

After such warnings have been given, the individual may knowingly waive these rights and agree to answer questions or make a statement (Albanese, 2013).

The right to legal counsel did not originate with the *Miranda* decision. It had actually been established by the Supreme Court as early as 1931 in the case of *Powell v. Alabama*. In that case, the conviction of the so-called Scottsboro Boys, nine young black men accused of raping two white women, was overturned by the court because the men were never provided the opportunity for legal counsel. Other cases since *Powell v. Alabama* have further established other rights regarding legal counsel.

For example, the court ruled that indigent defendants have the right to counsel, and that there is the right to have an attorney present during interrogation (*Escobedo v. Illinois*, 1964). Prior to the *Escobedo* case, in which a suspect, Danny Escobedo, was denied an opportunity to see his attorney (who was present in the police station during questioning), the police routinely blocked suspects' ability to be represented by counsel during interrogation. The court's decision in *Miranda* added specific warnings required at police interrogations to stop this kind of police conduct.

Since the *Miranda* decision, the Supreme Court has decided other cases in which the definition of an interrogation has been given and the court has addressed exactly what police questioning actually is. In general, the interpretation by the courts is that any words or questions by the police that are reasonably likely to elicit an incriminating response by a suspect qualify as an interrogation (Siegel and Worrall, 2012).

In order to ensure that the rights of suspects have been protected, most police departments use forms to show that suspects have signed off to guarantee they were given their Miranda warnings. In addition, a majority of police departments videotape interrogations and confessions. One study found that more than 60% of large police departments in the United States now videotape interrogations and confessions (Albanese, 2013). In a study conducted by the National Institute of Justice (Gelber, 1993), it was found that about 85% of police departments believed that videotaping improves the quality of interrogations. Such procedures help to ensure that suspects are given the Miranda warning, that they have not been coerced into giving false confessions, and that questioning has been done appropriately following proper procedures.

Both the Fourth Amendment and the Fifth Amendment have protected the rights of suspects. Furthermore, the interpretations of these amendments by the courts have done much to deter police misconduct, which helps to avoid false confessions and wrongful convictions. Although abiding by these court rules has provided special challenges to the police, when the proper procedures are followed in collecting evidence, the presentation of that evidence in court is enhanced.

Criminal Investigation and Intelligence

Never was the need for the intelligence community and law enforcement to form a symbiotic relationship greater than in the aftermath of the terrorists attacks of September 11, 2001. The many investigative and intelligence deficiencies identified through the numerous investigations and inquiries into the 9/11 attacks led to several conclusions as to what may have contributed to the lack of preemptive intelligence at the state and federal levels of law enforcement. The 9/11 Commission Report (National Commission on Terrorist Attacks, 2002) suggested that "although the 1995 National Intelligence Estimate had warned of a new type of terrorism, many officials continued to think of terrorists as agents of states, or as domestic criminals, i.e., Timothy McVeigh in Oklahoma City" (National Commission on Terrorist Attacks, 2002, p. 126).

On September 12, 2001, the president of the United States, George W. Bush, gave a speech to the nation. In that speech, President Bush exclaimed, "We will bring our enemies to justice or we will bring justice to our enemies" (Schmalleger, 2009, p. 12). At that time, the enemy was categorized as Islamic radicals. Outside of the federal system, state and local law enforcement was at a disadvantage as to how they would be able to identify the differences between peacefully practicing Muslims and Islamic radicals.

The process of conducting an investigation into a group of individuals who have been labeled a terrorist organization is a complex process that poses a great challenge for not only those in law enforcement, but also the intelligence community. The preliminary investigation and the intelligence gathering process, which is necessary in order for the case to reach the indictment stage of the criminal justice process, can be a pain-staking and tedious task. Intelligence analysis, in cooperation with the criminal investigative process, is a critical part of the process, and the intelligence analysts play a crucial role when helping law enforcement identify the criminal participants.

Law enforcement is traditionally more inclined to react to a crime rather than take proactive steps to prevent a crime. For example, in the case of a robbery, the police will respond and then investigate. Only if there are multiple robberies in a certain area, and a pattern is identified, will law enforcement attempt to take proactive steps to prevent future robberies.

It is usually when multiple crimes occur that criminal investigators can begin to develop a pattern, or a modus operandi (MO), that the criminal may follow. *Modus operandi*, loosely translated, means "a method of operation." To a criminal, an MO is a set pattern, or way, he or she prefers to commit his or her respective crimes. An MO can range from a burglar choosing to always break into his target locations from a rooftop to a murderer choosing a knife as his choice of weapon with which to commit murder. To a criminal, an MO is a comfort zone in which he or she feels safe in committing his or her criminal act.

Once a pattern is established, the next step in the investigative process is identifying the key components within the organization. This step is crucial if a criminal investigation is to have any success in attempting to dismantle the organization at all. By identifying and demonstrating developing trends in criminal behavior, while focusing on a particular crime group, criminal investigators can effectively prepare an investigative response plan intended to identify and, more importantly, target the threat.

Chalk and Rosenau (2004) advocate for strong analytical assessments, as they can prove to be invaluable tools for making recommendations pertaining to law enforcement strategies: "The analysis is intended to help inform debate on the advisability of creating dedicated information collection and surveillance body" (Chalk and Rosenau, 2004, p. 1).

The detection and investigation of crime, along with the pursuit and apprehension of criminals, require reliable intelligence. Without reliable intelligence, the investigator is limited to overt acts and volunteered information—and thus is severely handicapped in many areas.

The timeline below depicts identified criminal activity directed toward the United States, related to radical Islam, over a 12-month period. By analyzing the data outlined in the research, you can draw multiple conclusions as to the frequency, severity, and relevance to law enforcement of the criminal organization in question—that organization being the radical factions of Islam.

Figure 5.1 is a simplified visual of the level of criminal activity involving radical Islamic extremists. From a criminal investigator's perspective, the information shows

- Ten documented occurrences over a 12-month period
- September as the most active month
- Methods of attack varying from firearms to explosives
- American converts, or American Jihadists, joining the fold to engage in varying degrees of activity

Assessing analytical data and comparing them to related surveillance activity, in addition to any confidential informant information, can aid in the investigation moving from the preliminary stage to the actual proactive investigation stage. It is here, at this stage, that all of the aforementioned information can be disseminated and articulated to support the applications of search and arrest warrants, as well as wiretap affidavits that allow for the covert eavesdropping of telephonic and electronic devices being used by potential targets.

The key to police work, and in particular investigations, is information (Dempsey and Forst, 2010). Therefore, obtaining good

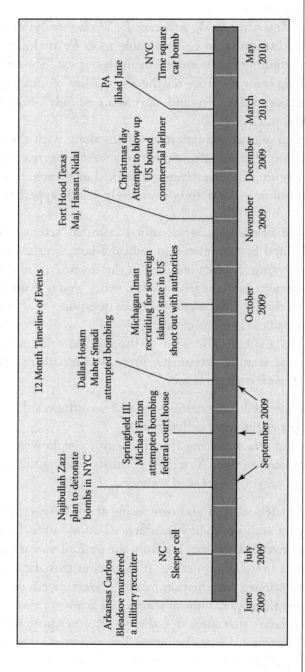

Figure 5.1 A simplified timeline showing how investigators may track the criminal activity of radical Muslim extremists over a 12-month period.

information is critical to a successful investigation. Information can come from complainants, victims, witnesses, the suspect, or all the various files of data kept by a police department. And all of this information can enhance and strengthen an investigation. Today, however, we can use computers to access information rapidly and efficiently. With the availability of millions of pieces of information through stored computer files and various databases, the trick is not related to finding information but to discerning which data are valuable and pertinent to the case that is being investigated. That is where tactical crime analysts and intelligence experts can play an increasingly important role in helping to solve crimes. In Chapter 6, we look more in depth at intelligence collection and the role intelligence analysts can play in solving crimes.

Questions for Discussion

1. Why is it so important for detectives to understand how evidence is collected?
2. Under what circumstances can warrantless searches be made?

Important Terms

Evidence: Evidence consists of legal proofs presented to the court in the form of witnesses, records, documents, objects, and other means, for the purpose of influencing the opinions of the judge or the jury toward the case of the prosecution or the defense.

Exclusionary rule: According to the exclusionary rule, evidence obtained as a result of an unreasonable or illegal search is not admissible in a criminal prosecution.

Exigent circumstances: Emergency or urgent circumstances.

Fruit of the poisonous tree doctrine: This rule prohibits the admission of evidence obtained as result of an illegal or initially tainted admission, confession, or search.

Good faith exception: The U.S. Supreme Court ruled that the exclusionary rule does not apply when the police relied in good faith on case law that was later changed by another judicial opinion or on a valid law or statute later declared unconstitutional, or on a search warrant that was later declared invalid even though originally signed by a judge.

Plain-view searches: Plain-view searches occur when the police are conducting a search pursuant to a search warrant and come across contraband or evidence they can plainly see but which they did not expect to find.

Procedural law: Aspect of the law that specifies the methods to be used in enforcing criminal law.

Stop and frisk: A frisk or a pat-down search of the outer garments of the suspect is permissible if the officer has reasonable suspicion that the suspect is engaging in criminal activity and may be dangerous.

Substantive law: Part of the law that creates and defines what conduct is criminal and which punishments should be imposed for violations of criminal laws.

Study Guide Questions

For questions 1–4, indicate whether the statement is true or false.

1. _____ The Fourth Amendment governs search and seizure evidence in a criminal case.
2. _____ Procedural law has to do with a body of laws governing how courts proceed with appointing judges.
3. _____ The importance of the Supreme Court's decision in *Mapp v. Ohio* is that illegally obtained evidence is inadmissible.
4. _____ A search does not require a search warrant if it is made incident to a lawful arrest.
5. A stop and frisk, or pat-down search, of a suspect requires
   a. Probable cause
   b. A search warrant
   c. Reasonable suspicion
   d. A judge's approval
6. The exclusionary rule prohibits the use of evidence that is
   a. Discovered in plain view
   b. Of little value
   c. Not obtained by crime scene investigators
   d. In violation of the Fourth Amendment

7. When evidence is obtained by illegal means and that evidence results in the finding of further evidence, then this situation will fall under

 a. Fruit of the poisonous tree doctrine

 b. Miranda warnings

 c. Stop and frisk rule

 d. Misconduct rule

8. A search and seizure is legal if

 a. The officer means well

 b. An individual gives the officer permission to search

 c. The police are trying to get evidence to prosecute a serial killer

 d. The police follow the rule of cutting corners in order to ensure a conviction

References

Albanese, J.S. (2013). *Criminal Justice*. 5th ed. Upper Saddle River, NJ: Pearson.

Bohm, R.H., and Haley, K.N. (2012). *Introduction to Criminal Justice*. 7th ed. New York: Glencoe/McGraw-Hill.

Carroll v. United States. 267 U.S. 132 (1925).

Chalk, P., and Rosenau, W. (2004). *Confronting the Enemy Within: Security Intelligence, the Police, and Counterterrorism in Four Democracies*. Santa Monica, CA: Rand.

Chimel v. United States. 395 U.S. 752 (1969).

Cole, G.F., and Smith, C.E. (2007). *The American System of Criminal Justice*. 11th ed. Belmont, CA: Thomson Wadsworth.

Dempsey, J.S., and Forst, L.S. (2010). *An Introduction to Policing*. 5th ed. Clifton Park, NY: Delmar.

Escobedo v. Illinois. 378 U.S. 438 (1964).

Fagin, J.A. (2012). *CJ: 2011*. Upper Saddle River, NJ: Pearson Educational.

Fagin, J.A. (2007). *Criminal Justice: A Brief Introduction*. Boston: Allyn and Bacon.

Florida v. Bostick. 501 U.S. 429 (1991).

Florida v. Jimeno. 500 U.S. 248 (1991).

Gelber, W.A. (1993). Videotaping interrogations and confessions. Rockville, MD: National Institute of Justice. Available at https://www.ncjrs.gov/App/Publications/abstract.aspx?ID=139962.

Hall, K.L., and Ely, J.W. (2009). *The Oxford Guide to United States Supreme Court Decisions*. 2nd ed. New York: Oxford University Press.

Harris v. United States. 390 U.S. 234 (1968).

Hess, K.M., and Orthmann, C.H. (2010). *Criminal Investigation*. 9th ed. Clifton Park, NY: Delmar Cengage Learning.

Kuykendall, J., and Roberg, R.R. (1982). Mapping police organizational change: From a mechanistic toward an organic model. *Criminology*, 20 (2), 241–256. Available at http://onlinelibrary.wiley.com/doi/10.1111/j.1745-9125.1982.tb00459.x/abstract.

Langworthy, R.H., and Travis, L.P. (1999). *Policing in America: A Balance of Forces*. 2nd ed. Upper Saddle River, NJ: Prentice Hall.

Mapp v. Ohio. 367 U.S. 643 (1961).

Miranda v. Arizona, 384 U.S. 436 (1966).

National Commission on Terrorist Attacks. (2002). *The 9/11 Commission Report: Final Report of the National Commission on Terrorist Attacks upon the United States*. Washington, DC: U.S. Government Printing Office.

Powell v. Alabama. 287 U.S. 45 (1931).

Schmalleger, F. (2009). *Criminal Justice Today*. 10th ed. Upper Saddle River, NJ: Prentice Hall.

Siegel, L.J., and Worrall, J.L. (2012). *Introduction to Criminal Justice*. 13th ed. Belmont, CA: Wadsworth.

Silverthorne Lumber Co. v. United States. 251 U.S. 385 (1920).

Terry v. Ohio. 392 U.S. 1 (1968).

Weeks v. United States. 232 U.S. 383 (1914).

Weston, P.B., and Lushbaugh, C.A. (2006). *Criminal Investigation*. 10th ed. Upper Saddle River, NJ: Pearson Prentice Hall.

Wolf v. Colorado. 338 U.S. 25 (1949).

PART III

INTELLIGENCE AND INTELLIGENCE ANALYSIS

6

AN INTRODUCTION
TO INTELLIGENCE

Chapter Outline

1. Criminal investigations
2. The crime analyst and the criminal investigator
3. Stages of the police intelligence process
4. How investigations are performed
5. Crime analysis
6. Criminal profiling
7. Geographical profiling
8. Time–event charting and link analysis

Learning Objectives for Chapter 6

1. Gain a better understanding of criminal investigations
2. Learn to view an investigation from the criminal investigator's perspective
3. Develop an understanding of the role of the intelligence analyst in a criminal investigation
4. Learn how intelligence plays a key role in criminal investigations
5. Learn some basic tools the intelligence analyst can use to contribute to a criminal investigation

A crime analyst's effort is what creates information, whether that information is "built" or "mined." A metaphor that works well is to see the analyst as a sculptor. Some sculptures are created by combining and molding pieces of clay, much as an analyst creates information by combining pieces of data. Other sculptures are created by chipping away extraneous pieces of stone to reveal a shape inside, much as an analyst filters out extraneous pieces of data to find the one that reveals a fact or truth.

Either way, the analyst's raw material is data, which might come from numerous sources. Out of this data, the analyst seeks to create information, which he then delivers to his "consumer"—the police agency. This information, once internalized, becomes knowledge that informs police action.

Christopher W. Bruce (2008)

Introduction

As we learned in Chapter 5, intelligence is the information that is the lifeblood of good police work. The detection and investigation of crime, along with the pursuit and apprehension of criminals, require reliable intelligence. Without reliable intelligence, the investigator is limited and the chances of a successful investigation are diminished. Today, we use computers to access information rapidly and efficiently. With the availability of millions of pieces of information through stored computer files and various databases, intelligence analysts and tactical crime analysts can access valuable, and often essential, information—information that can play a critical role in helping to solve crimes. In this chapter, we discuss how intelligence is gathered to assist investigators in the solution of crimes.

In this chapter, as well as in the chapters to follow, we discuss the importance of the role of tactical crime analysts as they work in conjunction with law enforcement to investigate and solve real-time crime. While we will examine in detail the actual process of tactical crime analysis in later chapters, what follows is an example of an actual event that highlights how crucial a fluid working relationship can be between the police investigator and the tactical analyst.

Date: June 14, 2014

Crime: Kidnapping

On June 14, 2014, the real-time center/tactical analyst was contacted by the city police department regarding a missing person/

possible kidnapping. The victim was a 15-year-old female, and the initial information supplied to law enforcement was that the victim had texted a relative pleading for help because a male had just put her in the trunk of a car and they were now driving on the highway.

Upon arrival by uniformed officers to the victim's home, the victim's sister told responding units that the victim had been talking to a male on social media and that the male was of a different race than she.* In addition, the sister advised that the victim may be in an online, romantic relationship with him.

After the preliminary investigation with the victim's family was concluded, the police investigator assigned to the investigation went to the real-time crime center and began to work the case leads with the tactical analyst. The investigator focused his attention on attempting to "ping"† the victim's cellular phone and, in doing so, discovered that it was hitting off a cellular tower in an adjoining state.

As the investigator was identifying the current location of the victim's cellular phone, the tactical analyst began a data search of the victim in an attempt to locate any of the victim's social media accounts. The analyst discovered on one such account that the victim had a social media friend, identified by moniker‡ only, who was a male that matched the race described by the victim's sister, and who listed his current state of residence as the same state the victim's cellular phone was pinging out of.

By using information now obtained from the social media account of the possible suspect, the tactical analyst was able to gather intelligence on the male based on his social media profile, moniker, and postings.

With the investigator working at the analyst's side, this information made the male a strong person of interest, primarily due to these facts now established:

- The male was of the same race described by the victim's sister.
- The male lived in the state that the victim's phone was currently pinging out of.

---

* Editor's note: This fact was crucial to the investigation, and more importantly, to the data mining that was required.
† Pinging of a cell phone means identifying the location of the cellular tower of the last signal the phone received.
‡ A moniker is a name a person may associate himself or herself with, being an actual name or an alias.

- The male was confirmed to have been in recent contact with the victim on her social media account.

As the investigation intensified, the investigator gave the analyst a phone number he wanted researched because it was the last incoming call the victim had received on her cell phone prior to her going missing.

For this data search, the analyst utilized several databases that analyzed information in relation to telephone numbers and persons associated with them. The information also focused on the history of the phone in question, in terms of it being documented in any official or public records database.

The analyst was also able to utilize a system that reverse dialed* into the cellular device being researched. The analyst was successful in being able to hear a prerecorded message that possibly identified, by moniker, the person who may have been currently in possession of the phone.

The analyst also searched the cellular phone through multiple social media accounts and discovered a social media account associated with the number. This account had a profile with a moniker the same as that on the prerecorded voice message.

The newly discovered information was given to the investigator, who, in turn, reached out to a police agency in the adjoining city and state that the victim's cell phone was pinging out of, and where the possible suspect listed as his state of residence on his social media account.

Upon receiving the information, the police agency in the adjoining city and state advised that they were, in fact, familiar with the suspect's moniker and that it was actually an alias. They provided the suspect's real name and date of birth. They further advised that the suspect had a lengthy criminal history, which included several sexual assaults. However, they were unable to provide a current residence since the suspect had no recent contacts with that law enforcement agency.

Once the suspect's actual identity and date of birth were given to the tactical analyst, she quickly data mined from multiple sources, both local and nationwide, and located the suspect's most recent address. This newly discovered address was also located within the adjoining state in

---

* Reverse dialing enables the analyst to dial into any cellular device without the knowledge of the holder of the phone in order to covertly listen to any prerecorded voice message.

question and within the jurisdiction of the police agency that had just passed along his actual name and date of birth.

Within an hour, the police agency from the adjoining state mobilized and responded to the rural area where the tactical analyst had identified the suspect's possible current address. Upon entry by uniformed officers, the victim was located inside the house with the male the analyst had identified. Once in custody, the suspect admitted to luring the underage victim to his house, against her will via social media, and having sexually assaulted her once there.

Investigators acknowledged that the tactical analyst was crucial in the identification of the suspect and in locating the victim before she was subjected to any further harm. In addition, it was acknowledged that the leads the tactical analyst rapidly data mined and supplied had directly contributed to the case leading to a swift conclusion—just 10 hours after the initial 911 call was made*.

In the following, Glenn Grana describes his years as a criminal investigator:

> During the course of my 21-year career in law enforcement, I had the opportunity to work in the Criminal Investigation Division (CID). CID was the unit that encompassed multiple subunits, all of which focused on a specific aspect of criminal investigations. I spent the majority of my time in CID working in three of these subunits: the narcotics squad, the warrant squad, and field investigations. Working in each of these units allowed me to focus on a specific aspect of criminal investigations, while keeping within the basics of the principles of the investigative process.
>
> While in the warrant squad, I had to follow the trail left behind by wanted suspects as they attempted to avoid detection and apprehension by law enforcement. We considered this the adult version of hide and seek, and as a result, leads as to the possible whereabouts of suspects were constantly being analyzed and researched.

---

* Geographically, the distance to drive from the victim's residence, where she was picked up by the suspect, to the suspect's residence in the adjoining state, was approximately six hours.

Additional research into the backgrounds of the suspects and their associates would ultimately lead to their whereabouts. Therefore, working in this unit required me to have the ability to research and follow up on leads that were being developed in the field as the search for suspects was ongoing. I also learned the art of surveillance, that is, observing locations for prolonged periods of time with the hope that the intended suspect would eventually show up. Acquiring keen surveillance skills would prove extremely beneficial as my career progressed into the field of narcotics investigation.

Field investigative units are located within the stations operated in various locations of an agency's jurisdiction of patrol, and outside of their headquarters. In the New York Police Department, for example, these would be called precinct detective bureaus. While working in field investigations, I carried out the role of the suit-and-tie investigator. Field investigations involved the investigations of a wide variety of crimes, crimes that ran the spectrum of the penal law from burglary, robbery, and sex crimes all the way down to lesser degree felonies and even, at times, misdemeanor crimes. Always, though, I needed to rely on the basic rules of investigation, which are described in detail in this chapter, as well as commonsense deduction abilities.

In field investigations, traditional investigative skills were practiced, such as interviewing of victims and witnesses, along with interrogation of suspects. The ability to testify as an expert witness in court hearings was also necessary, and I was called on to testify in a range of hearings, from suppression of the evidence hearings to written confession hearings to grand jury proceedings when the case was brought before a grand jury by an assistant district attorney for consideration of charges being levied.

It was during the 10 years I spent as a narcotics investigator that I was able to utilize all the aforementioned skills, while developing a high level of proficiency in the writing and execution of search warrants and the handling of confidential informants while acting in an undercover capacity making purchases of illegal narcotics. As my time in narcotics progressed, I was taught by more seasoned investigators the art of wiretap investigations.

Wiretap investigations involve the covert interception and monitoring of telephone calls made by high-level drug operatives. I learned how to perform the skills needed to successfully work such high-intensity and complex criminal investigations. The skills I learned involved such things as telephone line monitoring, which entails listening to and deciphering the conversations being intercepted. I also learned how to successfully perform all aspects of surveillance, from static surveillance (stationary surveillance of locations) to physical surveillance (the following of an individual to observe his or her criminal activity).

More importantly, I learned what type of evidence was needed to support these types of investigations—evidence that was almost always developed during an extensive preliminary investigative process. This preliminary process of investigation relied heavily on intelligence collection, examination, and dissemination, all of which were necessary to complete the affidavit required to present to a judge for his or her approval, granting the authority to eavesdrop on the intended target and the target organization.

To gain the level of proficiency and experience I achieved during my time in CID, I needed to have not only an understanding of how to conduct a basic criminal investigation, but also a solid understanding and ability to examine all aspects of intelligence.

It is crucial, therefore, for an intelligence analyst, especially one working in a real-time setting, such as a tactical crime analyst, to have a fluid working knowledge of criminal investigations. The tactical analyst needs to combine all of his or her skills related to analyzing critical intelligence in order to be an essential part of the investigative process. As you read on in this chapter, you will come to see the importance of both a working knowledge of criminal investigations and skills in analyzing intelligence.

Criminal Investigations

In order to conduct an investigation of a crime, the investigator or detective relies on intelligence. In assisting the investigator, the intelligence analyst concentrates on the collection and dissemination of information about criminals (Bruce, 2008). That is, the analyst may create physical, behavioral, or psychological profiles of offenders based on the crimes they have committed. Or the analyst might use investigative skills to compare possible suspects, research the modus operandi of a number of suspects, or create a profile of a serial offender.

It is important for intelligence analysts and tactical crime analysts to have an understanding of how a criminal investigation proceeds in order to be in the best position to provide the kind of intelligence investigators need to close cases.

To better understand the investigative process, it is useful to consider the essential qualities of a criminal investigator. According to Swanson et al. (2012), successful investigators have the following qualities:

1. Strong degree of self-discipline
2. Ethical and moral standards leading to using legally approved methods
3. Capable of winning the confidence of others
4. Not acting out of malice or bias
5. Always willing to include in their case documentation all evidence that may point to the innocence of a suspect—no matter how unsavory the character of that suspect
6. Knowledge that investigation is a systematic method of inquiry that is more science than art
7. Realization that investigations often require initiative and personal resourcefulness
8. Wide range of contacts across many occupations
9. Openness to consulting with experts from various fields to help move the investigation forward
10. Ability to use both inductive and deductive reasoning
11. Willingness to monitor their own use of inductive and deductive reasoning to try to avoid distortions and fallacies
12. Ability to learn something from every person they meet
13. Empathy, sensitivity, and compassion to do their job without causing undue anguish to others
14. Positive outlook that guards them against becoming callous and cynical

Knowing these essential qualities possessed by good investigators allows you to strive to have them.

Now, we can go on to talk about how criminal investigations are carried out.

How Investigations Are Carried Out

Of course, an investigation starts with a crime—and the report of a crime. Often, this means that a call has been placed to 911 or the police reporting an incident. For instance, let's use the example of a robbery that occurs just off a college campus. A student walking home from the university library at 10:00 p.m. is robbed of her backpack, which includes her purse and her laptop computer, and when she resists, she is pushed and falls to the sidewalk.

The student still has her cell phone and calls 911 and reports the incident. A police patrol officer in the vicinity arrives within 10 minutes to do a preliminary investigation. The actions taken by the first officer on the scene, usually a uniformed patrol officer, can be viewed as a preliminary investigation.

Typically, the preliminary investigation will include the following steps:

1. Interview victim as initial response.
2. Assess need for emergency care.
3. Secure the scene and control persons and evidence.
4. Issue a be on the lookout (BOLO).
5. Conduct neighborhood or vehicle canvass.
6. Process evidence and maintain the chain of custody of evidence.
7. Write an incident report.

During the preliminary investigation, the officer will be alert for people and cars leaving the crime scene or the immediate vicinity and note numbers and descriptions. In addition, the officer must determine whether a tactical situation exists. A tactical situation would exist if the person taking the student's backpack also abducted a friend of the victim or if the suspect broke into a nearby home and is armed with a weapon. That would necessitate that the responding officer call for backup or for the assistance of specialized units.

Furthermore, the initial officer must treat the location as a crime scene unless he or she determines otherwise. Also, if the suspect is still at the scene, he or she should be arrested and a search of his or her person should be conducted with weapons or other evidence seized. It is very important that the initial officer maintain control of the crime scene (Swanson et al., 2012). Not only does this mean making sure that the victim is safe and cared for and that evidence is secured, but it also means that all individuals at the scene are identified. Interviews should also be conducted with the victim and witnesses, but if the suspect has fled the scene, the officer should issue an all-points bulletin or a BOLO based on the description of the perpetrator provided by the victim or witnesses.

Finally, the responding officer must complete an incident report or an offense report. This report will include his notes, observations, and other information about the crime scene or incident. This report will be filed in the patrol division or referred to the investigative division for follow-up.

Follow-Up Investigation

A detective or criminal investigator may be assigned to a case and may even show up at the crime scene before the patrol officer leaves. In our example of a student who is robbed and assaulted, this occurrence may be so common that no investigation beyond the preliminary one takes place. However, if there has been a rash of such crimes in the vicinity of the campus, apprehending the offender or offenders may be a priority and a senior criminal investigator may be assigned to the case and assume responsibility for what happens from that point on.

In order to fulfill his or her responsibility for investigating the crime, he or she may conduct a visual inspection of the crime scene and develop a preliminary plan for the investigation. In addition, the senior investigator will decide what other services or resources are needed. For example, if the suspect was seen entering a nearby apartment building, the investigator may call for personnel to search the apartment building or ask for a search warrant if there is a suspect who has been identified as living in that apartment building.

Among the duties or procedures utilized by the senior investigator are interviewing the victim again or interviewing other witnesses, conducting or supervising the neighborhood canvass, interrogating the suspect if he or she is in custody, and searching for and collecting other evidence.

Evidence

There are three broad categories of evidence that investigators attempt to locate:

1. *Corpus delicti*: Evidence that will help substantiate the elements of the crime. For instance, the primary *corpus delicti* evidence in our example of the robbery of a backpack and laptop computer would be the backpack or laptop computer.
2. *Associative*: Evidence that connects a suspect to the scene or the victim, or connects the scene or victim to the suspect. For example, if a suspect is arrested after using a credit card belonging to the student whose backpack was stolen, the possession and use of the stolen credit card would connect the suspect to the scene and the victim.
3. *Tracing*: Evidence that helps to identify the offender. For instance, if the victim of our backpack robbery scuffled with the perpetrator and the perpetrator's wallet was dropped at the scene, the driver's license in the wallet could lead the police to the residence of the suspect, and that would help identify the offender.

Direct and Circumstantial Evidence

During a criminal investigation, there are two basic kinds of proof needed to establish the guilt or innocence of a suspect. One type of proof is direct evidence, and the other is circumstantial.

Direct evidence involves testimony by eyewitnesses who have information to offer about the crime through one of their five senses. That is, they have seen, heard, smelled, tasted, or touched something related to the crime and, perhaps, related to the suspect. There are two general categories of witnesses: those who come forward with the evidence willingly and those who are unwilling—or reluctant—witnesses. Circumstantial evidence, on the other hand, is evidence from which inferences can be drawn and include items such as physical evidence (Weston and Lushbaugh, 2006). Usually, circumstantial evidence includes weapons, blood, fingerprints, tool marks, documents, and dust, dirt, or other traces.

Standard operating procedure is for the first patrol officer at the scene of the crime to detain witnesses and other persons who might offer help. That officer must obtain adequate information about each witness or each person who may have information to contribute. That would mean getting names, addresses, and phone number so detectives can follow up. It also means getting a description of the perpetrator from witnesses and securing a more complete description of the facts of the crime. A canvass of the neighborhood or surrounding area may be undertaken by the initial officers on the scene or later by investigators.

Circumstantial evidence may be found at the scene and must be handled in such a way that the evidence is not compromised or contaminated. Any evidence found at the scene should be secured by the patrol officer or investigator.

Basic Investigative Leads and Informants

The biggest challenge in an investigation is when the offender is unknown. If the victim or witnesses can pinpoint a suspect, then the offender is known and the police can make an arrest. Cases involving named suspects are a high percentage of the cases cleared by arrest in any police department (Weston and Lushbaugh, 2006). It is the unknown offender who presents the biggest problem. In these cases, the investigator must develop the basic investigative leads to attempt to discover the identity of the perpetrator.

The basic lead, in many instances, comes from the victim. It is not always so much that a victim knows the offender, but the detective can develop a lead by learning more about the victim's activities just before the crime. A detective will want to make a list of those people who would benefit from the crime and who might have known about the victim and what he or she possessed (e.g., that a student walking home from the library would have a laptop computer in her backpack). Information from the patrol officer on the scene initially may result in further intelligence about possible suspects or vehicles in the area.

Fingerprints or other evidence at the scene may help confirm that a suspect was at the scene of the crime, and thus had opportunity to carry out the offense.

Another lead may come from the way in which the crime was committed. This is the *modus operandi*. In our running example in this chapter, if similar robberies were reported involving female students walking home from the library late at night with backpacks or laptop computers, the pattern may suggest a suspect, or information from previous such crimes can be combined to offer leads. Furthermore, recovered stolen property may be traced to the robber. Or, photos of arrested persons for similar crimes might be viewed by victims to see if an identification can be made.

Experienced investigators will avoid hunches or developing leads or suspects based on intuition. Instead, they realize that developing leads comes about best when investigators use their know-how, their cognitive processes, and their ability to work a case rapidly (Weston and Lushbaugh, 2006). The latter point is important. Time is of the essence in most criminal investigations because lapsed time diminishes the victim's or witnesses' memory, and provides an opportunity for the offender to dispose of the evidence, develop an alibi, or get away if he or she is fleeing the area.

Some leads turn out to be productive; others may be unproductive. But both require manpower and resources. However, there is no way to predict which are the valuable leads that will be useful versus those that will be a waste of resources.

Also, the fact that a suspect is named or identified by a victim or by witnesses does not mean that that person committed the crime or knows anything about it. Victims—and witnesses—can be mistaken, have their facts all wrong, or be attempting to cause trouble for some innocent party (Swanson et al., 2012). The integrity and ethics of the investigator play a key role in ruling out suspects when they are innocent, along with ruling in suspects when there is evidence suggesting guilt.

The Crime Analyst and Police Investigations

The preceding pages of this chapter have provided a quick overview of a criminal investigation. It is not meant to be exhaustive, and we will discuss further aspects of criminal investigation in future chapters.

But what has been written in this chapter simply serves as an introduction in order to highlight that the tactical crime analyst is part of an investigative team.

On a daily basis, officers and investigators encounter criminals, victims, and witnesses, as well as responding to dispatched complainants. Each individual, or location, has a relevant history; for example, individuals may have previous arrests, gang affiliations, social media postings, pawn shop activity, and relevant information linking them to unique crime trends. These data are stored in databases that require significant time to mine and disseminate. Without immediate access to this information, police personnel are hard pressed to make the quick connections and deductions necessary for effective policing. Real-time crime analysis provides officers in the field with pertinent information instantaneously.

Real-time crime analysis has proven to be an effective, proactive or reactive, crime fighting tool that aids in ongoing and follow-up investigations. In the past, officers returning from the field would sift through pages and pages of records to find information related to an investigation. Now, however, real-time crime analysis provides them with information pertaining to their investigations, and in some cases, even before they make it to the scene.

A real-time crime center gives the analyst the ability to monitor computer-aided dispatch (CAD) and work directly off dispatched jobs. This allows the analyst to begin a preliminary workup on CAD information, such as address of incident, vehicle data, and so forth, and prepare a data summary for the responding unit should they call for the information. In addition, the analyst can have direct communication with units via police radio, CAD messaging, 911 dispatchers, and telephone. The analyst utilizes multiple source databases, which allow the analyst to provide relevant information to officers in the field, usually within a matter of minutes. Real-time analysis is also an effective tool in the follow-up investigative process by conducting research on—and providing additional information for—solvability factor deduction.

Success stories, such as the one discussed below, are the best way to illustrate how the use of a real-time tactical analyst, or any intelligence analyst for that matter, can assist in the swift, successful conclusion to criminal investigations.

Case: Homicide

The tactical analyst was asked to research the history of a victim who sustained a gunshot wound to the head. Surveillance video showed the suspect riding a bicycle as he approached the victim. Holding the gun in his left hand while wearing a white glove on it, the suspect shot the victim. The suspect was last seen traveling in a southerly direction.

In addition to any intelligence that would indicate the victim having a dispute with anyone recently, the analyst was asked by homicide investigators to look into area gang members as possible suspects, focusing on any who may be left-handed.

Through the analyst's research, she was able to locate social media accounts for multiple gang members who occupied turf in the area of the homicide. After going through numerous gang members' accounts, the analyst located a social media account of a person of interest who was an active member of the gang who claimed that area as their own. The social media account, however, was under a moniker and not an actual name. The analyst noticed that on this social media account page, the newly developed person of interest had a photo of himself in a professional sports uniform, and the photo was tagged with the name of a local semiprofessional sports team.

The analyst researched the website of the sports team and found the current roster of players. As it turned out, the person of interest was an active member. This confirmed to the analyst that the gang member's social media account and the team roster belonged to the same individual. In addition, the team roster listed the individual by his real name and provided a photo instead of the moniker he used on his social media account. The analyst now had an actual name to research.

The analyst continued to view multiple photos of the person of interest from the sports team's website and discovered, in several of the live-action photos, that the person of interest appeared to be performing while favoring his left hand.

The analyst then reviewed a surveillance video of the suspect, right before he shot the victim, and noticed that the glove the suspect was wearing looked similar to the glove that the person of interest was wearing during the live-action game photos on the semiprofessional sports team's website. The analyst also compared the newly identified person of interest's social media photos to his photos with the semiprofessional sports team, and noticed that he fit the same muscular build as the suspect in the surveillance video.

In addition, now that the potential suspect was identified, and his gang affiliation confirmed, the analyst was also able to identify several potential witnesses through various gang-related intelligence and social media accounts. These witnesses included

- A gang member who had recently posted a photo of the deceased male
- A possible witness who was later identified and interviewed
- Three close associates of the suspect who also had gang affiliations
- An individual who was identified through corner store video footage of the actual homicide and turned out to be a witness to the homicide

The analyst sent all the intelligence and photos of the person of interest to the investigator.

The homicide investigator advised the analyst that by using her identification and a photo of the person of interest, he was able to create a photo array.* As a result of the photo array, the investigator was able to gain a positive identification of the individual as the person who was the shooter. The individual was eventually charged with murder.

Success stories like this one not only serve to describe the investigative and analytical process used by the tactical crime analyst, but also help to clarify any misconception that may exist that the tactical analyst may lack an investigative mindset.

Confidential Informants

What has not been written about so far, and should be mentioned, is that informants also provide information to investigators. There are various kinds of informants that prove of value at times to investigators. There are those who expect to be paid or to receive some kind of consideration, or they may cooperate with detectives for other reasons.

---

* A photo array is a series of six photographs of individuals with similar features, with one photo being a photo of the suspect; it is used by law enforcement in an attempt to make an identification of a potential suspect.

Nonetheless, informants can pass along valuable intelligence that may lead to the identification of a suspect. Furthermore, police investigations rely on surveillance, sting operations, photo lineups, and live lineups—all with the intention of helping to identify suspects.

Role of Databases in Investigations

But there is also the use of databases that allow investigators to close off some lines of inquiry, encourage the continuance of others, or suggest new lines of investigation (Swanson et al., 2012). There are myriad databases available to the police these days, especially to the crime analyst or intelligence expert who knows how and when to access those databases. Available databases are international, national, multistate, state, or regional.

Among the national databases are the following:

- *AEXIS* (Arson, Explosives, and Incident System). Run by the Bureau of Alcohol, Tobacco, Firearms, and Explosives (ATF). This database contains information on arson, bombs, and misuse of explosives, including incident characteristics that can be useful in determining patterns, trends, and motives.
- *NIBIN* (National Integrated Ballistics Information Network). Also operated by the ATF, this database helps to determine if firearms are related to other cases.
- *NDPIX* (National Drug Pointer Index). This database from the Drug Enforcement Administration (DEA) alerts participating agencies of investigative targets they have in common.
- *NamUs* (National Missing and Unidentified Persons System). Administered by the National Institute of Justice, this database is designed to help track missing persons or identify human remains.
- *NCIC* (National Crime Information Center). Maintained by the Federal Bureau of Investigation (FBI), this database consists of 19 files, which include the National Sex Offender Registry, Unidentified Person File, Missing Persons File, U.S. Secret Service Protective File, Foreign Fugitive File, Gang File, Supervised Release File, and Identity Theft File.
- In addition to national databases, there are state and local databases that contain information about millions of offenders, as

well as missing persons, driver's license and vehicle registration information, state and local court information, Department of Corrections offender and inmate tracking, sexual predator tracking, and various other kinds of information.

Many police departments now have intelligence units that help to produce real-time, immediately actionable information. While the sophistication of individual intelligence units may vary from city to city or state to state, these departments can provide information that is invaluable in a criminal investigation.

While it may be the investigative department or the detective bureau that requests information from the intelligence unit (which are called by a variety of names, including fusion centers, intelligence units, and real-time crime centers), it is the responsibility of the intelligence unit to make sure that appropriate, supportive, and useful information is provided to crime investigators.

Charles R. Swanson and his colleagues (2012) propose that there is a continuous six-step process used by intelligence centers. Those six steps are as follows:

1. Planning and direction. The intelligence process requires a focus and direction for the intelligence effort. This could mean that the focus at a particular time might be on the solution of a series of crimes, a current hostage situation, the reexamination of a cold case, or preventing homicide in a section of the city.
2. Collection. Raw data are collected by the intelligence unit, but these raw data must be analyzed and refined so that usable information is relayed to the police unit in need of data.
3. Processing. In this step, the raw data are analyzed, which may mean that information is indexed, sorted, and filed in meaning ways that will allow for rapid retrieval and immediate usefulness to investigators or other police personnel.
4. Analysis and production. Data that have been processed are translated into a finished intelligence report. The data should be scrutinized for timeliness, reliability, validity, and relevance. The crime analyst in the intelligence unit must combine data into a finished product that informs the user of the

analyst's assessment of events and the implications of that
assessment (Swanson et al., 2012).
5. Dissemination. Ultimately, after collecting data, analyzing it,
   and producing a finished report, one must disseminate it to
   the officer or department that requested it.
6. Reevaluation. The receiving officer or department must provide feedback so that the intelligence unit can be constantly
   striving for improvement. Often, the finished product leads
   to new questions or problems that lead back to step 1 and a
   recycling of the six steps.

Intelligence Reports

There are any number of reports that an intelligence unit can produce
for a police department. But, among the many kinds of reports that an
intelligence unit could provide for criminal investigators, perhaps the
four most important are criminal profiles, geographic profiles, time–
event charts, and link analysis.

Criminal Profiles

Although criminal profiling is a staple of television shows such as
Criminal Minds, profiling has only been around since the 1960s. Howard
Teten was the first FBI agent to come up with a profile for the FBI.
Prior to joining the FBI in 1962, Teten worked for the San Leandro
Police Department in California. He was appointed as an instructor in
applied criminology at the National Police Academy in Washington,
D.C., but showed an interest in offender profiling and included some of
his theories about profiling in his applied criminology course.

Teten studied under, and was inspired by, Dr. Paul Kirk, who in
1937 became head of the University of California–Berkeley's criminology program. Kirk became well known for investigating the bed-
room in the Dr. Sam Sheppard case in the 1950s and later testifying
in the retrial of that case. Howard Teten was also inspired by the work
of Dr. Hans Gross and Dr. James Brussel. Dr. Brussel was a psychia-
trist whose criminal profile of a serial bomber in New York City in the
1950s led to the arrest of the man the media designated as "The Mad
Bomber" (Winerman, 2004).

It was Teten's work with the FBI that advanced the development of profiling in the 1970s and led to the establishment of the FBI's Behavioral Science Unit (BSU). Since renamed the Behavioral Research and Instruction Unit (BRIU), it continues to provide services to other law enforcement agencies during investigations.

Criminal profiling, by definition, means developing a psychological portrait of an unknown offender. While criminal profiling has come under criticism in the past few years because of a lack of scientific rigor, research continues to play a role in advancing the scientific base for criminal profiling.

These days, profiling rests, sometimes uneasily, somewhere between law enforcement and psychology (Winerman, 2004). As a science, it is still a relatively new field with few boundaries or definitions. Its practitioners don't always agree on methodology or even terminology. The term *profiling* has caught on among the general public, largely due to movies like *The Silence of the Lambs* and TV shows like *Profiler*. But the FBI calls its form of profiling "criminal investigative analysis," one prominent forensic psychologist calls his work "investigative psychology," and another calls it "crime action profiling" (Winerman, 2004).

Despite the different names, all of these tactics share a common goal: to help investigators examine evidence from crime scenes and victim and witness reports to develop an offender description. The description can include psychological variables such as personality traits, psychopathologies, and behavior patterns, as well as demographic variables such as age, race, or geographic location. Investigators might use profiling to narrow down a field of suspects or figure out how to interrogate a suspect already in custody.

"In some ways, [profiling] is really still as much an art as a science," says psychologist Harvey Schlossberg, PhD, former director of psychological services for the New York Police Department (Winerman, 2004, p. 66). But in recent years, many psychologists—together with criminologists and law enforcement officials—have begun using psychology's statistical and research methods to bring more science into the art.

To date, there is a lack of scientific evidence in support of the techniques used in criminal profiling, and the proclaimed successes of criminal profilers. The unscientific basis of profiling calls into question the validity of the methods it has spawned, and the ways in which these methods are used today. Academic evaluation and criticism promote the need for further research and scientific research on whether profiling can be a useful tool in criminal investigations (European Association of Psychology and the Law, 2011).

Some empirical evaluations of criminal profiling have been conducted. Two studies attempted to profile stranger rapists' criminal histories from their crime scene behavior, and both reported some limited success (Abumere, 2015). A study that tried to predict the characteristics of burglars from their crime scene behavior also achieved some success in predicting criminal demographics and previous criminal history (Abumere, 2015). These studies have searched for relationships between criminal characteristics and actions at the behavioral level. There are several researchers (such as Craig Bennell at Carleton University in Ottawa, Canada) who are studying the effectiveness of offender profiling.

Geographical Profiling

The term *geographic profiling* was coined by D. Kim Rossmo, a former detective inspector with the Vancouver Police Department. While studying for his doctorate, Rossmo conceived of the idea of using geographic profiling to target the residence of offenders, and he was instrumental in developing the first software package to be able to do this.

The premise of geographic profiling is that given a sufficient number of crimes, with adequate information for analysis, a probabilistic map of the area in which the offender's residence is located can be calculated (Swanson et al., 2012).

Although designed to analyze the locations of a connected series of crimes to determine the most likely area of offender residence, geographic profiling allows investigators and law enforcement officers to more effectively manage information and focus their investigations. Although there have been anecdotal successes with geographic profiling, there have also been several instances where geographic profiling has either been wrong in predicting where the offender lives or works or been inappropriate as a model (Paulsen, 2006). Thus far, none of the geographic profiling software packages have been subject to rigorous, independent, or comparative tests to evaluate their accuracy, reliability, validity, utility, or appropriateness for various situations. As Swanson et al. (2012, p. 200) point out, "As in the case of other recently developed investigative technologies, geoprofiling is in a state of transition as refinements are developed. It is not a perfect tool, and its capabilities can be decreased if the number of cases in a series are roughly less than 5 or the crime linkage is inaccurate."

Time–Event Charting and Link Analysis

Follow-up investigations often result in the accumulation of significant amounts of data. As a result, financial transactions, relationships, places, events, telephone calls, and other data can be obscured and their importance overlooked, resulting in an unnecessarily lengthened or even truncated investigation. Software has been generated that creates a variety of charts, saving investigative time and effort for other uses. Two commonly used investigative tools to offer shortcuts for crime investigators are time–event charting and link analysis.

A time–event chart depicts in graphic form the chronology of an individual's or a group's activities. A time–event chart is simply a timeline that offers investigators a way to focus on individual incidents in order to develop a general, graphic overview of a crime. In this sense, a time–event chart answers the question "What were this individual's activities leading up to a crime?"

Link analysis refers to analyzing relationships among people or organizations and is used to find matches in data for known patterns of interest, find anomalies where known patterns are violated, and discover new patterns of interest.

In intelligence work for police departments and investigators, one of the major goals of data mining is to discover patterns, links, and relationships hidden in the data. By discovering relationships—links—intelligence analysts may be able to provide detectives with valuable leads in unsolved cases.

As this chapter clearly indicates, intelligence is essential in modern police work, especially in criminal investigations. Given the importance of an intelligence unit being part of the investigative team, Chapter 6 will go into more detail about how intelligence is collected.

Questions for Discussion

1. What do you see as fundamental characteristics of a criminal investigator?
2. What should be the mindset of the intelligence analyst when assisting in a criminal investigation?

Important Terms

Circumstantial evidence: Evidence from which inferences can be drawn and may include physical evidence, such as weapons, blood, fingerprints, tool marks, documents, and dust, dirt, or other traces.

Corpus delicti: Evidence that will help substantiate the elements of the crime.

Criminal profiling: Developing a psychological portrait of an unknown offender.

Direct evidence: Evidence from the testimony by eyewitnesses who have information to offer about the crime through one of their five senses.

Fusion center: Name for some police department intelligence units; they may also go by other names, such as intelligence unit or real-time crime center.

Geographic profiling: Developing a probabilistic map of the area in which the offender's residence is located.

Intelligence: Data available to, collected by, or disseminated through the intelligence analyst or the tactical crime analyst.

Intelligence analysis: Continually evaluating and analyzing data in order to provide the most useful possible information to police officers.

Link analysis: Analyzing relationships among people or organizations; used to find matches in data for patterns of interest in investigations.

Modus operandi: Particular method or manner in which an offender carries out crimes.

Real-time crime center: Room in which the intelligence analyst or tactical crime analyst has at his or her disposal a bank of computers and extensive websites and data banks that allow access to and analysis of intelligence in order to provide practical and useful on-the-spot information to police officers in the field. May also be called a fusion center or intelligence unit.

Time–event chart: Graphic depiction of the chronology of an individual's or a group's activities.

Study Guide Questions

For questions 1–4, indicate whether the statement is true or false.

1. _____ The intelligence analyst's raw material is data.

2. _____ It could be argued that the lifeblood of criminal investigation is information.

3. _____ It is unimportant for intelligence analysts and tactical crime analysts to have an understanding of how a criminal investigation proceeds.

4. _____ The first police officer on the crime scene is usually the intelligence analyst.

5. A successful criminal investigator often possesses the following qualities *except* for
   a. Strong degree of self-discipline
   b. Ethics and integrity
   c. Lack of concern for winning the confidence of others
   d. Never acting out of malice or bias

6. One of the duties of the patrol officer when he is the first officer on the crime scene is to
   a. Interview the victim
   b. Order a cup of coffee
   c. Call for backup
   d. Arrest any unwilling witnesses

7. Associative evidence is any evidence that
   a. Discovers all of the known associates of the suspect
   b. Connects a suspect to the crime scene or the victim
   c. Has valid fingerprints
   d. Leads to the arrest of other suspects

8. There are many databases available to the intelligence analyst, and these databases can help

    a. Pinpoint the identity of the perpetrator

    b. Encourage some lines of inquiry

    c. Zero in on the actual residence of the offender

    d. Create an infallible portrait of the offender's personality

9. Criminal profiling is

    a. As much an art as a science

    b. Always right on the mark

    c. A technique that has been perfected through rigorous research

    d. Useful in many criminal investigations

References

Abumere, I. (2015). Criminal profiling. Available at http://www.academia.edu/2333675/Effectiveness_of_Criminal_Profiling.

Bruce, C.W. (2008). Fundamentals of crime analysis. In S.L. Gwinn, C.W. Bruce, J.P. Cooper, and S. Hicks (eds.), *Exploring Crime Analysis: Readings on Essential Skills*. Overland Park, KS: International Association of Crime Analysts, pp. 7–32.

European Association of Psychology and the Law. (2011). Fact sheet: Criminal profiling. Available at http://itssimple.ca/forensicgroup/wp-content/uploads/Factsheet_Criminal_Profilingbackup.pdf.

Paulsen, D.J. (2006). Connecting the dots: Assessing the accuracy of geographic profiling software. *Policing: An International Journal of Police Strategies and Management* 29(2): 306–334.

Swanson, C.R., Chamelin, N.C., Territo, L., and Taylor, R.W. (2012). *Criminal Investigation*. 11th ed. New York: McGraw-Hill.

Weston, P.B., and Lushbaugh, C.A. (2006). *Criminal Investigation*. 10th ed. Upper Saddle River, NJ: Pearson Prentice-Hall.

Winerman, L. (2004). Criminal profiling: The reality behind the myth. *Monitor on Psychology* 35(7): 66–69.

7

INTELLIGENCE AND THE
TACTICAL ANALYST

Chapter Outline

1. Intelligence perspective
2. Case study: A robbery investigation
3. Intelligence process
4. Case study: Assisting in an out-of-state murder investigation
5. Intelligence analyst
6. Intelligence-led policing
7. Case study: Shots fired
8. Intelligence and the terrorist threat

Learning Objectives for Chapter 7

1. Understand the intelligence perspective
2. Learn the five-step intelligence process
3. Develop an understanding of how the intelligence analyst contributes to investigations
4. Gain an understanding of intelligence-led policing
5. Learn the role of intelligence in the terrorism threat

Intelligence is the product of systematic gathering, evaluation, and synthesis of raw data. It is information that has been analyzed to determine meaning and relevance.

U.S. Department of Justice (2003, p. 4)

Introduction

A shooting takes place, and the call is made to 911. The 911 operator immediately creates a "job" card, a computer incident entry unique to the call, and within seconds the shooting call is dispatched to a uniformed patrol unit. In addition to the radio dispatch, the job card, or computer incident, is also sent to the marked unit's car computer.

From an intelligence perspective, in terms of general suspect description, location of incident, and possible vehicle involvement, intelligence that can aid and assist the responding units is usually sent over the radio in order to make the responding officers aware of the particulars of the incident as they respond. For the most part, this is usually the only intelligence the responding units can rely on until they arrive on scene and can ascertain what actually happened.

Tactical analysts working in real-time crime centers (RTCCs) have the capabilities to also monitor those dispatched calls and read the job cards as they are sent to the responding units. It is here that the tactical analysts can begin the process of rapid data mining of the intelligence that is being sent in order to ascertain the possible "who, what, when, where, why, and how" that can help paint the picture of what may have just occurred and then relay that intelligence to the responding patrol units—sometimes even before they arrive on scene.

But before tactical analysts even become involved to this extent, they need to fully understand what is meant by the term *intelligence* and how intelligence differs from information. Data mining from bits and pieces of information being dispatched over the police radio or written on a 911 job card is only useful if that information can be turned into viable intelligence that the responding officers can use to help them better understand the situation they are being confronted with.

Since information is based on a set of collected facts, the intelligence process takes these facts and then uses them, as data, to make informed predictions.

In addition to having to understanding the intelligence process, and with RTCCs increasing throughout the country, there needs to be a better understanding of the analysts who data mine from these centers, because they are now an integral part of the real-time process.

Real-Time Crime Centers

In 2005, the New York City Police Department (NYPD) opened its $11 million RTCC. The center was designed to have analysts working cohesively with sworn law enforcement in a technologically driven environment for the purpose of data mining intelligence in real time from multiple data sources and then sending those results out to the field to assist officers with their investigations. At the time when the NYPD's RTCC opened, then police commissioner Raymond Kelly stated that technology combined with good old-fashioned police work can ultimately create a safer community (D'Amico, 2006).

Joseph D'Amico, commanding officer of the NYPD's RTCC, added, "The Real Time Crime Center (RTCC) of the NYPD is a centralized data hub that rapidly mines information from multiple crime databases and disseminates that information to officers in the field" (NYC Global Partners Innovation Exchange, 2010, p. 1).

With the advent of RTCCs, the need to train traditional crime analysts in the field of intelligence analysis became clearly evident. A hybrid form of traditional analysis was needed to address the skill set required to rapidly data mine information and intelligence and disseminate it to a third party. Enter the tactical analyst, and with the tactical analyst, the need for that analyst to fully understand the intelligence process.

Case Study: Robbery Investigation

A tactical analyst, working in an RTCC, received a request from a police investigator in the field to try to identify a male who was known on the street by the nickname of "Big Red." The request was in relation to a robbery that occurred approximately five minutes earlier. During the robbery, the suspect being sought had just stolen two handguns. The need to identify this suspect was urgent.

The tactical analyst utilized social media to tentatively identify the suspect and, as a result, did in fact find a social media account associated with an individual who also utilized the nickname of Big Red as a social media moniker. Ironically, as the tactical analyst was capturing photographs and intelligence from the social media account, the account was suddenly deleted.

The tactical analyst was able to use the information she found on the just-deleted social media account to do an in-depth analysis into the history of the individual identified as the account holder. The tactical analyst discovered that in this individual's criminal history, there were several incidents of criminal conduct similar to the robbery of the two guns that was currently being investigated.

The tactical analyst sent her intelligence findings, along with the individual's photo, to the investigator handling the robbery investigation, and he, in turn, used the photograph to create a photo array. A photo array is a photo lineup that law enforcement uses to show victims of crimes a series of photographs, including one that may be the possible suspect, for identification purposes.

As a result, the individual who was identified by the tactical analyst was identified by the victim as the male who stole the handguns. As a result of the positive identification, an arrest warrant was issued for the suspect—Big Red—for robbery.

The most important fact to note here is that it took less than 10 minutes for the analyst to make the identification once the call was made from the field to the RTCC.

The tactical analyst in this case had been trained to rapidly data mine from several data resources as she looked for information that she could turn into credible intelligence for the field investigator. More importantly, she fully understood the intelligence process.

Intelligence Process

Also known as the intelligence cycle, the intelligence process focuses on turning information into intelligence, hopefully, in most cases, actionable intelligence. Actionable intelligence is intelligence that can be used to initiate activity in the field. Keep in mind, however, that intelligence is not always 100% accurate, but when it is properly processed and disseminated, it is the process most advantageous to those involved in the decision-making process.

The intelligence process may look different at times, especially in terms of the sequence of events, but depending on how it is used, the key components usually do not deviate that much.

Five-Step Intelligence Process

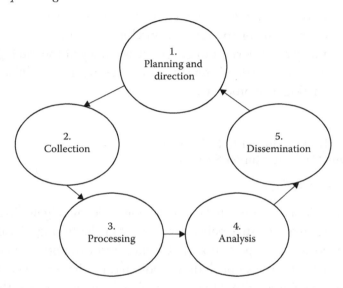

- *Step 1: Planning and direction.* Step 1 involves identifying the need for intelligence. This step clarifies the request that calls for intelligence and helps define how the results will be presented.
- *Step 2: Collection.* The second step involves collecting information and data that relate to the subject in question. This step usually involves a mass collection of information and the review of previous intelligence; both new and old information need to be vetted—given a careful and critical examination—for relevance, significance, and accuracy.
- *Step 3: Processing.* The third step involves filtering all of the collected information into a usable and organized format that can be analyzed for relevance and priority.
- *Step 4: Analysis.* In this step, the intelligence is analyzed. This means that the information collected is converted into actual intelligence that can now be disseminated in various forms.

- *Step 5: Dissemination.* This step has multiple layers to it in regard to information sharing. It must be decided to whom the intelligence will be disseminated, and how much of it will be shared. Dissemination typically involves the release of the findings by written correspondence, verbal briefing, or any form that seems like a proper way to communicate the factual results of the weighed and analyzed intelligence.

There is a possible step 6: reevaluation. Sometimes there needs to be a continued analysis of the released intelligence, and in a follow-up process, it may be important to gauge the accuracy of the intelligence, the need for more in-depth review, or the re-creation of finished, or updated, intelligence products.

Case Study: Assisting with the Identification of an Out-Of-State Murder Suspect

Step 1: Planning Stage

A crime analyst was contacted by a local homicide investigator in regard to assisting an out-of-state police department in identifying a local individual who was a suspect in a double murder in the other state. The crucial piece of modus operandi, as indicated by the investigator, was that the homicide appeared to be drug related, and it appeared that the homicide suspect had been robbed by local drug dealers. This suspect was from the state in which the analyst currently worked, and that was why the request was made from the out-of-state police agency. The analyst discussed the case directly with the out-of-state police investigator.

In this case, it was determined that the need to examine local intelligence on the possible murder suspect might help to ascertain the local suspect's associates, who could turn out to be accomplices in the homicide.

Step 2: Collection Stage

The out-of-state investigator gave the analyst the information that an unknown female, who could only be identified by the apparent nickname "Jeannie," was a major heroin distributor within the other state for the past year. This woman who went by the name of Jeannie was a close associate of the male, who was initially arrested for the double murder. The out-of-state investigator sent the analyst a link to a social media page for the female, hoping that the analyst would be able to identify her.

In this case, we see the collection of information involved a nickname and a social media link on the possible second suspect. However, the information had yet to been deemed relevant.

Step 3: Processing Stage

In examining the social media page, the analyst found no photos of actual people on the page, and no information indicating who the account belonged to. However, the analyst was able to locate a post from the previous year where the account holder referred to an actual "named person" as mom, and it was stated in a social medium posting that she would see "mom" on a street within the jurisdiction of the police agency in which the analyst worked.

The analyst now had an actual name to work with. The analyst was able to research that name in multiple databases and was able to locate a female with the same name who lived on the street mentioned in the social media posting. The analyst then researched the background of this female and found her to have two daughters.

In this step, the tactical analyst not only collected intelligence, but also processed it for relevance. It was found to be very relevant.

Step 4: Analysis Stage

The analyst researched both daughters and found one to have a local arrest history. The analyst also located a police-documented field interview form (FIF). This is a form in which a police officer documents street contacts they had during their shifts. The daughter was listed on the FIF, along with a male cousin of hers. The officer also documented on the FIF the male cousin's prior local jail inmate number. The analyst researched the cousin's history and found that he had spent five years in state prison for drug possession, and that he also had a violent arrest history.

The collected information was analyzed for relevance and converted into actual intelligence that could be used for investigative purposes.

Step 5: Dissemination Stage

The information collected and analyzed by the tactical analyst was enough to indicate to the analyst that the now-identified female with the social media account and the nickname Jeannie had a real name, and she had contact with individuals prone to violence and narcotics activity. With the collected and documented intelligence, the analyst created an intelligence product that also included a police jail photograph of the female taken from a previous local arrest. The analysis report was sent to the out-of-state police investigator.

The out-of-state investigator contacted the analyst and confirmed with her that the intelligence and identification was, in fact, the second murder suspect who had previously been known only by Jeannie. The investigator also confirmed that this female was also a major narcotics dealer in her state, thus further tying her into the drug-related double murder.

The Intelligence Analyst

David Moore in a 2007 paper on critical thinking and intelligence analysis states that intelligence analysts are engaged in an intellectual pursuit (Moore, 2007). "They are trying to solve puzzles, resolve uncertainties, discover the nature and meaning of things that others would keep secret," Moore writes. "They must have the entire intellectual apparatus to help them identify the problem, assess the parts they know and the parts they do not, come up with an explanation of what is going on, and then express it in a way that others, including an audience not steeped in their own techniques, can understand" (Lowenthal, 2007, p. ix).

In the example previously discussed related to the out-of-state investigator and Jeannie, it was easy to see how the ultimate goal of the analyst was to data mine information and produce intelligence that directly responded to an initial request. Intelligence analysts are a critical component in the intelligence process since they are the ones tasked with completing each stage of the process. More importantly, however, they need to be extreme analytical thinkers in terms of processing the information and formulating conclusions.

When performing these functions in a real-time setting, the tactical analyst is required to rapidly data mine information gleaned from 911 dispatched crimes in progress. This process of rapid data mining accelerates the stages of the intelligence process because the information needs to be converted to actionable intelligence, and relayed to the field, as soon as possible. In some cases, tactical analysts are also multitasking several requests at once—strongly suggesting that the analyst must possess a confident, capable, analytical skill set.

Analyst Responsibilities

Regardless of whether the analyst is acting in the capacity of an intelligence analyst or a real-time tactical analyst, the roles and responsibilities attached to his or her duties remain the same. Those include

- Collection
- Evaluation
- Analysis
- Conclusions based on analysis
- Product development and distribution
- Follow-up

Intelligence-Led Policing

Intelligence-led policing often focuses on threats. And intelligence-led policing usually centers on the elimination of specific threats. The process of intelligence-led policing begins with information derived from the field but, once put through the intelligence process, produces intelligence deemed actionable for operational purposes. At this point, strategic decisions are made to deal with the now-identified threat.

The National Criminal Intelligence Sharing Plan Global Intelligence Working Group (GIWG) issued a report in 2005 that defined intelligence-led policing as "the collection and analysis of information to produce an intelligence end product designed to inform law enforcement decision-making at both the tactical and strategic levels" (U.S. Department of Justice, 2003, p. 4). Furthermore, Carter and Carter (2009, p. 16) stated that "intelligence-led policing is multijurisdictional, threat-driven, and strategic. It predominantly focuses on criminal enterprises such as terrorism, violence, and organizational crime and the conditions that support them."

Case Study: Shots Fired

Information Derived from the Field

The police responded to a shots fired call. Upon arrival, they found recently spent (fired) 12- gauge shotgun casings located in front of the home and noticed the front door was wide open. Officers entered the home to check for victims and found no one inside. They did find, in plain view, evidence of possible narcotics packaging. Information derived from the scene was written into an FIF and forwarded to the intelligence center in an attempt to identify the person(s) associated with the location and to see if the location posed an actual threat.

Intelligence Derived through the Intelligence Process: The Threat Identified

The intelligence analyst was able to data mine information on the location and discovered that a recent domestic incident report (DIR) documented that a male by the name of David Smith was currently staying at the location, and it was reported by the complainant that this man was involved in the sale of drugs at the location as well.

The analyst, through a rigorous data mining process, discovered a social media account associated with David Smith. The social media account had multiple photos of him holding a shotgun and a handgun. Keeping in mind that the responding officers had found spent shotgun casings in front of the location immediately after a 911 shots fired dispatched call, the analyst concluded that this was pertinent intelligence that she could directly link to the location and the David Smith who lived there. The analyst crated an intelligence product that synopsized the intelligence on the location, the man residing in the home, and its relevance to a shots fired call. The photos of the man holding the weapons were also placed on the product prior to it being disseminated throughout the law enforcement community.

Strategic Planning Based on Developed Intelligence

The police department's narcotics unit was then tasked to develop a case in which they could strategically target the location, which was now deemed a threat associated with shootings, weapons, and drug sales. Narcotics was able to utilize the intelligence produced by the intelligence analyst as actionable intelligence in their investigation. Part of their strategic plan was to introduce a confidential informant into the location in an attempt to purchase narcotics. This plan proved successful, and as a result, a search warrant was written that contained aspects of the intelligence provided by the intelligence analyst, and used as part of the probable cause.

The search warrant was executed, and officers found David Smith in the home, along with a shotgun, a handgun, cocaine, and heroin.

This case illustrates intelligence-led policing, as it started with information derived from the field and used that information to develop actionable intelligence that was then used to strategically deal with the identified threat. The analyst's intelligence resulted in an arrest and confiscation of contraband.

Intelligence and the Terrorist Threat

As defined in Title 18, Section 2332b of the U.S. Code of Federal Regulations, the federal crime of terrorism is an offense that "is calculated to influence or affect the conduct of government by intimidation or coercion, or to retaliate against government conduct" (FBI 2015, p. 1).

In general, terrorism is the unlawful use of force and violence against persons or property to intimidate or coerce a government, the civilian population, or any segment thereof, in furtherance of political or social objectives.

The terrorist attacks that occurred on September 11, 2001, opened America's eyes to a new kind of threat to the nation's security. Radical extremist—terrorists—introduced themselves to the American people by means that had not been seen on American soil since December 7, 1941, when Japan attacked the Pearl Harbor naval base in Hawaii. As in the 2001 attack and other attacks that continue to today, many questions linger—not only about the attack itself, but also about the background of the attackers and the countries that would support such a murderous attack. The intelligence community, in particular, found itself to be at a major crossroads.

The aftermath of the 9/11 attacks exposed a glaring deficiency as to the level of interagency intelligence sharing and cooperation, particularly in the areas of radical terrorist groups (U.S. Department of Justice, 2003). Inadequate, or nonexistent, relationships enabled members of radical organizations to basically hide in plain sight.

The radicalized enemy here in America seeks to accomplish the same objectives as their international brothers, by instilling fear through violence. They live among us unassumingly. We may have encountered them unknowingly during our daily routines, such as riding the bus while they may be sitting beside us or dining together in the same public restaurant. They are trained to blend into our society and do so with ease. They are polite, engaging, and even courteous as they covertly watch and learn all they can about our vulnerabilities and weaknesses. They patiently wait until the time is right to engage in criminal activity in order to exploit the openness of our free society. It is only through the intelligence process, and intelligence-led policing, that law enforcement can create credible intelligence intended to identify these individuals, groups, and potential soft-target locations.

On February 9, 2011, then U.S. secretary of homeland security Janet Napolitano testified before the U.S. House of Representatives Committee on Homeland Security in reference to understanding the homeland threat landscape. During her testimony, Secretary Napolitano stated,

> Since 9/11 the terrorist threat facing our country has evolved significantly in the last ten years, and continues to evolve, so that, in some ways, the threat facing us is at its most heightened state since those attacks. This fact requires us to continually adapt our counterterrorism techniques to effectively detect, deter, and prevent terrorist acts. (Department of Homeland Security, 2011, p. 1)

In 2010, the International Association of Chiefs of Police (IACP) held its annual conference in Orlando, Florida. The main speaker was Robert Mueller, then director of the Federal Bureau of Investigation. During his speech, Director Mueller spoke specifically of the continued growth of radical terrorism in America. According to Director Mueller, "Threats from homegrown terrorists are of great concern. These individuals are harder to detect, easily able to connect with other extremists on the internet, and, in some instances, highly capable operationally" (Mueller, 2010, p. 1).

Chalk and Rosenau (2004, p. iii), in a report for the RAND Corporation, advocate for strong analytical assessments, as they can prove to be an invaluable tool for making recommendations pertaining to law enforcement strategies. Chalk and Rosenau state, "The analysis is intended to help inform debate on the advisability of creating dedicated information collection and surveillance body."

The intelligence process described in this chapter, whether worked by federal, state, or local law enforcement, is the most accurate methodology and process that can effectively address the identification of the terrorist threat.

Intelligence: Post-9/11

The need to share intelligence resources and to turn untrusting relationships among certain law enforcement agencies into trusting ones took a decidedly sharp turn immediately after the terrorist attacks that occurred on September 11, 2001. Prior to 9/11, intelligence and information sharing among law enforcement agencies from the federal and state levels was virtually nonexistent. This glaring deficiency in intelligence sharing among those sworn to protect was one of the main reasons the intelligence community decided to focus their attention on positive efforts to improve their intelligence sharing with each other.

From these efforts, certain acts and plans were created to assist with interagency cooperation and intelligence sharing among federal, state, and local law enforcement agencies. Those acts and plans included the following:

- USA Patriot Act (2001): Provides appropriate tools required to intercept and obstruct terrorism. One key component, in terms of intelligence gathering, was the provision requiring information sharing while targeting terrorist organizations.

- Homeland Security Act (2002): Designed to consolidate several federal agencies under one governing body. These were primarily intelligence-led agencies, and they were also required to share information at multiple levels.
- National Criminal Intelligence Sharing Plan (2003): Created by the GIWG to provide an intelligence sharing plan model.
- 9/11 Commission Report (2004): Also known as the National Commission on Terrorist Attacks, this report is a government study on the details of what led to the terrorist attacks on September 11, 2001. It gives several recommendations relating to the continued need for information and intelligence sharing among law enforcement at every level of government.

The common denominator that can be found within this select group of examples is intelligence, and the need for information and intelligence to be shared among those organizations that utilize intelligence to investigate crime.

Questions for Discussion

1. How does the intelligence analyst best make sure that intelligence is actionable?
2. What does the analyst do during the analysis stage of the five-step intelligence process?

Important Terms

Actionable intelligence: Intelligence that can be used to initiate activity in the field.

Five-step intelligence process: Process that involves planning and direction, collection, processing, analysis, and dissemination.

Global Justice Information Sharing Initiative: In the fall of 2002, in response to the IACP's proposal to create the National Criminal Intelligence Sharing Plan GIWG, the U.S. Department of Justice, Office of Justice Programs (OJP), authorized the formation of the Global Justice Information Sharing Initiative. The initial meeting of the GIWG was held in Atlanta, Georgia, in 2002, and the mission statement of the newly formed group was stated as "The GIWG mission is to develop, build, and support the creation of the National Criminal Intelligence Sharing Plan, which will provide law enforcement agencies with the ability to gather, analyze, protect, and share credible and timely information and intelligence to identify, investigate, prevent, deter, and defeat criminal and terrorist activities, both domestically and internationally, as well as protect the security of our homeland and preserve the rights and freedoms of all Americans."

Intelligence-led policing: Collection and analysis of information to produce an intelligence end product designed to inform law enforcement decision-making at both the tactical and strategic levels.

Intelligence process: Also known as the intelligence cycle, the intelligence process focuses on turning information into intelligence, especially actionable intelligence.

Real-time crime center: Center designed to have analysts working cohesively with sworn law enforcement in a technologically driven environment for the purpose of data mining intelligence in real time from multiple data sources and then sending those results out to the field to assist officers with their investigations.

Terrorism: Unlawful use of force and violence against persons or property to intimidate or coerce a government, the civilian population, or any segment thereof, in furtherance of political or social objectives.

Study Guide Questions

For questions 1–3, indicate whether the statement is true or false.

1. _____ Once a call has come into a police department, the tactical analyst can begin the process of rapid data mining of the intelligence that is being sent in order to ascertain the possible "who, what, when, where, why, and how" of a criminal event.

2. _____ The RTCC has been described as a centralized data hub that rapidly mines information from multiple crime databases and disseminates that information to officers in the field in a criminal investigation.

3. _____ It is not important for the tactical analyst to understand the intelligence process.

4. The intelligence process focuses on turning information into
   a. Good police department press releases
   b. Propaganda
   c. Probable cause
   d. Actionable intelligence

5. The five-step intelligence process *does not* involve
   a. Planning and direction
   b. Sharing initial data with the mayor
   c. Collecting information
   d. Analyzing information

6. The intelligence analyst's responsibilities include
   a. Choosing the best site for a new jail
   b. Collecting data from prisoners
   c. Product development and distribution
   d. Analyzing odds for football games

7. Intelligence-led policing often focuses on
   a. Threats
   b. Protecting businesses from cybercrime
   c. International copyright violations
   d. Gambling violations

References

Carter, D.L., and Carter, J.G. (2009). Intelligence-led policing: Conceptual and functional considerations for public policy. *Criminal Justice Policy Review* 20(3): 310–325.

Chalk, P., and Rosenau, W. (2004). Confronting "the enemy within" security intelligence, the police, and counterterrorism in four democracies. Santa Monica, CA: RAND Corporation. Available at http://www.rand.org/content/dam/rand/pubs/monographs/2004/RAND_MG100.pdf.

D'Amico, J. (2006). Stopping crime in real time. *Police Chief Magazine* 73(9): 1.

Department of Homeland Security. (2011). Testimony of Secretary Janet Napolitano before the U.S. House of Representatives Committee on Homeland Security, Understanding the homeland threat landscape—Considerations for the 112th Congress. Available at https://www.dhs.gov/news/2011/02/09/secretary-napolitanos-testimony-understanding-homeland-threat-landscape.

FBI (Federal Bureau of Investigation). (2015). Terrorism. Washington, DC: FBI. Available at https://www.fbi.gov/about-us/investigate/terrorism/terrorism-definition.

Lowenthal, M.M. (2007). Foreward. In D.T. Moore, Critical thinking and intelligence analysis. Occasional paper no. 14. Washington DC: National Defense Intelligence College. Available at http://www.au.af.mil/au/awc/awcgate/dia/ndic_moore_crit_analysis_hires.pdf.

Moore, D.T. (2007). Critical thinking and intelligence analysis. Occasional paper 14. Washington, DC: National Defense Intelligence College. Available at http://www.au.af.mil/au/awc/awcgate/dia/ndic_moore_crit_analysis_hires.pdf.

Mueller, R. (2010). IACP 2010: FBI director Robert Mueller talks terrorism, training, technology, and trust. San Francisco: PoliceOne. Available at http://www.policeone.com/federal-law-enforcement/articles/2834806-IACP-2010-FBI-Director-Robert-Mueller-talks-terrorism-training-technology-and-trust/.

NYC Global Partners Innovation Exchange. (2010). Best practice: Real-time crime center: Centralized crime data system. New York: NYC Global Partners Innovation Exchange. Available at http://www.nyc.gov/html/unccp/gprb/downloads/pdf/NYC_Safety%20and%20Security_RTCC.pdf.

U.S. Department of Justice. (2003). The national criminal intelligence sharing plan. Global justice information sharing initiative. Washington, DC: U.S. Department of Justice. Available at http://www.it.ojp.gov/documents/National_Criminal_Intelligence_Sharing_Plan.pdf.

8

COLLECTING INTELLIGENCE

Chapter Outline

1. Investigation
2. Sources of information and intelligence
3. Interplay between the intelligence analyst and the criminal investigator
4. Databases

Learning Objectives for Chapter 8

1. Gain a better understanding of the interplay between the criminal investigator and the intelligence analyst
2. Begin to understand the use of databases in criminal investigations
3. Develop an initial understanding of the number of possible databases that can be accessed by the intelligence analyst to assist in criminal investigations

Information is the most valuable commodity in the world. It's more valuable than money, for with it one can make money. It's more valuable than power. It's more valuable than goods, for with it one can build, acquire, and improve goods. In any business, in any industry, in any part of the world, the right information is absolutely priceless.... Businesses invest a great deal of money, time, and resources in the quest to acquire information—information about their products, and how to improve them; information about their competitors, and what they're up to; information about customers and what they want; information about the business itself, and how its various divisions are doing. Governments rise and fall on information—information about the opinions and attitudes of their citizens; information about allies; information about enemies. Information wins wars, builds cities, heals the sick, enriches the poor, and—most relevant to our purposes—solves and prevents crimes.... Such is the case with crime analysts. Crime analysts provide information to police agencies about crime, disorder, calls for service, police activities, and other areas of police interest, all with the goal of helping the agencies do their jobs better ... the analyst's raw material is data, which might come from numerous sources. Out of this data, the analyst seeks to create *information*, which he then delivers to his "consumer"—the police agency.

Bruce (2008, pp. 7–8)

Introduction

When investigators arrive on the scene of a crime, some information will be available to them. For instance, the first responders to the scene—typically patrol officers—will have secured that scene helping to prevent contamination of the evidence and locating and identifying witnesses and suspects. Normally, that will mean that the criminal investigators will have access to a number of sources of information. Those sources will include the victim, any evidence left behind by the perpetrator(s), witnesses to the crime, and, perhaps, even one or more suspects.

This sometimes considerable amount of information may be all the investigator needs in order to solve the crime and arrest a suspect. However, more often than not, there will be insufficient evidence to lead to an arrest and the suspect will not be known or identified. In this situation, the investigator or detective will need to draw on other sources of information to begin the process of investigating the crime and pursuing the criminal. In this sense, the investigator must rely on intelligence.

As you learned in previous chapters, intelligence is the information or data that are collected and evaluated. For an investigation to make any progress, the intelligence that comes to the investigator must be reliable and relevant. While the investigator has the usual sources of information—victim's statement, forensic evidence, and witness statements—often other intelligence is required for the blossoming of an investigation. This is where the intelligence analyst and the tactical crime analyst play a critical role.

Interplay between the Intelligence Analyst and the Criminal Investigator

As the role and importance of the intelligence analyst increase, in a certain sense, there is a synergy and a merging of roles between the investigator and the analyst. In a perfect police department, the investigator and analyst would think along the same lines as both work in tandem to investigate a crime. While the detective is on the scene in the beginning and has access to his or her direct sources of information, the intelligence analyst is away from the actual crime scene but can access numerous sources of intelligence while taking new data fed to him or her by the investigator and helping to connect the dots between a crime and a criminal offender.

The investigator feeds information that he gathers in the field to the analyst, who can use previously collected and warehoused intelligence to, in turn, send data back to the investigator to help move the investigation in appropriate directions.

The interplay between the intelligence analyst and the investigator may start even before the detective arrives on the scene. A skilled intelligence analyst will begin accumulating information valuable to the detective early in the process. For example, if the crime is the armed robbery of a convenience store, the analyst can determine quickly a number of pieces of information for the investigator:

- The name of the convenience store
- The owners of the store
- Whether there have been previous robberies at this store
- The outcomes of previously reported crimes at the store
- Whether suspects were identified in previously reported crimes at the store and whether arrests were made
- The names of previous suspects or arrestees
- The addresses of those previous suspects or arrestees

By arriving at the scene with this kind of intelligence, the investigator can interview victims and witnesses with a more informed perspective and ask more probing questions. But from that point on, the investigator can provide feedback to the analyst and can ask more pointed questions of the analyst. For instance, the investigator may want to know

- What other robberies have occurred in the area recently?
- Is there a pattern to the robberies over the past few months or longer?
- What weapons were used in other robberies in the vicinity?
- Who were the suspects in those recent robberies?
- What are the residence addresses of all previous suspects in local robberies?
- Do any of those suspects have a record of robbery arrests or convictions?
- Which known criminals live in the vicinity of this and previous robberies?
- What photographs are available of previous suspects?
- Do these photographs resemble the description of the perpetrator(s) in this current robbery?

By obtaining answers to these kinds of questions, the investigator can determine the next steps in the investigation. He may determine that interviews should be conducted of previous suspects of local robberies to check on alibis and movements around the time of the latest crime. In addition, he may decide to solicit information from other police officers who work in the vicinity of the robbery or from confidential informants in the area who may be able to share important information.

Sources of Information

In addition to statements from victims and witnesses, and information from other police officers and informants, detectives can work with intelligence analysts to review sources of information available in databases.

Some of the databases offering treasure troves of information are the following:

- *Department of Motor Vehicles (secretary of state)*: To obtain driver's licenses, vehicle registrations, and photos.

- *Department of Corrections*: To track convicted felons and determine their incarceration or parole status; photos from the time of incarceration are often available.
- *Stolen property databases*: For instance, *Trace* is the largest database of property reported stolen to U.S. law enforcement agencies. This database holds millions of serial numbers of stolen goods from thousands of police agencies that can be searched to identify goods that are recovered.
- *Federal, state, and local court information*: The database *PACER* hosts millions of case file documents and docket information for all district, bankruptcy, and appellate courts. Furthermore, most state and local felony courts maintain a database, but there are databases that cover the entire United States. An example is *Corra's Nationwide Criminal Records Database*, a powerful search of more than 200 million records nationwide, including the District of Columbia, which includes criminal records from statewide repositories and archives, departments of correction, local county information, traffic violations and infractions, and administration of court records. This database also includes the nationwide Sex Offender Registry search.
- *Probation, parole, and supervised release data*: There are state and local databases that track offenders who have been placed on probation or are on parole.
- *Prosecutorial information*: Transactional Records Access Clearinghouse (TRAC) has a database for hundreds of millions of federal charges and convictions. There are federal databases that list health and safety convictions, elder abuse convictions, and prosecutions by the Environmental Protection Agency.
- *Gang-related tracking*: The National Gang Intelligence Center (NGIC), operated by the Federal Bureau of Investigation (FBI), integrates gang intelligence from across federal, state, and local law enforcement on the growth, migration, criminal activity, and association of gangs that pose a significant threat to the United States. The NGIC supports law enforcement by sharing timely and accurate information and by providing strategic and tactical analysis of intelligence. The databases of each component agency are available to the NGIC, as are

other gang-related databases, permitting centralized access to information about gangs.

- *Sexual predator tracking or Sex Offender Registry*: The FBI has on its website the National Sex Offender Public Website, which provides access to the latest information from all 50 states, the District of Columbia, Puerto Rico, Guam, and numerous Indian tribes for the identity and location of known sex offenders.

Besides state and local systems and databases, there are also non-profit and private sources of information about suspected or known criminal figures, groups, and businesses, as well as terrorism. For instance, one such database is operated by the Association of Law Enforcement Intelligence Units (LEIU). Another is *LeadsOnLine*, a private subscription service used by more than 1600 law enforcement agencies (Swanson et al., 2012). This service provides access to transactions from thousands of reporting businesses, including scrap metal processors, secondhand stores, Internet drop-off stores, pawnshops, and eBay.

In addition, there are social network sites, such as *FaceBook*, *MyYearbook*, *Twitter*, *Pinterest*, *LinkedIn*, and *Classmates*, that contain personal profiles and often valuable personal details about where people live, work, and vacation, along with information about friends, associates, and love interests.

As can be readily seen, there are a plethora of databases and sources of intelligence and data these days. The intelligence analyst and the tactical crime analyst must be aware of the many sources of useful data in order to be of the most help to law enforcement.

In Chapter 9, we introduce the concept of data mining and using information accessed from computers and the Internet to give police investigators and police administrators actionable intelligence.

Questions for Discussion

1. What do you see as fundamental characteristics of a criminal investigator?
2. What should be the mindset of the intelligence analyst when assisting in a criminal investigation?

Important Terms

Data: Information, especially facts or numbers, collected to be examined and considered as useful for the investigation of a crime or for analyzing crime trends.

Database: Set of data grouped together in one location in a computer. A computerized database is much like an electronic filing cabinet of information arranged for easy access or for a specific purpose.

Intelligence: Data available to, collected by, or disseminated through the intelligence analyst or the tactical crime analyst for use by a police agency.

Intelligence analysis: Continually evaluating and analyzing data in order to provide the most useful possible information to police officers.

Study Guide Questions

For questions 1–3, indicate whether the statement is true or false.

1. _____ The intelligence analyst's raw material is data.
2. _____ Crime analysts provide information to police investigators about crime, suspects, or other persons of interest in a criminal investigation.
3. _____ The intelligence analyst's data only come from one source.
4. For an investigation to make any progress, the intelligence that comes to the investigator must be
   a. Able to name the criminal offender
   b. Absolutely accurate
   c. Reliable and accurate
   d. Obtained with a search warrant
5. There should be an interplay between the criminal investigator and the intelligence analyst so that data are
   a. Kept secret by the analyst
   b. Only relayed when the investigator is stumped
   c. Shared back and forth
   d. Obtained based on databases that the investigator is familiar with

6. Some of the databases potentially offering valuable information to move an investigation forward may come from
   a. The Department of Motor Vehicles
   b. The Department of Corrections
   c. Stolen property databases
   d. All of the above

References

Bruce, C.W. (2008). Fundamentals of crime analysis. In S.L. Gwinn, C.W. Bruce, J.P. Cooper, and S. Hicks (eds.), *Exploring Crime Analysis: Readings on Essential Skills*. Overland Park, KS: International Association of Crime Analysts, pp. 7–32.

Swanson, C.R., Chamelin, N.C., Territo, L., and Taylor, R.W. (2012). *Criminal Investigation*. 11th ed. New York: McGraw-Hill.

9

DATA MINING AND ANALYZING INTELLIGENCE

Chapter Outline

1. What is data mining?
2. Understanding data mining
3. Computer-based transaction processing
4. Analytical systems
5. Software available for criminal justice data mining
6. What kinds of relationships can data mining software find?

Learning Objectives for Chapter 9

1. Understand data mining
2. Learn how crime data are analyzed
3. Begin to understand how to explore large databases
4. Explore examples of data mining

A major challenge facing all law enforcement and intelligence-gathering organizations is accurately and efficiently analyzing the growing volumes of crime data. For example, complex conspiracies are often difficult to unravel because information on suspects can be geographically diffuse and span long periods of time. Detecting cybercrime can likewise be difficult because busy network traffic and frequent online transactions generate large amounts of data, only a small portion of which relates to illegal activities. Data mining is a powerful tool that enables criminal investigators who may lack extensive training as data analysts to explore large databases quickly and efficiently.

Chen et al. (2003, p. 50)

Introduction

What Is Data Mining?

Data mining, sometimes called data discovery or knowledge discovery, is the process of analyzing data from different perspectives and summarizing them into useful information. On a more technical level, data mining is the process of finding correlations or patterns among many fields in large relational databases (McCue and Parker, 2003).

For the most part, data mining tells us about very large and complex data sets. And these days, there are many large, complex data sets available. For instance, in Chapter 8 we listed some data sets—or databases—that are often used by law enforcement. For instance, one large database is the motor vehicles department (or secretary of state) in your state. If, for example, you live in Illinois, the secretary of state in Illinois manages one of the largest computer databases in the state, keeping track of approximately 8.7 million drivers, 11 million registered vehicles, 466,000 corporations, 230,000 limited liability entities, 159,000 registered securities salespersons, and 16,000 investment advisor representatives. This one database illustrates something that most of us know—or, at least, realize on some level: there is far more information available than anyone can digest, let alone analyze, without a computer. And that amount of information is growing every day. The reason for that is simple, because nearly every one of our transactions leaves a data signature that someone (or more likely some computer) is capturing and storing.

The sheer scale and volume of the data collected by businesses and the government defy our imagination; it is beyond our sense-making capabilities (Furnas, 2012). To try to determine relationships and patterns, therefore, is often too complex to figure out by trying to look at the data. For instance, using our example of the Illinois secretary of state, if you wanted to find a relationship between licensed drivers who had their license suspended during the years 2008 and 2012 and who drove a Chevy Impala, you could not possibly determine this by hand; you could find such relationships, though, with data mining.

In other words, data mining is used to simplify and summarize the data in a manner that we can understand and use. For example, we are all familiar with the way Amazon.com or Netflix utilize data mining, although you may not have known that these companies were using data mining techniques. However, every time you log in to Amazon to look for a book or a DVD, you will see on the website that Amazon knows exactly what you previously looked at, what you previously bought, and what you might like to buy this time. Netflix does exactly the same thing, recommending what movie you would probably enjoy watching next. MasterCard and Visa use data mining to target you for deals or advertising. Most such major companies use sophisticated data mining software to track your data.

How Does Data Mining Work?

Large-scale information technology (IT) has been evolving for years. In fact, the term *information technology* is so common that it is used in every large organization. Yet, when we typically use the term, we usually are referring to the IT department of a business or university. We say, "I should call IT to come and fix my computer" or "See if IT can install the new software we ordered." But we generally no longer question exactly what the term *information technology* means.

For our purposes, IT is the use of any computers, storage, networking, and other physical devices, infrastructure, and processes to create, process, store, secure, and exchange all forms of electronic data. The term *information technology* was coined by the *Harvard Business Review* in order to make a distinction between purpose-built machines designed to perform a limited scope of functions and general-purpose computing machines that could be programmed for various tasks (Applegate et al., 1988). As the IT industry evolved from the mid-twentieth century, it encompassed transistors and integrated circuits, while our computing capabilities make giant leaps forward.

IT usually includes several layers of physical equipment (hardware), virtualization and management or automation tools, operating systems, and applications (software) used to perform essential functions. User devices, peripherals, and software, such as laptops, smartphones, or even recording equipment, can be included in the IT domain. IT can also refer to the architectures, methodologies, and regulations governing the use and storage of data. But it is important for you to be aware that IT has over the past two decades been evolving into separate transaction and analytical systems.

A transaction processing system (TPS) supports the processing of a company's or organization's business transactions. For instance, the TPS of a university helps perform such tasks as enrolling students in courses, billing students for tuition, and issuing paychecks to faculty. In addition, the TPS associated with a university's large employee and faculty pension fund may assist stockbrokers in executing buy and sell orders while also helping with accounting for the transaction (Mahar, 2003).

TPSs keep an organization running smoothly by automating the processing of the voluminous amounts of paperwork that must be handled daily. These systems, if we again use the example of a large university, include the accurate recording of transactions, as well as control procedures usually used in paychecks, invoices, customer statements, payment reminders, tuition bills, and student schedules (Mahar, 2003).

The TPS of an organization may be far reaching, extending completely throughout the organization, linking together the entire financial system.

Computer-Based Transaction Processing

Computer-based TPSs are often considered the "bread and butter" of the management information system application. No matter how nervous upper management in a medium to large organization is about spending in the information system area, it knows that it cannot pull the plug on its TPS and survive. Actually, many large companies have had computer-based TPSs since the 1950s. Most TPSs have been and still are mainframe oriented. IBM equipment and their compatibles currently claim the lion's share of the transaction processing marketplace (Mahar, 2003).

Although many companies consider TPS to be their most important computer application, a surprisingly large number of firms have not carried computer-based information processing far beyond the transaction processing stage. TPSs in many organizations today are used in this way as competitive weapons. Additionally, the move from dumb terminals to intelligent microprocessor-based workstations is expected to alter transaction processing in other ways, such as by distributing certain traditionally mainframe-based centralized transaction processing functions closer to their own offices or departments.

As indicated, the TPS supports the processing of an organization's many transactions. This includes accounting for the transactions on its records, as well as providing support activities such as sending out payment reminders. Recently gaining competitive advantage has become a TPS concern in some firms, especially those that are working to tie customers and suppliers together more closely with the organization's TPS via electronic linkages.

Role of Information Technology and Transaction Processing

For many businesses, a transaction refers to an exchange of goods or services for money. The earliest TPSs were manual systems. A clerk would record transactions in a journal or on numbered, multipart forms. These transactions would later be transferred manually to a central system of handwritten records or file folders responding to individual customers or suppliers. These records would be set up to trigger statements to customers or checks to suppliers. Many small businesses still operate with manual TPSs; however, inexpensive and easy-to-use computer technology is finding its way into more small businesses (Mahar, 2003).

Analytical Systems

On the other hand, and at the same time, IT has been developing analytical systems. One strategy for extracting meaning from large amounts of investigative information is the use of data mining applications. Data mining systematically searches information to identify relationships and patterns. Although data mining has been used effectively in private industry for a number of years, law enforcement has trailed in the application of this technology. As an interesting comparison, data mining techniques in the commercial environment have allowed retailers to know more about purchasing habits than what the police know about criminal suspects.

To explore the use of data mining within criminal justice, particularly criminal investigations, data mining software analyzes relationships and patterns in stored transaction data. Data mining software consists of sophisticated search programs, advanced statistical techniques, and innovative graphics features. Search programs used in data mining software provide users with the ability to make queries that use varied search criteria and repeatedly redefine those criteria to make searches as useful as possible. By using data mining software, investigators can initiate database searches and link analyses that extract information describing relationships between persons, events, and other aspects of criminal activities. Data mining systems provide users with graphic displays that make it easier to see the detected relationships or patterns.

A typical law enforcement data mining application might attempt to identify a suspect when the only available information is a crime report and a vehicle description. An investigator could initiate a query of a regional network database to obtain information that would identify a suspect. Data mining software would then search information compiled by all agencies participating in the network. The vehicle description contained in the crime report submitted by one agency might match an entry in a field interview report submitted by a different agency. The field interview report might indicate the vehicle was seen a short distance from the crime scene at a time close to the time of the crime, and that its driver had been questioned and provided a name and address. Data mining software could then be used to determine the involvement of the now-identified suspect in other crimes. Without the advantage of data mining software, information from the crime report and the field interview information might never be found or linked.

The 2002 "D.C. sniper" (or "beltway sniper") case investigation illustrates the difficulty in searching massive amounts of information available to law enforcement agencies. Because the various shootings in this case took place in Washington, D.C., Maryland, and Virginia, multiple law enforcement agencies were compiling information, resulting in the availability of a large amount of data in various systems. Review of the investigation revealed that information on the vehicle used by the snipers had been previously reported by law enforcement agencies, but the volume of data and their storage in disparate systems precluded timely searches. Data mining addresses this kind of problem.

Software Available for Data Mining in Criminal Justice

Several types of analytical software systems are currently available for use in the criminal justice system. For example, the following sections cover some categories of software that are suitable for criminal justice and law enforcement applications,

Statistical

Statistical Analysis System (SAS) is a software suite that can mine, alter, manage, and retrieve data from a variety of sources and perform statistical analysis on them. SAS provides a graphical point-and-click user interface for nontechnical users and more advanced options.

Machine Learning

Machine learning and data mining often employ the same methods and overlap significantly. Machine learning, by definition, is a type of artificial intelligence (AI) that provides computers with the ability to learn without being explicitly programmed. Machine learning focuses on the development of computer programs that can teach themselves to grow and change when exposed to new data.

The process of machine learning is similar to that of data mining. Both systems search through data to look for patterns. However, instead of extracting data for human comprehension—as is the case in data mining applications—machine learning uses those data to improve the program's own understanding. Machine learning programs detect patterns in data and adjust program actions accordingly. For example, Facebook's News Feed changes according to the user's personal interactions with other users. If a user frequently tags a friend in photos, writes on his wall, or "likes" his links, the News Feed will show more of that friend's activity in the user's News Feed due to presumed closeness.

Machine learning and data mining can be generally distinguished as follows:

- Machine learning focuses on prediction, based on *known* properties learned from the training data. (The data used to construct or discover a predictive relationship are called the training data set. Most approaches that search through training data for empirical relationships tend to overfit the data, meaning that they can identify apparent relationships in the training data that do not hold in general. A test set is a set of data that is independent of the training data, but that follows the same probability distribution as the training data.)

• Data mining focuses on the discovery of (previously) *unknown* properties in the data. This is the analysis step of knowledge discovery in databases.

The two areas overlap in many ways: data mining uses many machine learning methods, but often with a slightly different goal in mind. On the other hand, machine learning also employs data mining methods as "unsupervised learning" or as a preprocessing step to improve learner accuracy. Much of the confusion between these two research communities comes from the basic assumptions they work with: in machine learning, performance is usually evaluated with respect to the ability to reproduce *known* knowledge, while in knowledge discovery and data mining (KDD), the key task is the discovery of previously *unknown* knowledge. Evaluated with respect to known knowledge, an uninformed (unsupervised) method will easily be outperformed by supervised methods, while in a typical KDD task, supervised methods cannot be used due to the unavailability of training data.

Trying to detect specific patterns of crime and criminal behavior is extremely challenging. Crime analysts can spend countless hours sifting through data to determine whether a crime fits into a known pattern and to discover new patterns. Once a pattern is detected, the information can be used to predict, anticipate, and prevent crime.

A machine learning method called "Series Finder" was developed by Wang et al. (2013) to assist the police in discovering crime series. Initially, Series Finder was trained to detect housebreak patterns, and it "learned" how to do this using historical data from one police department's crime analysis unit. (Whether you are doing simple multiplication or a complicated calculus problem, you must use a predetermined set of rules, called an *algorithm*, to solve it. An algorithm includes a finite number of steps to solve any given problem.) The algorithm used in Series Finder tries to construct a modus operandi (MO) of the offender. As Series Finder grows the pattern from the database, the MO for the pattern becomes better defined.

Neural Network

The simplest definition of a neural network, more properly referred to as an artificial neural network (ANN), is provided by the inventor of one of the first neurocomputers, Dr. Robert Hecht-Nielsen. He defines a neural network as "a computing system made up of a number of simple, highly interconnected processing elements, which process information by their dynamic state response to external inputs" (Borhanazad, 2014).

ANNs are processing devices (algorithms or actual hardware) that are loosely modeled after the neuronal structure of the mammalian cerebral cortex, but on much smaller scales (University of Wisconsin-Madison, n.d.). A large ANN might have hundreds or thousands of processor units, whereas a mammalian brain has billions of neurons with a corresponding increase in magnitude of their overall interaction and emergent behavior.

The Artificial Neural Network System for Classification of Offenders in Murder and Rape Cases project developed two software prototypes that demonstrate developed algorithms for analyzing and comparing large databases of crime data. The Computer-Aided Tracking and Characterization of Homicides (CATCH) and CATCHRAPE software applications analyze homicide data and sexual assault data, respectively. Both applications are similar, although they analyze different databases. CATCH was developed to provide crime analysts with enhanced means for interpreting large databases of crime data. These databases store a large number of crimes, with each case described in great detail. The huge volumes of information collected for crimes during investigations make it difficult to compare a crime with other crimes by the investigators alone. CATCH uses advanced algorithms to facilitate the comparison of crime data to find crimes that have similar patterns.

What Kinds of Relationships Can Data Mining Software Reveal?

Generally, any of four types of relationships are sought:

1. Entity extractions
2. Clusters
3. Associations
4. Sequential patterns

Entity Extractions

Entity extraction identifies particular patterns from data, such as text, images, or audio materials. It has been used to identify a person's addresses, vehicles, and personal characteristics, which means that entity extraction can provide basic information for crime analysis.

In criminal justice, as in other fields, such as business, there is a need for collecting and understanding web information about a real-world entity—a person of interest or a suspect, for example. For most of us, if we want to find out more about a person, we use a search engine. However, if you do a Google or Yahoo search to learn more about an individual (say, Mark Robinson, to pick a name at random), you will get 174 million hits. To learn more about the particular Mark Robinson you might be interested in would mean that you would have to scroll through thousands of web pages. Even if Google or any other search engine could find all the relevant web pages about Mark Robinson, how long would it take you to sift through all these pages to get a complete view of who Mark Robinson is? A few hours? A few days? Maybe. But it might take even longer.

Entity extraction works at solving this problem. Microsoft came up with EntityCube to help to search and browse summaries of entities, including people, organizations, and locations.

Software such as EntityCube or Rosette Entry Extractor (REX) automatically mine from billions of web pages to extract entity information and detect relationships, covering a spectrum of everyday individuals and well-known people, locations, conferences, journals, and organizations.

Clusters

A cluster is a subset of objects that are similar. Clustering is the process of grouping data into a set of meaningful subclasses, called clusters. For example, in the insurance industry, you may want to group together certain policy holders, say, for instance, all policy holders with high average claim requests and payouts. By identifying this cluster, you can decide how to target that group to reduce its claims.

In criminal justice, crime analysts have started helping detectives and other law enforcement officers to speed up the process of solving crimes. More specifically, a data mining approach using clustering-based models can help in the identification of crime patterns. But providing that help has not been easy because the data related to crime and criminals are often scattered in various databases and around the Internet. Some data are kept confidential, while other data are public information. Data about county prisoners are usually found in the county or the sheriff's sites. However, data about crimes related to narcotics or juvenile cases are often more restricted. Similarly, information about sex offenders is made public to warn others in the area, but the identity of the victim is often not accessible. Thus, as a data miner, the analyst has to deal with various issues—and databases—to mine crucial data for detectives.

Furthermore, sheriffs' offices and police departments may use a computerized reporting system, or they may still use the traditional paper-based crime reports. Whether these crime reports are computerized or paper, they almost always contain certain basic information: the type of crime, the date and time of the crime, the location of the crime, the names and addresses of the victims, the names and addresses of the witnesses, and the name and address of the suspect. Additionally, there is the narrative or description of the crime and MO, both of which are usually in the form of text. That is, police officers and detectives use free text to record certain facts, observations, and conclusions. This is information that cannot be included by checking boxes on a police department form. While some information can be stored in computer databases as numeric, character, or date fields of tables, the observations and conclusions are often stored as free text.

And therein lies the challenge in data mining crime data. Combing through hundreds or thousands (or even more) of crime reports to locate data (such as a descriptions of crime perpetrators or the names of suspects) to gather them into data mining categories is not always an easy job. And that's where clustering in data mining comes in. A cluster is a group of crimes or people or other kinds of data that are similar and may represent a geographical region, a hot spot of crime, or a possible crime pattern.

Clustering algorithms in data mining are equivalent to the task of identifying groups of records that are similar between themselves but different from the rest of the data. In some instances, clusters will be useful for identifying a crime spree committed by one person or a group of suspects. Given this information, the next challenge is to find the variables providing the best clustering. These clusters will then be presented to the detectives to "drill down" (meaning move to another, often lower or more basic, level of analysis) using their expertise as detectives.

However, clustering requires a skilled crime analyst who is aware that data mining is sensitive to the quality of input data. What that means is that law enforcement officers' reports may be inaccurate or have missing information, or that the data entry step was flawed because names or locations were misspelled, for instance. The skilled and experienced data miner must have a good knowledge of clustering, and know what software will perform the tasks that he or she requires, all the while working closely with a detective, at least in the initial phases of the investigation (Nath, 2006).

Associations

In data mining, association rules are useful for analyzing and predicting customer behavior. They play an important part in shopping basket data analysis, product clustering, catalog design, and store layout. For example, if a grocery store wished to sell more 1-liter bottles of Coke, they could examine transactions by customers who bought 1-liter bottles of Coke. By data mining associations, they might discover that customers who bought 1-liter bottles of Coke often bought 15-ounce bags of Lay's Classic Potato Chips. Once this association is understood, the store could send out coupons for Lay's Classic Potato Chips and offer a sale on potato chips. They could, then, be relatively certain that the sales of Coke would increase.

While the use of data mining and association rules has nothing to do with selling either Coke or potato chips in criminal justice, the goal of crime data analysis in law enforcement is to identify and visualize associations among criminal networks. For example, findings that 80% of individuals released from a particular prison were subsequently involved in automobile thefts within six months of leaving that prison would be valuable information for the police to have. Similarly, if a crime analyst determined that there was a strong association between young white men in their twenties who applied to purchase a handgun from a national chain store and rejection of that transaction with a subsequent murder, this information could lead to preventative efforts that might save lives.

The Associate Wizard (developed by Microsoft) is one example of software that helps a crime analyst create a data mining model using the Microsoft Association Rules algorithm. Such mining models are particularly useful for creating recommendation systems. How this works is that the Microsoft Association Rules algorithm scans a data set comprised of transactions or events, and finds the combinations that frequently appear together. There can be many thousands of combinations, but the algorithm can be customized to find more or fewer, and to retain only the most probable combinations.

This kind of association analysis can potentially be used to address several problems, including predicting who is likely to commit certain crimes and when these crimes might take place. Association rule mining can be used to generate rules from a crime data set based on the frequent occurrence of patterns to help lead to recommendations for preventive action. But, in general, discovering association rules helps investigators to recognize mutual implications among criminal occurrences.

Sequentials

Sequential pattern mining is a data mining approach that is concerned with finding statistically relevant patterns between data examples where the values are delivered in a sequence. There are several key traditional computational problems addressed within this field. These include building efficient databases and indexes for sequence information, extracting the frequently occurring patterns, comparing sequences for similarity, and recovering missing sequence members. In general, sequence mining problems can be classified as *string mining*, which is typically based on string processing algorithms, and *itemset mining*, which is typically based on association rule learning. String mining has to do with understanding the sequence in a data set, identifying individual regions or structural units within each sequence, and then assigning a function to each structural unit. Itemset mining is used for discovering regularities between frequently co-occurring items in large transactions. For example, by analyzing the records of parolees, a rule can be produced that reads, "If a parolee finds a full-time job within one month of being released from prison, he or she is likely to keep his appointments with his parole officer."

Frequent sequence mining is used to discover a set of patterns shared among objects that have between them a specific order. For instance, a retail shop may possess a transaction database that specifies which products were acquired by each customer over time. In this case, the store may use frequent sequence mining to find that 40% of its customers who bought the first volume of *Lord of the Rings* came back to buy the second volume a month later. This kind of information may be used to support directed advertising campaigns or recommendation systems. In criminal justice, frequent sequence mining could help determine the interval between certain types of crimes and the sequence of criminal offenses by offenders involved in burglary offenses. (The question to be asked and, hopefully, answered by the crime analyst might be, after a home break-in during which a violent crime occurred, what other crimes occurred, in what sequence, and with what time lapse between those offenses?) In effect, a huge number of possible sequential patterns are hidden in databases, and it is the job of crime analysts to mine those sequential patterns.

Summing Up

Data mining is the process of analyzing data from different perspectives and summarizing it into useful information. A crime analyst, using data mining, can extract useful information from very large and complex data sets. In Chapter 10, we further explore practical intelligence applications.

Questions for Discussion

1. What might be some new and unique applications of data mining in police work?
2. What might be some of the challenges of data mining for the intelligence analyst?

Important Terms

Association rules: In data mining, association rules are useful for analyzing and predicting the behavior of individuals.

Data mining: Process of analyzing data from different perspectives and summarizing them into useful information. Data mining systematically searches information to identify relationships and patterns.

Clustering: Process of grouping data into a set of meaningful subclasses, called clusters.

Entity extraction: Data mining approach that identifies particular patterns from data, such as text, images, or audio materials. In criminal justice, it has been used to identify person's addresses, vehicles, and personal characteristics.

Information technology: Use of any computers, storage, networking, and other physical devices, infrastructure, and processes to create, process, store, secure, and exchange all forms of electronic data.

Machine learning: Type of AI that provides computers with the ability to learn without being explicitly programmed. Machine learning generally focuses on the development of computer programs that can teach themselves to grow and change when exposed to new data.

Sequential mining: Data mining approach that is concerned with finding statistically relevant patterns within databases.

Transaction processing system: Supports the processing of a company's or organization's business transactions.

Study Guide Questions

For questions 1–3, indicate whether the statement is true or false.

1. _____ Data mining is essential in criminal justice because trying to determine relationships and patterns within databases is often too complex to figure out in other ways.

2. _____ One strategy for extracting meaning from large amounts of investigative information is the use of video game applications.

3. _____ To find out information about almost any suspect, an intelligence analyst need only "Google" that person's name.

4. To comb through many large databases to find useful information in an investigation, the crime analyst may find similarities through
   a. Entity extraction
   b. Clustering
   c. Associations
   d. Sequential pattern mining

5. In criminal justice, frequent sequence mining could help determine the interval between certain types of crimes and the _____ of criminal offenses.
   a. Sequence
   b. Violence
   c. Motivation
   d. Economic variables

References

Applegate, L.M., Cash, J.I., and Mills, D.Q. (1988). Information technology and tomorrow's manager. *Harvard Business Review* 66(6): 128–136.

Borhanazad, H. (2014). Artificial neural network, part I. ResearchGate. Available at http://www.researchgate.net/publication/262936797_ARTIFICIAL_NEURAL_NETWORK_PART_1.

Chen, H., Chung, W., Xu, J., Wang, G., Chau, M., and Qin, Y. (2003). Crime data mining: A general framework and some examples. *IEEE Computer* 37(4): 50–56.

Furnas, A. (2012). Everything you wanted to know about data mining but were afraid to ask. *The Atlantic*. Available at http://www.theatlantic.com/technology/archive/2012/04/everything-you-wanted-to-know-about-data-mining-but-were-afraid-to-ask/255388/.

Mahar, F. (2003). Role of information technology in transaction processing system. *Information Technology Journal* 2: 128–134.

McCue, C., and Parker, A. (2003). Connecting the dots: Data mining and predictive analytics in law enforcement and intelligence analysis. *Police Chief* 70(10): 115–119.

Nath, S.V. (2006). Crime pattern detection using data mining. In *International Conference on Web Intelligence and Intelligence Agent Technology Workshops*, Hong Kong, pp. 41–44.

University of Wisconsin-Madison. (n.d.). A basic introduction to neural networks. Department of Computer Science, University of Wisconsin-Madison website. Available at http://pages.cs.wisc.edu/~bolo/shipyard/neural/local.html.

Wang, T., Rudin, C., Wagner, D., and Sevieri, R. (2013). Learning to detect patterns of crime. In H. Blackiel, K. Kersting, S. Nyssen, and F. Zdezny (Eds.). *Machine Learning and Knowledge Discovery in Databases*, pp. 515–530. Springer. Available: http://link.springer.com/chapter/10.1007/978-3-642-40994-3_33.

PART IV
CRIME ANALYSIS

10

HISTORY AND TYPES OF CRIME ANALYSIS

Chapter Outline

1. History of crime analysis
2. Different types of contemporary law enforcement analysis
3. Categories of crime analysis
   a. Tactical crime analysis
   b. Strategic crime analysis
   c. Administrative crime analysis
   d. Police operations analysis
4. Tactical crime analysis
   a. Definition
   b. Descriptions
   c. The tactical crime analyst working in a real-time crime center
   d. Training of the tactical analyst
5. Strategic crime analysis
   a. Definition
   b. Description
6. Administrative crime analysis
   a. Definition
   b. Description
7. Police operations analysis
   a. Definition
   b. Description

Learning Objectives for Chapter 10

1. Gain an understanding of the history of crime analysis
2. Be able to place crime analysis in a historical context

3. Understand the major types of crime analysis
4. Be able to differentiate the goals and purposes of each type of crime analysis

In 1829, Sir Robert Peel, in bringing about the London Metropolitan Police in London, England, developed a set of principles for good policing. One of these principles was "to recognize always that the test of police efficiency is the absence of crime and disorder, and not the visible evidence of police action in dealing with them" (Reith, 1956). In other words, Peel believed that it wasn't arrests or use of force that made for good, effective policing. It was that the police would prevent crime and disorder in the first place, rather than deal with responding to and solving crimes.

Introduction

The earliest use of the term *crime analysis* can be found in the second edition of O.W. Wilson's book *Police Administration* (1963). In this book, Wilson, who was the superintendent of the Chicago Police Department from 1960 to 1971, as well as serving as police chief in other cities, writes,

> The crime-analysis section studies daily reports of serious crimes in order to determine the location, time, special characteristics, similarities to other criminal attacks, and various significant factors that might help to identify either a criminal or the existence of a pattern of criminal activity. Such information is helpful in planning the operations of a division or district. (Wilson, 1963, p. 103)

Even though the term *crime analysis* might not have been used prior to Wilson's use of it in 1963, it seems likely that the practice of crime analysis actually goes back to the nineteenth century, although some criminal justice historians might effectively argue that it dates back to the beginning of society. While that is debatable, and while it depends on how you define *crime analysis*, it seems more certain that August Vollmer, who has been called "the father of American policing," seemed to be describing some of the early uses of crime analysis when he talked about pin mapping, the regular review of police reports, and the formation of patrol districts based on crime volume (Oliver, 2008). Serving as chief of police in Berkeley, California, from 1905 to 1932, Vollmer was an innovator who was among the first police chiefs to introduce police radios, fingerprints, modus operandi, and beat analysis by saying that "on the assumption of regularity of crime and similar occurrences by area within a city and thus determine the points which have the greatest danger of such crimes and what points have the least danger" (Stering, 2008, p. 49).

But we can go back even farther to trace the beginnings of crime analysis. Rudimentary forms of crime analysis can be discovered in the work of the London Metropolitan Police, founded by Sir Robert Peale in 1829. By the 1840s, the London Metropolitan Police designated some officers as detectives, but in 1877, the Criminal Investigations Department (CID) was formed and 200 detectives were hired; and hundreds more were hired and assigned to police districts within the city of London by 1883. However, in the 1840s, the few detectives who were assigned to different boroughs in London were likely using some "modern" methods of crime analysis to link different crimes into patterns (Strickland, 2013). In addition, the concept of modus operandi and classifying offenses and crimes based on modus operandi was taking place in the second half of the nineteenth century (Strickland, 2013).

Between 1973 and 1977, the Law Enforcement Assistance Administration (LEAA) published a series of manuals on crime analysis. Recognizing the growing importance of crime analysis, it became one of the four facets of the LEAA's Integrated Criminal Apprehension Program (ICAP).

Then, in the 1990s, there was a surge of activities related to crime analysis. Herman Goldstein, professor emeritus at the University of Wisconsin–Madison Law School, published his book *Problem-Oriented Policing*. Problem-oriented policing is a policing strategy that involves the identification and analysis of specific crime and disorder problems, in order to develop effective response strategies. Goldstein suggested replacing what he termed the reactive, incident-driven "standard model of policing" with problem-oriented policing—an approach requiring police to be proactive in identifying underlying problems that can be targeted to reduce crime and disorder at their roots (Weisburd et al., 2008). Goldstein's model was expanded in 1987 by John E. Eck and William Spelman into the SARA model for problem-solving.

Eck and Spelman (1987) developed a 12-step model of what problem-oriented policing agencies should do:

1. Focus on problems of concern to the public.
2. Zero in on effectiveness as the primary concern.
3. Be proactive.
4. Be committed to systematic inquiry as a first step in solving substantive problems.
5. Encourage the use of rigorous methods in making inquiries.
6. Make full use of the data in police files and the experience of police personnel.
7. Group like incidents together so that they can be addressed as a common problem.
8. Avoid using overly broad labels in grouping incidents so separate problems can be identified.
9. Encourage a broad and uninhibited search for solutions.
10. Acknowledge the limits of the criminal justice system as a response to problems.
11. Identify multiple interests in any one problem and weigh them when analyzing the value of different responses.
12. Be committed to taking some risks in responding to problems.

Eck and Spelman (1987) indicate that under the traditional system of policing, a patrol officer might answer repeated calls to a certain problem area or "hot spot" and deal only with each individual incident. Under problem-oriented policing, however, that officer would be encouraged to discover the root cause of the problem and come up with ways of solving it. The goal would be to find a cure for the ailment instead of merely treating the symptoms. Eck and Spelman also point out that there is a difference between community-oriented policing and problem-oriented policing. The main focus of community-oriented policing is improvement of the relationship between law enforcement and the citizens, while problem-oriented policing depends on information from the citizens and a good relationship with the community.

In 1990, the International Association of Crime Analysts (IACA) was founded, and a year later it held its first conference. Today, the IACA has more than 2500 members from 45 different countries. The IACA offers an annual training conference, and the conference, held in different cities around the United States, features several days of training in crime analysis and policing topics. In 2011, the IACA offered its first annual international symposium in Vancouver, British Columbia. The purpose of the symposium each year is to bring crime analysis training to different parts of the globe. In addition, the IACA's Professional Training Series provides classes in the fundamentals of crime analysis, crime mapping, computer applications, tactical analysis, problem analysis, and special topics at different locations around the United States. Hundreds of analysts have attended Professional Training Series classes over the last four years.

The IACA also features a Certified Law Enforcement Analyst (CLEA) credential that has been available since 2005. The CLEA allows police departments to feel confident that an IACA CLEA possesses a demonstrated proficiency in crime analysis skills.

The California Department of Justice has also provided a certificate program in crime analysis; however, this certification program began in 1992—13 years before the certificate program offered by IACA. Offered through various California universities and colleges, such as California State University, Fullerton, the Crime and Intelligence Analysis Certificate provides specialized training in how to identify and define crime trends, identify crime problems and patterns, and use research and analysis to create tactics and strategies that lead to an effective police response. Graduates receive a certificate from the California Department of Justice designating them as a Certified Crime and Intelligence Analyst. The certification is generally recognized in other states.

In 1994, the CompStat program began in the New York City Police Department (NYPD). CompStat may be short for *computer statistics* or *comparative statistics*—nobody can be sure which according to its inventor, NYPD deputy commissioner Jack Maple (Dussault, 1999). CompStat is a performance management system that is used to reduce crime and achieve other police department goals. The program emphasizes information sharing, responsibility and accountability, and improving effectiveness. It includes four generally recognized core components:

1. Timely and accurate information or intelligence
2. Rapid deployment of resources
3. Effective tactics
4. Relentless follow-up (PERF, 2013)

The most widely recognized element of CompStat is its regularly occurring meetings where department executives and officers discuss and analyze crime problems and the strategies used to address those problems. Often, department leaders will select commanders from a specific geographic area to attend each CompStat meeting.

In the early 1990s, crime was a central concern for New York City residents, and the issue of crime played a prominent role in the city's 1993 mayoral election. Lou Anemone, the NYPD's chief of department (top uniformed officer) in 1994, said that during the early 1990s, "there was very bad violent crime and pervasive fear of crime in the community, and this likely contributed to Mayor David Dinkins' loss to Rudy Giuliani in 1993" (PERF, 2012, p. 3). After his victory at the polls, Mayor Rudy Giuliani, along with his pick for police commissioner, Bill Bratton, laid out his vision for New York City; they would make the city safe, reduce fear of crime, and improve the overall quality of life.

Commissioner Bratton thought there were some problems to making New York City safer. One problem was that crime statistics were collected for the Federal Bureau of Investigation (FBI)—not for timely crime analysis. Another problem was that the NYPD did not have any broad, police department–wide focus on preventing crime (PERF, 2013). And, it was also recognized within the NYPD that it was dispatchers at headquarters who were the lowest-ranking people in the department, who, in effect, controlled field operations. All police officers seemed to be spending most of their time responding to 911 calls. There was literally no free time for officers to focus on crime prevention (PERF, 2012). This situation wasn't unique to New York City. Police officers in many cities were answering emergency calls and responding to crimes that had already been committed. Furthermore, their effectiveness was judged in terms of response times, arrest statistics, and clearance rates. For the most part, the police were simply not held accountable for preventing crime. And that went against the basic dictum of Sir Robert Peel in 1830 London. Peel said back then that his police should be responsible *not* for arrests so much as for preventing crime (Archbold, 2013). In the 1920s in Berkeley, California, Chief of Police August Vollmer said the same thing (Oliver, 2008). But most police departments had forgotten what was the most fundamental tenet of the two most influential founders of modern policing—that prevention was a key to effective policing.

Perhaps Bratton remembered what Peel and Vollmer said about the duties of the police. Maybe not. Anyway, Bratton and his command staff wanted to change the focus of the NYPD and begin to pay attention to crime prevention. With that goal in mind, they created and implemented a new data-driven performance measurement system they eventually called CompStat. Chief Bratton described the earliest version of CompStat as a system to track crime statistics and have police respond to those statistics. The new focus on crime prevention and implementation of CompStat represented a major shift for the NYPD. Instead of dealing with reducing police corruption, which they had done since the 1970s, now it was time to ask an important question: How can we reduce crime? There may have been a prevailing belief that in New York City—as well as elsewhere—the police couldn't do anything about crime (PERF, 2013). It seemed clear to Bratton and his commanders that the community wanted the police to do something about the high crime rate.

The four core components of CompStat were developed by NYPD deputy commissioner Jack Maple, whom *New York Magazine* called "perhaps the most creative cop in history" (Horowitz, 2013). With the principles of CompStat in place, the NYPD began exploring methods to gather and share timely intelligence. To start mapping crime, the department received money from the New York City Police Foundation for the purchase of mapping materials. However, because of the huge volume of crime, leaders quickly decided that a computerized mapping program was required. Jack Maple purchased a computer from Radio Shack, and the name *CompStat* was born (Horowitz, 2013). The NYPD began to make use of their own crime statistics and track indicators of problems, such as the locations of crime victims and gun arrests.

By 1996, the NYPD—for the first time in its history—was using crime statistics and regular meetings of key enforcement personnel to direct its enforcement efforts. Since then, the commanders of the NYPD—and other police departments around the country—watch weekly crime trends with the same hawk-like attention private corporations pay to profits and loss. Crime statistics have become almost every police department's bottom line. It's the best indicator of how the police are doing precinct by precinct and citywide.

As the NYPD honed in on solving crime problems, CompStat became less of a numbers discussion and more of a tactical and strategic discussion (Smith and Bratton, 2001). Moreover, police administrators realized that CompStat shouldn't analyze just the performance of precinct commanders, and began including detectives and representatives from narcotics and other specialized units. By bringing in detectives and officers from specialized units, there was much more focused direction in all NYPD departments. And as the number of people who attended CompStat meetings grew, the NYPD made use of larger meeting spaces and adopted more sophisticated computer systems (PERF, 2012).

Overall, CompStat was not just a regular meeting and a new use of technology. Rather, it was a larger system of management, and that contributed to significant changes within the NYPD's organizational structure and culture.

The use of tactical and strategic planning that came with CompStat began to pay off with crime declines under Commissioner Ray Kelly, and when Commissioner Bratton took charge of the NYPD, he made it widely known that he had set a target of cutting crime by an additional 10% in his first year (PERF, 2013). With CompStat in place, he met and surpassed that goal, with a drop of 12% (PERF, 2013). The next year, significant declines continued, and crime dropped in every one of New York City's 76 police precincts. From 1993 to 1998, homicides dropped 67%, burglary was down 53%, and robberies were down 54% (PERF, 2013). There may have declines in many other cities, but in no American city were the crime declines more dramatic than in New York City.

Consequently, following its success in New York, police agencies large and small throughout the country began using CompStat, hoping to replicate the NYPD's success (PERF, 2013). In a number of cases, former NYPD officials brought CompStat to other agencies when they were hired as police chief. For example, Bill Bratton implemented CompStat in the Los Angeles Police Department (LAPD), John Timoney brought CompStat to Philadelphia and updated it in Miami, Gary McCarthy expanded CompStat significantly in Chicago, and Edmund Hartnett brought it to Yonkers, New York.

The successes brought about by CompStat were not just reflected in lower crime rates. Many law enforcement leaders recognized that CompStat could help focus attention and resources on crime and the causes of crime, which then could lead to better deployment plans. CompStat also proved to be a helpful tool to demonstrate that police resources are monitored and used effectively. And, furthermore, many agencies report that CompStat has improved information sharing within their organization (PERF, 2013). Some agencies use CompStat to assess overtime, budgets, use of force, citizen complaints, and other measures of police work for which the public and government leaders hold police agencies accountable. CompStat and the accountability that comes with it can help chiefs drive organizational change.

In 1997, the National Institute of Justice (NIJ) Crime Mapping Research Center (CMRC) was founded. Now called the Mapping and Analysis for Public Safety Program (MAPS), it supports research that helps agencies use geographic information systems (GIS) to enhance public safety. The program examines

- How to use maps to analyze crime
- How to analyze spatial data
- How maps can help researchers evaluate programs and policies
- How to develop mapping, data sharing, and spatial analysis tools

The NIJ established the CMRC using funds from the Omnibus Appropriations Act of 1996. The center surveyed police departments to determine how they used analytic mapping in policing and began developing training programs to enhance the ability of police departments to use spatial maps and data sets. In 2002, CMRC evolved into the NIJ's MAPS program.

MAPS funds research that uses GIS, statistical analysis, and analysis of spatial data to help police agencies and departments more effectively deploy officers, make better use of public safety resources, develop stronger crime policies, and have a greater understanding of crime (NIJ, 2013).

A year after MAPS was developed by the NIJ, the NIJ started the National Law Enforcement & Corrections Technology Center's (NLECTC) Crime Mapping and Analysis Program. At the core of the NLECTC system is the idea of linking research with practice. The NLECTC system is the conduit between researchers and criminal justice professionals in the field for technology issues. NLECTC works with criminal justice professionals to identify urgent and emerging technology needs, while the NIJ sponsors research and develops best practices to address those needs. NLECTC centers demonstrate new technologies, test commercially available technologies, and publish results—all with the intent of linking research with practice.

Originally created in 1994 as a program of the NIJ's Office of Science and Technology, the NLECTC system plays a crucial role in enabling the NIJ to carry out its critical mission to assist state, local, tribal, and federal law enforcement, corrections, and other criminal justice agencies in addressing their technology needs and challenges (Justice Information Technology Center, 2012).

It was the development of LEAA's ICAP, the research and writing leading to the SARA model for problem-solving, the founding of the IACA, the invention and refinement of the CompStat program, the MAPS, and NLECTC's starting of the Crime Mapping and Analysis Program that brought about a proliferation of crime analysts and crime analysis units. Of course, these developments couldn't have taken place without advancements in technology. Today, the technology and the interest in crime analysis have brought about many crime analysis units in police departments.

Classification of Crime Analysis

As law enforcement agencies were beginning to use technology and develop CompStat programs similar to those used in the NYPD and LAPD, police agencies decided they needed to be more aware of public safety analysis or simply police analysis. In general, when police departments began to initiate technology and intelligence analysis units, they were interested in processing techniques and products that would provide information and support for the various missions of those agencies. Chief among those missions were running efficient and effective police departments and reducing crime. These necessarily morphed into crime analysis units or centers. Usually, crime analysis functions are assigned to one of four classifications:

1. Tactical crime analysis
2. Strategic crime analysis
3. Administrative crime analysis
4. Police operations analysis

Tactical Crime Analysis

Tactical crime analysis is a term that describes the daily identification and analysis of emerging or existing crime patterns. It is the study of recent criminal incidents and activity by examining characteristics such as how, when, and where crime occurs to develop patterns, trends, and potential suspects.

Tactical crime analysis offers a police agency the ability to allocate resources in a most efficient manner. There is something called the 6/68 rule. This states that there are a small amount of offenders (6%) committing the majority of criminal activity (68%). Tactical crime analysis helps police agencies to focus on these priority and prolific offenders by conducting analysis on serial crime. For example, tactical crime analysts help to find serial criminals using data, mapping, or more complex calculations. Identifying that a serial criminal is engaging in regular crime incidents, the tactical crime analyst may be able to predict the next day, date, time, and location of the next offense in the series. Furthermore, the analyst may be able to predict the offender's residence location. This all leads to intelligence that police officers can use in their crime fighting operations.

Tactical crime analysis focuses on information from recent crimes reported to the police. "Recent" can refer to the last few months or longer periods of time for specific ongoing problems. Tactical crime analysis also focuses on specific information about each crime, such as method of entry, point of entry, suspects' actions, type of victim, and type of weapon used, as well as the date, time, location, and type of location. Field information, such as suspicious activity calls for service, criminal trespass warnings, and persons with scars, marks, or tattoos collected by officers, is also considered in the analysis. Although quantitative analysis is often conducted once a pattern has been identified, qualitative analysis—that is, critical thinking and content analysis—is used to identify patterns and trends initially (Boba, 2001).

Goals of Tactical Crime Analysis

Four goals of tactical crime analysis are (1) linking cases together and identifying crime patterns and trends as soon as possible, (2) analyzing patterns discovered to identify potential suspects of a crime or crime pattern, (3) notifying the police department about the existence of patterns and suspects as soon as possible, and (4) working with the police agency to develop the best tactics to address the pattern and clear the case (Boba, 2001).

The Tactical Crime Analyst Working in Real Time

When working in real time, especially at a real-time crime center, analysts who work directly with their law enforcement counterparts do so from a tactical perspective. With law enforcement working as a paramilitary organization, analysts assigned to real-time centers, working in concert with law enforcement, should follow a para–law enforcement ideology.

In the following, Glenn Grana explains the role of tactical analysts:

> In the agency where I work as a tactical analyst supervisor, I am often asked what a tactical analyst does?
>
> My response is that a tactical analyst is an analyst who can rapidly data mine, and analyze information and intelligence from multiple data sources, while applying his or her understanding of the theories and practices that law enforcement follow in order to create a unique analytical process that works as a real-time

extension of the investigative process. When successful, this creates a symbiotic relationship between the two parties. This comes down to a mutual understanding.

Analysts working tactically, as tactual analysts, must shadow certain procedures that law enforcement implement as a working protocol, such as working within the prescribed investigative process and understanding the rules of evidence, to cite two examples. However, this can only work if the tactical analyst fully understands his or her law enforcement counterpart's methodology and ideology, and, in turn, the law enforcement counterpart fully understands him or her.
The tactical analyst needs to have:

- A basic understanding of law enforcement principles
- An understanding of criminal behavior
- Experience in crisis management protocol (in order to assist during crisis situations)
- A grasp of the real-time process of investigations

On the other hand, law enforcement needs to understand the analytical process and the intelligence available to the analyst.

Understanding is key to tactical analysts doing their job, mainly because crime analysts are primarily civilians who, unlike their law enforcement partners, have not been trained to multitask during a real-time or crisis situation. The need—and urgency—for immediate information, and actionable intelligence, is crucial to the successful handling of real-time situations. Training, therefore, for both the analyst and law enforcement, is critical in order for both parties to achieve the success needed to work together to establish a fluid investigative process.

While traditional crime analysis often relies on the analyst to methodically pour over data in order to form conclusions relevant to crime patterns or trends, this process, while frequently effective, is also time-consuming. The analysts working in a tactical role, in real time, need to rapidly data mine, analyze, and disseminate information and intelligence as the situation, crime, or investigation is unfolding. Time is of the essence in most situations.

Understanding the process of investigation that their law enforcement counterpart is following would help to expedite the analytical process. Having a basic understanding as to what investigative process the investigator is following can help the tactical analyst in the data mining of relevant information and transitioning that information into actionable intelligence. Once the relevant intelligence is forwarded to the investigator, it helps to keep the investigative process moving or, depending on what the information revealed, change the course of the investigation in order to set it on a more focused path. This can occur when the analyst understands the investigative mindset of the investigator he or she is assisting.

Tactical Analysis, Crisis Management, and Negotiation

For five years, Glenn Grana was assigned to the Sheriff's Hostage Response Team (HRT) as a hostage negotiator negotiating situations ranging from suicidal individuals to barricaded gunmen holding hostages. Regardless of the situation, the process of negotiation relied heavily on the use of intelligence on the subject, situation, or location, to help him best maneuver the negotiation to a successful resolution.

From a crisis management perspective, whether the analyst is involved in a hostage situation, an active shooter situation, or some other crisis, success is measured simply in terms of the life you save. One of the most critical stages in the crisis management process—particularly in terms of the success of crisis negotiations and tactical operational planning—is the analytical stage; the stage in which intelligence is mined, disseminated, prioritized, and eventually relayed to the lead negotiator or crisis team leader.

By introducing a tactical analyst into the team as a working component related to the law enforcements crisis management protocol, you can create a position that combines the analytical strengths of the tactical analyst with the negotiating strengths of the crisis negotiator. What is most important here is the tactical analyst's ability to rapidly data mine and analyze information obtained from multiple data sources, while—at the same time—applying their understanding of the theories and practices that law enforcement crisis managers follow. If successful, it will create an analytical process unique to the needs of crisis management.

If a crisis management team is willing to consider utilizing the skills of a tactical analyst, the process should begin with both parties acknowledging a mutual understanding of each other's skill sets, abilities, and roles in order to achieve the comfort zone necessary to create a cohesive working, and trusting, relationship. Mutual understanding leads to that comfort zone.

What the Tactical Analyst Needs to Understand

In order to step into a role as a valuable member of a crisis management team, a tactical analyst needs to have an understanding and working knowledge of

- Criminal behavior
- Crisis management protocol
- The "real-time" process of crisis negotiations

On the other hand, in order to accept the contributions of the tactical analyst, the crisis manager needs to understand

- The analytical process
- The intelligence available to the analyst

The ultimate goal during any crisis situation is to achieve a successful resolution. For this to occur, the negotiation process needs to focus on the root cause of the crisis. Regardless of whether the motivation is emotionally, politically, or criminally driven, identifying the subject's true reason for creating the situation is critical. Therein lies the importance of the intelligence process.

Crisis Management Protocol

The crisis management protocol is a set of guidelines or procedures that define and regulate a police department during a crisis. If a police department has a Hostage Recovery Team (HRT), for instance, the protocol indicates the roles and responsibilities of various officers during a crisis. A crisis could mean that one or more individuals are suicidal, barricaded, hostage-taking, or engaged in terrorist activities.

Often a protocol will provide the incident commander with negotiators who have been specifically trained and equipped to diffuse critical incidents involving suspects who are involved in the crisis activities. The trained negotiator seeks to accomplish their assigned task by persuasion, thus minimizing the need for the use of force; yet, they also continually provide the field and tactical (SWAT) commanders with intelligence should a tactical solution be required.

By using a tactical analyst in support of the intelligence gathering process, information and actionable intelligence would be readily available once it is rapidly data mined by the analyst who has been cross-trained in the skill set involving the negotiation process.

> *Primary negotiator*: The duties of the primary negotiator in a crisis event are to establish contact with the suspect(s) and deal exclusively with that suspect(s) until relieved.
>
> *Secondary negotiator*: The secondary negotiator monitors all conversations between the primary negotiator and the suspect and/or hostages.
>
> *Intelligence officer*: The member assigned to intelligence gathering is charged with the responsibility of gathering intelligence on the suspect and/or hostage(s) for the negotiators, the team leader, the tactical (SWAT) commander, and the incident commander. He or she also debriefs those who may have tactical or intelligence information relating to the critical incident.

Prior to the advent of today's technology, intelligence gathering was a tedious, time-consuming process that did not always yield the most up-to-date intelligence on the subject. By injecting an analyst who is tactically trained to multitask, and trained to rapidly data mine through a crisis, information that may have been lost in previous years can now be located, analyzed, and disseminated more rapidly.

Tactical Analyst Training Is Crucial

Crime analysts are primarily civilians who, unlike their law enforcement partners, have not been trained to multitask during a real-time crisis. If the decision is made to utilize tactical analysts during a crisis management situation, training should be made part of the protocol.

Devising a training curriculum that introduces, and incorporates, the skills of the tactical analyst, and negotiator, into the crisis management process helps to build the level of trust needed between the two in order for there to be a fluid exchange of intelligence during an actual crises situation. Most crisis teams (often called either SWAT teams or hostage teams) have monthly scheduled training days where they go over scenarios, train on equipment, and discuss the latest techniques and technology. Incorporating the analyst into the training can help build the level of trust and respect needed to establish a strong cohesive relationship.

Training also helps when comparing the roles and responsibilities of the tactical analyst to those of the crisis manager or negotiator. In comparing the two roles, both analyst crisis manager/negotiator can find common ground in what both expects to achieve during a crisis.

Hostage/Crisis Negotiator

The negotiator's first priority, at the beginning of a negotiation, is to gather information. The negotiator must find out

- Who the subject is
- What the possible motive is
- Who are any other persons associated with the situation that could help shed light on the subjects' motives and intents

Most importantly, the negotiator needs to pay close attention to the hostage-taker's responses, mannerisms, and general attitude, in order to form a psychological profile of the subject.

Tactical Analyst in a Crisis Situation

The tactical analyst gathers information through data mining and uses critical thinking based on

- Information
- Research
- Theory

This helps the tactical analyst in creating a profile of the subjects' criminal behavior.

But, both the analyst and the negotiator/crisis manager need to gather information to help them create a profile of the subject—whether that profile is a psychological profile or a profile based on past criminal behavior.

If successfully cross-trained, the tactical analyst, engaged in a crisis management situation, can effectively data mine for critical pieces of intelligence that can be crucial to identifying

- The mindset of the subject
- The motive of the subject
- Ways to effect a resolution

Training of the Tactical Crime Analyst

With any type of cross-training for crime analysts who are assigned to work in tactical, real-time situations, the goal is to create a hybrid form of crime analysis, that is, crime analysis that merges the traditional skills of the crime analyst with the investigative skill set of a sworn investigator. One way to do this is for crime analysts to work with their law enforcement partners to create a training course that mirrors the curriculum of an established investigator's course.

Using this curriculum as a guide, specific topic instruction (incorporating such areas as interviewing and interrogation, rules of evidence, etc.) can be taught to the analyst by a seasoned investigator with the emphasis on how each specific block of instruction would directly relate to the tactical analyst's role.

In New York, for example, most law enforcement agencies follow a Department of Criminal Justice Services Basic Investigator School Curriculum, which, over the course of two weeks, is composed of several different blocks of instruction designed to teach a newly promoted police investigator the tools needed to conduct a proper criminal investigation.

Here is a sampling of topics and class hours as taught in the Basic Investigator School Curriculum:

- Case Management/Basic Investigative Techniques and Canvassing: 3 h
- Interview and Interrogation: 12.5 h

When looking to combine the curriculum for the investigator's course with a newly developed training curriculum for the tactical analyst, a certified instructor can see the value of applying certain relevant subject matter. When this is done correctly, the subject matter, combined with case studies specifically related to situations that would utilize a tactical analyst, becomes an effective learning tool.

The following is an example of how the aforementioned listed topics relate to the role of the tactical analyst:

- Case Management/Basic Investigative Techniques
  - Tactical analysis calls for managing and collecting relevant information and transitioning that into actionable intelligence for the use of investigators in the field.
- Interview and Interrogation
  - Tactical analysis calls for close interaction with investigators in the field, and as such, there needs to be a cohesive exchange of information between the analyst and the investigator. Knowing how to extract viable information, as the investigation progresses, is crucial to the data mining process, particularly when sorting through several databases looking for specific information and intelligence that can be sent to officers in the field in an expedient manner.

The goal of this type of training is to help analysts gain insight into the investigative process and develop a better understanding of their role as they support a criminal investigation.

Mutual Understanding

In law enforcement, achieving investigative success is a process that can be measured in many different ways. One of the most critical stages in this process is the analytical stage, the stage in which intelligence is mined, disseminated, prioritized, and eventually relayed to the investigator.

Training—and understanding—two different mindsets is a two-way street once an agency makes the decision to work with a real-time crime center utilizing tactical analysts. To this point, the law enforcement partner should also gain a better understanding as to the role of the tactical analyst, primarily, what the tactical analyst brings to the table in terms of being an asset to the investigative process.

In the following, Glenn Grana gives his thoughts on teaching:

> Coming from a law enforcement background made it easier for me to walk into a classroom of seasoned investigators and suggest to them they include the use of a tactical analyst in their investigative process. Having come from the same world as them brought some credibility to my reasoning; however, even with that I found some of the more tenured investigators still expressing reservations about relying on a civilian analyst as they worked a case.
>
> The comment I heard most was "I like to knock on my own doors and gather my own intelligence," to which my response would always be, "I want you knock on your own doors, too; however, the tactical analyst is there to help narrow down the number of doors you need to knock on."
>
> Then, I state it very simply: the main reason to include a tactical analyst in your investigation is to
>
> 1. *Decrease* the amount of time spent working on preliminary investigations
> 2. *Increase* proactive time working on the investigation. I emphasize that less office time equals more time in the field.
>
> I further point out that the tactical analyst is an investigative aide, if you will, an extension of the investigative process that, if used correctly, can help keep you—the investigator—in the field as the analyst on the intelligence side follows up on leads developed in the field.
>
> As long as the relationship between the analyst and investigator is a collaborative effort, the flow of information between the two should be a fluid process that helps create a level of trust between the two.
>
> Introducing the sworn side to the skill set of the analyst and the resources the analyst has at his or her disposal goes a long way toward building that trusting relationship. I find that establishing a presentation that illustrates the abilities of the analyst, which I

combine with the resources they utilize with case studies and success stories, will show the sworn side the value the analyst brings to investigations. The goal is to have the investigators come away with a confident understanding of what the analyst can do, how the analyst understands the investigative process, and the value he or she brings to their investigations.

Case Study

The tactical analyst was contacted by homicide investigators regarding the homicide of a known gang member. The victim was shot with a sawed off shotgun in the parking lot of an apartment building.

The analyst was advised that the suspect drove a red Mercedes Benz and was given a license plate number. The analyst ran the plate through a vehicle registration database and found it to be registered to a female. However, the suspect was male.

The analyst also learned that intelligence was developed that the suspect was known by a nickname on the streets. More importantly, the analyst was given a possible first name of the suspect. The analyst data mined the nickname, the actual first name, and the vehicle license plate through a database that data mines from multiple data resources. The search yielded more than 600 results.

Understanding that a homicide investigation has its best percentage of success within the first 48 hours of when the crime was first committed, and based on her training and knowledge of the investigative process, the analyst was able to rapidly sift through the 660 results and quickly locate a documented traffic stop of the suspected vehicle.

This traffic stop occurred in a town that adjoined the jurisdiction where the murder was being investigated. The analyst also discovered that on that particular vehicle traffic stop, a male was arrested who gave the same first name as the first name she was given that might belong to the murder suspect.

After reviewing the traffic stop arrest report, the analyst now had a first and last name to research. The analyst discovered the person arrested in the traffic stop was currently in a street gang, as was the homicide victim, and that this newly identified male also matched the physical description of the suspect.

This intelligence, along with a photo of the now-identified male, was sent to the homicide investigators. Utilizing the intelligence given to them by the analyst, the investigators created a photo array. Included in that photo array was the photo of the male that the tactical analyst sent to the investigators. That male was positively identified as the shooter by multiple witnesses.

The collaborative effort between the homicide investigators and the tactical analyst, along with the timeliness of the suspect information being relayed, data mined, and sent back as actionable intelligence, resulted in the identification of an originally unknown murder suspect within five hours of the murder being committed. More importantly, the tactical analyst was now viewed as a viable asset to the homicide unit, and as a result, her position was permanently assigned to homicide to work exclusively within that unit.

Strategic Crime Analysis

Strategic crime analysis furnishes information concerning long-range problems. Strategic crime analysts provide data relative to long-term increases or decreases in crime (crime trend data). They also prepare crime statistical summaries—often referred to as exception reports since they reflect deviations from the norm—and provide resource acquisition and allocation information.

Strategic crime analysis involves the study of crime and law enforcement information integrated with sociodemographic and spatial factors to determine long-term "patterns" of activity, to assist in problem-solving, and to research and evaluate responses and procedures.

In general, strategic crime analysis consists primarily of quantitative analysis of aggregate data. That usually means monthly, quarterly, or yearly compilations of information, such as crime, calls for service, and traffic information analyzed in aggregate (as a collection or a whole) form. That is, general categories such as date, time, location, and type of incident are analyzed instead of qualitative data, such as narrative descriptions of incidents. Variables including race, class, sex, income, population, location, and location type are examined, along with law enforcement information in the analysis process.

Goals of Strategic Crime Analysis

The two primary goals of strategic crime analysis are (1) to assist in the identification and analysis of long-term problems, such as drug activity or auto theft, and (2) to conduct studies to investigate or evaluate relevant responses and procedures.

Concerned with operational strategies that seek solutions to ongoing problems, strategic crime analysis can provide information for resource allocation purposes, including optimized patrol scheduling and configuration of patrol zones. Its purpose is to identify crime activities and patterns, identify community conditions, provide police service more effectively and efficiently by matching demands for service with actual delivery, reduce or eliminate recurring problems, and assist in community policing or problem-oriented policing.

Examples of strategic crime analysis include crime pattern analysis (examination of the nature and distribution of crime within an area), crime control methods analysis (investigation of crime control methods and techniques to determine their usefulness), and general profile analysis (identification of the typical characteristics of perpetrators of certain types of crimes).

Administrative Crime Analysis

Administrative crime analysis concerns itself with the presentation of interesting findings of crime research and analysis based on legal, political, and practical concerns to inform audiences within the law enforcement administration, the city government, and citizens.

Administrative crime analysis is different from the previous types of analysis that we have discussed in that it refers to the presentation of findings rather than to statistical analysis or research. The decision of what information to present and how is the primary focus of administrative crime analysis. The purpose and the audience of the information determine what is presented, but the primary purpose of administrative crime analysis is to inform audiences. These audiences may vary from one situation to the next, which is why the type and quantity of information will vary as well. Audiences can be police executives, city council, media, citizens, and neighborhood groups, or all of these.

Examples of Administrative Crime Analysis

Examples of administrative crime analysis tasks include grant writing, feasibility studies, and the preparation of special research projects. In general, administrative crime analysis is not focused on the immediate or long-term reduction or elimination of a criminal pattern or trend. An example of administrative crime analysis is to post information on the police department's website to inform citizens and the community about an issue. Besides citizens, the audience of a police department's website may well include police personnel, businesses, victims, criminals, and the media. Thus, the type of information presented on the website can include crime trends, police department policy changes, and other updates useful to the community.

Sometimes, the analyst will conduct a study into a police department's own operations, procedures, and policies. This kind of analysis is imperative to the operation of a department because it ensures that the department is operating efficiently and effectively. Administrative analysis often includes the presentation of findings to the police administration and to government officials. But the police administration and public officials may ask for statistics or data to be sure they are leading the department or the city in the right direction. Much like investigative analysis, administrative analysis tasks can range from small scale, like determining if burglaries declined during a prevention initiative, to large scale, like conducting a workload analysis to determine if staffing is adequate and if departmental resources are being efficiently deployed.

Other examples of administrative crime analysis could include tracking nuisance calls for service to the police department, generating press releases and other public information materials concerning crime patterns and crime prevention, and researching new technologies and services available to police.

Police Operations Analysis

Police operations analysis describes the study of a police department's policies and practices. This could include studying a department's allocation of personnel, money, equipment, and other resources. The operations analyst might try to decide the best way to divide a city into beats, the optimal allocation of officers per shift, or whether the agency can justify a request for more police officers.

However, many operations decisions are based on long-term crime trends within a department's jurisdiction. For instance, a police department might wish to identify the appropriate staffing of the agency given its workload and the community demographics and crime levels. Or, a police department, recognizing that the city has had a number of new liquor licenses granted to bars and restaurants, might desire to deploy more officers later in the evening if there are more drunk and disorderly complaints or other public nuisance problems that have become more frequent.

Four Types of Crime Analysis

With a better understanding of the four types of crime analysis— tactical crime analysis, strategic crime analysis, administrative crime analysis, and police operations analysis—we can now move on in the next chapters to discuss in more detail the types of tasks, duties, and specific analysis required in each of the four categories of crime analysis.

Questions for Discussion

1. What would you consider some crime analysis techniques that were likely used hundreds of years ago?
2. Which type of crime analysis seems most interesting to you? Why?

Important Terms

Administrative crime analysis: Presentation of interesting findings related to crime research and analysis based on legal, political, and practical concerns to inform audiences within the law enforcement administration, the city government, and citizens.

CompStat: Performance management system that is used to reduce crime and achieve other police department goals. It emphasizes information sharing, responsibility and account-ability, and improving effectiveness.

Hot spot: Certain problem area in a city where there has been repeated calls to the police.

Police operations analysis: Study of a police department's policies and practices. Often, it concerns itself with studying a department's allocation of personnel, money, equipment, and other resources.

Problem-oriented policing: Policing strategy that involves the identification and analysis of specific crime and disorder problems, in order to develop effective response strategies.

Strategic crime analysis: Analysis that has to do with developing data to better understand long-term increases or decreases in crime.

Tactical crime analysis: Daily identification and analysis of emerg-ing or existing crime patterns. It is the study of recent crimi-nal incidents and activity by examining characteristics such as how, when, and where crime occurs to develop patterns, trends, and potential suspects.

Study Guide Questions

For questions 1–3, indicate whether the statement is true or false.

1. _____ The police operations analyst might try to find the best way to divide the city into beats.
2. _____ One of the first uses of the term *crime analysis* occurred in a 1963 book by August Vollmer.
3. _____ CompStat can help focus attention and resources on crime and the causes of crime.
4. Crime analysis functions are generally assigned to all but which one of these classifications:
   a. Tactical crime analysis
   b. Strategic crime analysis
   c. Administrative crime analysis
   d. Arson crime analysis
5. The IACA was founded in
   a. 1840

b. 1890
c. 1940
d. 1990
6. The most widely recognized element of CompStat is its
   a. Regularly occurring meetings
   b. Yearly board meetings
   c. Conferences in Hawaii
   d. Smoke-filled backroom get-togethers
7. Crime declines in New York City may be attributed to
   a. Aggressive stop and frisk policies
   b. Concerts in Central Park
   c. Introduction of CompStat
   d. Mass incarceration
8. The NLECTC's Crime Mapping and Analysis Program was started in 1998, and it provides for
   a. Scientific and technical support to rural police departments
   b. Support for the transfer and adoption of technology into practice by law enforcement and corrections agencies, courts, and crime laboratories
   c. Distributing military equipment to small police departments
   d. Recruiting crime analysts from Russia
9. The tactical analyst needs to have
   a. A basic understanding of financial laws
   b. An understanding of managerial principles
   c. Experience in crisis management protocol
   d. A grasp of the economic forces that drive crime

References

Archbold, C.A. (2013). *Policing: A Text/Reader*. Thousand Oaks, CA: Sage.

Boba, R. (2001). Introductory guide to crime analysis and mapping. Report to the Office of Community Oriented Policing Services. Cooperative Agreement 97-CK-WXK-004. Washington, DC: U.S. Government Printing Office.

Dussault, J. (1999). Jack Maple: Betting on intelligence. *Government Technology*. Available at http://www.govtech.com/magazines/gt/Jack-Maple-Betting-on-Intelligence.html?page=2.

Eck, J.E., and Spelman, W. (1987). *Problem Solving: Problem-Solving Policing in Newport News*. Rockville, MD: National Institute of Justice.

Goldstein, H. (1990). *Problem-Oriented Policing*. New York: McGraw-Hill.

Horowitz, C. (2013). Remembering Jack Maple. *New York Magazine*. Available at http://nymag.com/nymetro/news/crimelaw/features/5087/.

Justice Information Technology Center. (2012). About NLECTC. Gaithersburg, MD: Justice Information Technology Center. Available at https://www.justnet.org/About_NLECTC.html.

NIJ (National Institute of Justice). (2013). Mapping and analysis for public safety. Washington, DC: National Institute of Justice, Bureau of Justice Programs. Available at http://www.nij.gov/topics/technology/maps/pages/welcome.aspx.

Oliver, W.M. (2008). August Vollmer. In J. Bumgarner (ed.), *Icons of Crime Fighting*. Vol. 1. Westport, CT: Greenwood Press, 83–116.

PERF (Police Executive ResearchForum). (2012). PERF survey shows widespread use of many technologies in policing. Washington, DC: Police Executive Research Forum.

PERF (Police Executive Research Forum) (2013). *CompStat: Its origins, evolution, and future in law enforcement agencies*. Bureau of Justice Assistance. Washington, DC: Police Executive Research Forum.

Reith, C. (1956). *A New Study of Police History*. London: Oliver and Boyd.

Smith, D.C., and Bratton, W.J. (2001). Performance management in New York City: CompStat and the revolution in police management. In D.W. Forsythe (ed.), *Quicker Better Cheaper? Managing Performance in American Government*. Albany, NY: Rockefeller Institute Press, 453–482.

Stering, R. S. (2008). *Police Officer's Handbook: An Analytical and Administrative Guide*. Sudbury, MA: Bartlett and Jones.

Strickland, J. (2013). *Introduction to Crime Analysis and Mapping*. Colorado Springs, CO: Simulation Educators.

Weisburd, D., Telep, C., Hinkle, J., and Eck, J. (2008). *Effects of problem-oriented policing on crime and disorder*. National Institute of Justice. Available at https://www.ncjrs.gov/pdffiles1/nij/grants/224990.pdf.

Wilson, O.W. (1963). *Police Administration*. New York: McGraw-Hill.

11

TACTICAL CRIME ANALYSIS

Chapter Outline

1. Introduction
   a. Recap what tactical crime analysis is
   b. What does tactical crime analysis entail?
      i. Identify emerging crime patterns as soon as possible
      ii. Analyze carefully any crime patterns
      iii. Notify the police department or agency about the identified pattern
      iv. Work with the police department or agency to address the identified pattern
2. Identify emerging crime patterns
   a. Daily review of crime reports
   b. Comparison of crime reports with those in the past—last week, month, year, or three to five years
   c. Crime mapping
   d. Statistical comparisons
   e. Qualitative research
3. Carefully analyze any emerging patterns
   a. Identify commonalities of criminal events
      i. By searching databases
   b. Identify the who, what, when, where, and how factors that are common
   c. Use an inductive model
4. Notify the police department or agency about the existence of a pattern
   a. Predict future criminal events
   b. Work with detectives to address the pattern
   c. Use spatial and temporal analysis
5. Work with the police department or agency to develop the best tactics to address the pattern

    a. Wrap up
    b. A few words about the next chapter

Learning Objectives for Chapter 11

1. Gain an understanding of crime patterns
2. Be able to differentiate between seven types of crime patterns
3. Identify the crime analyst's role in crime patterns
4. Be aware of different ways of addressing crime patterns

> Tactical crime analysis involves pattern detection, linkage analysis for suspect–crime correlations, target profiling, and offender movement patterns. The main difference between strategic and tactical crime analysis is the timeliness of the data. Strategic crime analysis usually involves data covering at least a yearlong period, whereas tactical crime analysis uses data collected during several days.
>
> **Goldsmith et al. (2000, p. 5)**

Introduction

As you learned in Chapter 11, tactical crime analysis involves analyzing data to develop information on the who, what, and where of crime; in other words, it's about identifying crime patterns and helping a police department or investigators within a police department to better understand a crime pattern or problem and develop the most effective response.

According to Philip Canter (2000), crime analysis has two broad functions: strategic and tactical. Strategic crime analysis will be discussed in Chapter 12, but tactical crime analysis will be the focus of this chapter. Canter (2000) goes on to say that tactical crime analysis involves pattern detection, linkage analysis for suspect–crime correlations, target profiling, and offender movement patterns. In other words, tactical crime analysis involves

- Identifying emerging crime patterns as soon as possible
- Analyzing carefully any identified crime patterns

- Notifying the police department or agency about the identified pattern
- Working with the police department or agency to address the identified pattern

Identifying Emerging Crime Patterns

Pattern detection occurs when offenses are reported during a relatively short period of time and the crime analyst is able to identify common attributes among those offenses. The most likely common attributes would include the type of crime (e.g., all were armed robberies), modus operandi (MO) (all of the crimes involved a man who initially feigned an illness in a convenience store), and type of weapon used (each armed robbery of a convenience store involved a .22-caliber handgun).

Additionally, a crime pattern can occur over a large geographic region, say a whole county, or it may be confined to a relatively small area, perhaps a neighborhood encompassing four blocks. When a crime pattern occurs in a relatively small area, it is referred to as a "hot spot" or a cluster.

The tactical analysis of crime patterns is a primary responsibility of crime analysts at police agencies around the United States and, indeed, around the world. Every day, analysts search databases and mine data in an effort to link cases by the key factors we just mentioned above, and then disseminate information about known and newly discovered patterns to fellow police personnel. This analysis improves the safety of communities by facilitating police response, which can, in turn, prevent and reduce crime. While the pattern identification process is reasonably standardized, there is a diversity of perspective on what constitutes a crime pattern (Gwinn, 2011). Unfortunately, the profession lacks a common language, and the terms *crime pattern, crime series, hot spot, crime trend,* and *crime problem* are often used interchangeably (Gwinn, 2011).

Standards and Definitions Related to Crime Patterns

Given this lack of a common language, before we go any further in discussing the identification of crime patterns, it is important to review standards and definitions as promulgated by the Standards, Methods, and Technology (SMT) Committee of the International Association of Crime Analysts (IACA).

In 2011, the IACA chartered the SMT Committee to begin to define "analytical methodologies, technologies, and core concepts relevant to the profession of crime analysis" (Gwinn, 2011). The resulting report, entitled "Crime Pattern Definitions for Tactical Analysis," began to set standards not only for crime analysis definitions but also for procedures (Gwinn, 2011). The goals of the report, which was called a white paper, were to standardize the definition of a crime pattern, differentiate crime pattern types, and define and illustrate each of the different crime pattern types (Gwinn, 2011).

What Is a Crime Pattern?

According to the IACA report "Crime Pattern Definitions for Tactical Analysis," a crime pattern is a group of two or more crimes reported to or discovered by police that are unique because they meet each of the following conditions:

1. They share at least one common factor; that common factor could be the type of crime; the behavior of the offenders or victims; the characteristics of the offender(s), victims, or targets; the property taken; or the locations of the occurrence of the offenses.
2. There is no known relationship between the victim(s) and the offender(s); this means that it is a stranger-on-stranger crime.
3. The shared common factor or factors make the set of crimes notable and distinct from other criminal activity occurring within the same general date range (say, a week or a month).
4. The criminal activity is typically of limited duration—ranging from a week or more to as long as a month or several months.
5. The set of related crimes is treated as one unit of analysis and is addressed through focused police efforts and tactics (Gwinn, 2011).

What a Crime Pattern Is Not

Again, according to the IACA, a crime pattern is not a crime trend. A trend is a persistent, long-term rise or fall in temporally based data (Gwinn, 2011). Knowing about crime trends is valuable because it can alert the police and the community to increases or decreases in the amount of criminal offenses.

However, crime trend analysis does not examine shared similarities between specific crime incidents. For example, when a local police department reports that homicides in the city have increased by 14% over the past year, this is not reporting a crime pattern. Sometimes such reports give no information as to any common factors among the homicides, the victims, or the offenders. A crime pattern report would indicate commonalities. Therefore, a crime trend is not a crime pattern.

Also, a crime pattern is not a chronic problem. Ron Clarke and John Eck have defined a crime problem as "a recurring set of related harmful events in a community that members of the public expect the police to address" (Clarke and Eck, 2003, p. 7). Based on this definition, a crime pattern would technically be classified as a *type* of crime problem; however, it would differ from a crime pattern in these important ways:

1. Scope and length: A crime problem is chronic in duration and persistent in frequency with occasional acute spikes; a crime pattern is short term and acute in frequency.
2. Nature of activity: A crime problem is related to "harmful events" that may include crime, safety, disorder, or quality of life concerns; on the other hand, a crime pattern is limited to a specific set of reported crimes.
3. Response: A crime problem requires specialized, strategic responses that often involve multiagency and community collaboration; a crime pattern usually requires routine operational tactics carried out primarily by the police agency responsible for that jurisdiction (Gwinn, 2011).

A crime pattern is not just defined by numbers and a summary report of crimes that are similar in some characteristics and occur in roughly the same location. Nor is a crime pattern simply a cluster of incidents on a map. A crime pattern is identified through a systematic, deductive analytical process, subsequently communicated to police agencies via some form of bulletin (Gwinn, 2011). The bulletin clearly and succinctly describes the critical elements of the pattern and highlights any notable implications for action. More specifically, crime pattern bulletins typically include analytical elements such as a geographic profile, a temporal profile, a list of potential suspects matching physical or MO descriptions, or other information that has value for an investigation or for a response seeking a solution.

Crime Pattern Types

What are the common shared elements that are necessary to define a set of crimes as a pattern?

According to Gwinn (2011), there are seven common types of crime patterns. These types are not mutually exclusive, and sometimes they overlap. Therefore, when a crime analyst is examining a crime pattern that does not seem to fit neatly in one category, the analyst should categorize the pattern as the type that appears most applicable based on the characteristics of the crimes involved and the nature of the most appropriate potential police response.

The seven primary crime pattern types are as follows:

1. Series: A group of similar crimes thought to be committed by the same individual or group of individuals acting in concert. An example of a series crime pattern would be five home invasions in upper-middle-class neighborhoods in a suburban community. In each, either one person was at home or the home was empty. The two white males observed by the home owner or by neighbors were in their 20s, wearing uniforms of a utility company, and threatening residents with handguns. They were seen leaving the area in a blue Honda Civic.

2. Spree: A group of similar crimes thought to be carried out by the same individual or group, but with a high frequency within a relatively short period of time. The crimes are so frequent that they appear continuous. For example, a rash of thefts from automobiles parked on a certain street in a five-block area occurring during a seven-hour period would be called a spree. In this spree, all of the cars are broken into by smashing a driver's side window, and the offenses all happen during a period of time from 8:00 p.m. one evening until 3:00 a.m. the next morning.

3. Hot prey: A group of crimes committed by one or more individuals, involving victims who share similar physical

characteristics or engage in similar behavior. An example of a hot prey crime would be this series of crimes: five homeless men in an area comprising 10 square blocks are beaten with baseball bats over a two-month time frame.

4. Hot product: A group of crimes committed by one or more individuals in which a unique type of property is targeted for theft. A hot product example would be when, over a three-month period of time, more than 20 new construction homes are broken into and copper wiring and bathroom fixtures are stolen.

5. Hot spot: A group of similar crimes committed by one or more individuals at locations within close proximity to one another. An example of a hot spot would be eight daytime burglaries that take place in a large condominium development during a few weeks. No one was home in any of the condominiums that were broken into, and different items were stolen in each break-in. There were differences in the method of entry and the location of the door or window that was chosen for entry.

6. Hot place: A group of similar crimes committed by one or more individuals at the same location. A hot spot is different from a hot place. An example of a hot place would be seven armed robberies that take place at three different banks that are all located on the same street within a mile of each other.

7. Hot setting: A group of similar crimes committed by one or more individuals that are primarily related by type of place where crimes occurred. A hot setting could be illustrated by a series of robberies of 24-hour service stations that all have convenience stores. More than a dozen such robberies take place at these service stations throughout the city. In each, one person is working alone late at night and different types of weapons are used to force the attendant to empty the cash register. In some of these robberies, the lone person working the service station is beaten or shot, while in others there are only threats.

The Crime Analyst's Task in Identifying Emerging Crime Patterns

The primary task of the crime analyst is to identify an emerging crime pattern as soon as possible. Beyond that, though, it is part of his or her job to decide which of the seven types of patterns it is, because this makes the succeeding steps in the tactical crime analysis process easier.

To identify each type, the analyst must study daily crime reports and determine which belong to the crime pattern that is her focus. If she believes it is a crime series, then she may assume that the same individual or individuals are responsible for each one. By studying the crime reports of offenses that seem to fit in this series, she may determine if it is one or more than one individual, and begin to develop a profile of the likely individual(s) responsible. Also, she can begin to make predictions about when the next offense is likely to take place.

On the other hand, if the analyst believes it is a hot product pattern, then she must identify the product and learn where that product is available so she can predict the next target for a burglary of that product.

By studying crime reports and determining the category of the crime pattern, the crime analyst will be able to move on to the next step in the tactical crime analysis sequence.

Analyzing Carefully the Crime Pattern

To analyze the crime pattern carefully, the crime analyst studies reports and may even have to contact patrol officers or detectives to ask for more information. It is important to categorize the crime pattern, but it is also very important to pull together all of the available and relevant information in order to know as much as possible about the crime pattern, to be able to make predictions about future crime events, and to be able to offer a profile of the offender or offenders.

Let's take an example of a series crime pattern that was featured in the "Crime Pattern Types" section. In this example, there are a series of home invasions in two upper-middle-class neighborhoods in a suburban community. They all take place during the day, and two males, dressed in what appear to be utility company uniforms, go into homes to rob them. The culprits have been identified as two white males in their 20s, who wield handguns and make their escape in a blue Honda Civic.

Having identified this as a series crime pattern, the analyst can use some inductive reasoning to begin to develop a useful profile. If they are daytime burglaries, then the young men are either unemployed or work night shifts. If they are carrying handguns, then they may have recently purchased or acquired these guns. If they are driving a blue Honda Civic, then the car may be registered to one of them. Given this beginning formulation, the analyst can begin to query available databases to try to learn about men in their mid-20s who might live within a several-mile radius. They could have been recently paroled, so parole databases can be reviewed. The motor vehicle department or secretary of state database can be checked for Honda Civics registered to people in the area. By putting together this kind of intelligence, when the crime analyst reports about this crime pattern, she can add other information that will be helpful to detectives who are investigating this series.

Notify the Police Department about the Identified Pattern

Having identified a crime pattern and gathered more data to give the police as much information as possible, it is then time to send a bulletin or report to the police department.

The way crime pattern intelligence is communicated can vary, and that variety of formats can be related to the pattern that has been discovered by the analyst. Here are three examples of the way an analyst can report his results:

1. *Repeat incident location report*: This is a standardized weekly report to provide more information for various units in the police department when the analyst has identified repeat incident complaints at the same location. The report will generally consist of addresses that meet a particular threshold (e.g., a minimum of four calls for service) within a designated time period (such as over a period of four weeks). Other information that may be included in this report might be the dates of previous calls for service, the time of day for each call, the type of call, the disposition of the call, the case number, and the name of the officer(s) that responded.

2. *Crime report data variables used for pattern analysis*: This report is more like a request for help than the identification of an actual crime pattern. The analyst will, in this communication, have a list of recommended variables to be included in future

police reports to enhance crime pattern analysis. For instance, the analyst may ask that police reports in the future give the time of day and the names of any people (whether complainants or witnesses) interviewed.

3. *Crime pattern bulletin*: This report summarizes the relevant information of crimes that have been linked together as a pattern. Although bulletins will vary in their style and format, each will contain basic information in order to alert other units within the police department of the essential information about the crime pattern. A bulletin may consist of maps, graphs, addresses, or descriptions or profiles of suspects.

Tools for Analyst Communication

While tactical crime analysts may develop their own format for reports and bulletins, there is software developed to help crime analysts create a crime analysis bulletin.

For instance, Microsoft MS Access 2000 is such a program. It can track "customers" that request the bulletins, multiple crime analysts or bulletin creators, and multiple crime series, trend, spree, clusters, or patterns as needed by the police department or agency. This bulletin maker product was modeled after an MS Excel version that was developed by the Phoenix Police Department.

Some police units within police departments, such as the Crime Analysis Unit in the Criminal Investigations Bureau of the Chesapeake Police Department in Virginia, have developed a series of bulletins and reports—each with different functions. Since the Crime Analysis Unit is responsible for providing detailed and timely crime analysis to all levels of the Chesapeake Police Department, including command personnel, supervisors, detectives, and patrol officers, information from the Crime Analysis Unit gets disseminated in different formats.

For instance, "crime bulletins" identify specific crime problems. "Crime alerts" indicate that crime problems previously identified in a crime bulletin are continuing or increasing. "Crime leads" detail information relating to the identification of suspects in criminal cases or information related to serial crimes committed by the same suspects. In addition, the Crime Analysis Unit puts out specialized crime studies and statistical reports.

Some crime analysts also create and disseminate maps depicting crime hot spots and aerial imaging using the latest mapping technology. Or they may update and maintain statistics and mapping for the various other units, such as a drug offender program. Still other tactical crime analysts may be responsible for monitoring new laws in their state and for keeping up with emerging technology within the field of crime analysis.

Work with the Police to Address the Crime Pattern

Having communicated the existence of a crime pattern through a bulletin or report, the tactical crime analyst's job is not necessarily complete. Often, he or she will work with other units within the department to come up with strategies to address the crime pattern. But, first, the analyst is in the position that he or she is giving up control over the process. In effect, having issued a report or a bulletin, the process gets turned over to the operational units. The operational units may elect not to have the analyst continue to work as part of a team crafting a strategic response. Then, again, the operational unit—whether a patrol unit, a detective unit, or a drug program— has to work with whatever information or intelligence is passed on to them, regardless of its quality or operational relevance (Bruce and Ouellette, 2008). Four things may happen at this point. The operational unit may discover that the analyst failed to turn over sufficient information or the information is somehow faulty. In other words, one thing that may happen is that nothing happens: the intelligence is not actionable. The second thing that could take place is that while the information may be actionable, the police agency has no process in place to do anything with the intelligence. So, no action takes place. Third, the operational unit may take the intelligence and develop strategies—but without further assistance from the crime analyst. Or, fourth, the crime analyst is seen as a valuable member of the team to help develop strategies for dealing effectively with the crime pattern.

Providing Actionable Information

It has been pointed out that crime analysts cannot provide actionable information if they do not have the time, training, or tools to implement the latest methods in data querying, spatial analysis, temporal analysis, forecasting, publications, and a host of other crime analysis skills (Bruce and Ouelette, 2008). To remain at peak performance, a crime analyst or crime analysis unit needs the following:

- Adequate staffing: The IACA defines adequate staffing as 1 analyst per 1500 Uniform Crime Reports Part I crimes (agencies with fewer than 1500 Part I crimes should have at least part-time analysts). Agencies with fewer analysts run the risk that they will miss some patterns or will be unable to fully analyze crime and disorder issues (Bruce and Ouellette, 2008).
- Time: The 1:1500 ratio assumes each analyst will have 40 hours a week to devote to crime analysis. Appointing analysts and loading them up with nonanalytic duties will almost certainly doom a program to inadequacy.
- Initial and ongoing training: An initial round of basic training for new analysts should be supplemented with annual classes and professional conference attendance (Bruce and Ouellete, 2008).
- Proper equipment: Necessary equipment includes modern computers; software for data analysis, statistics, and publications; and a geographic information system (GIS).

Getting Analysts out of the Office

A good first step in orienting the crime analysis unit toward an operational focus is to make sure crime analysts leave the office sometimes. Bruce and Ouellette (2008) point out that no good analysis comes out of an ivory tower or a cloistered computer room. Instead, analysts must

- Have a true understanding of the nature of crime, criminals, and the social dynamics of the jurisdiction in which they work
- Know what types of information operational units find valuable
- Understand what tactics and strategies have a realistic chance of success

- Plug themselves into the informal intelligence exchange that happens on the ground level of any agency, discovering relevant facts that do not always make it into police reports
- Get the insight of officers, detectives, and community members in the analysis process

If a police officer comes to the job of crime analyst, he or she may already have much of this knowledge. However, many crime analysts were civilians first—not police officers or detectives. Therefore, the analyst who comes from a civilian background should take steps to develop these resources, but new analysts will likely need the support and encouragement of police department leaders to get out of the office now and then. Police agencies should encourage crime scene visits, ride-alongs, participation in offender interviews, and a regular, open exchange of information, intelligence, and ideas between analysts and investigators.

Array of Tactics and Strategies

In many police departments, the typical and usual response to any identified crime pattern, crime series, hot spot, crime trend, or crime problem is the directed patrol (Bruce and Ouellette, 2008). A directed patrol is focused patrol; that is, patrol resources are concentrated at the times and in the places with the highest risks of serious crime. The hypothesis is that the more patrol presence that is concentrated at the hot spots and "hot times" of criminal activity, the less crime there will be in those places and times (Sherman and Weisburd, 1995). Unfortunately, in some agencies it is often the only response. Directed patrols can be valuable for certain issues and can lead to both suppression of crime and apprehension of offenders (Bruce and Ouellette, 2008). However, there is a much larger list of potential responses at an agency's disposal.

As Bruce and Ouellette (2008) point out, tactical analysis and the identification of crime patterns require tactical responses—fast, effective responses that stop a crime pattern or series in its tracks. Generally, this is accomplished through one of three means:

1. Apprehending offenders
2. Hardening potential targets
3. Suppressing underlying opportunities for crime

What is the correct approach for a particular crime pattern? That depends on the characteristics of the pattern, as determined by the analysis. There is likely no existing published model for analysis-based tactical action, but Table 11.1 suggests several tactics based on the focus of the pattern and the tactical avenue a police department might choose to pursue.

As is seen in Table 11.1, the police department response could change based on the focus (whether location, offender, or target) and based on which tactical avenue (apprehension, target hardening, or suppression) is selected by the department. For example, if the crime analyst has a good description of the suspect, or if the analyst was actually able to identify the offender by name and address, the department might well choose apprehension as the best tactical avenue. The options

Table 11.1   Police Tactics based on Focus of the Pattern

	TACTICAL AVENUE		
FOCUS	APPREHENSION 1	TARGET HARDENING	SUPPRESSION
Location: limited locations for next offense; small target area	Rapid response Silent alarms Stakeouts Hidden cameras Channeling	Security surveys Alarms	Security guards or dogs Directed patrols Phantom cars Checkpoints Closures Visible cameras
Offender: strong offender description or name; good physical evidence	Traditional evidence-based investigation Surveillance Suspect-oriented patrol General community and madia information	General community and media information	Profile interview patrols
Taget: limited number of potential targets; targets easy to identify and reach	Decoys Controlled buys	Property identification Bulletins to potential victims	Market disruption
None: broad geography; no suspect; large number of available targets	Planned response Informants	Warning signs Community organization General community and media information	Saturation patrols

Source: Bruce, C.W., and Ouellette, N.F., Closing the gap between analysis and response, *Police Chief* LXXV(9), 2008. Available at http://www.policechiefmagazine.org/magazine/index.cfm?fuseaction=display_arch&article_id=1604&issue_id=92008.

if apprehension is desired would include traditional evidence-based investigation to gather evidence against this suspect, surveillance of the suspect, patrol oriented toward awareness and tracking of the suspect, or providing community and media information to locate the suspect.

Encouraging Initiative throughout the Police Department

Given that a pattern has been identified, the police department leadership should disseminate information throughout several units while encouraging initiative at the following levels of their organizations:

- Patrols: Patrols should review crime analysis information and implement what tactics and strategies they can to address a particular issue. These might include suspect-oriented patrols, profile interview patrols, directed patrols, talking to informants, and warning members of the community.
- Investigators: Investigators can group related crimes, prioritizing those that are part of a pattern or series, and implement such effective tactics as surveillance, stakeouts, and controlled buys.
- Supervisors: Supervisors should plan and direct more resource-intensive tactics, such as decoys, saturation patrols, and planned response.

The Ideal Is a Formal Response Process

Ideally, a police department will support the development of a formal response process that ensures that something is done about emerging crime patterns. A few law enforcement agencies allow the crime analysis unit to recommend assignments, and officers are expected to follow these crime analysis unit assignments unless a supervisor countermands them.

For instance, the Shawnee, Kansas, Police Department has a program known as Crime Analysis Directed Enforcement (CADE). In CADE, the crime analyst determines directed patrol locations by location and shift. In Cambridge, Massachusetts, the Crime Analysis Unit can assign "park and walks," which are essentially directed patrols, to route officers.

Such policies and procedures place a lot of power into the hands of analysts, but they can generate resentment within the police department if not handled carefully. This suggests another reason for crime analysts to leave their computer screens behind and get to know officers in other units.

In other police departments, established groups of officers who are given assignments by crime analysts spend their shifts intervening in patterns and problems. These officers are detached from regular patrol so as not to be distracted from their missions with routine calls. One name given to these officers is "impact teams." Another name applied to them by some police departments is the "split-force model." This term means that the department has divided its operations divisions into regular operations units (that respond to calls) and tactical-action or problem-solving units. Chief Gary Gemme of the Worcester, Massachusetts, Police Department instituted such an approach in 2005, and the agency's Community Impact Division has since been credited with solving several crime patterns (Bruce and Ouellette, 2008).

But such models are not limited to large police departments. For instance, the Redmond, Washington, Police Department created a ProAct Unit with five officers and a detective. The ProAct Unit was to specifically intercede in auto-related crime. They use offender intelligence from the crime analysis unit as their "to-do list."

It might be said that the mother of all formal response development methods is CompStat. As you have learned already in Chapter 10, CompStat was established by the New York City Police Department in the 1990s, and it involves getting all of the decision-makers in the department in a room on a regular basis, reviewing current activity, deciding what to do about it, and reviewing success or failure at subsequent meetings. CompStat-style systems go under many alternative names and acronyms, so much so that Lincoln, Nebraska, chief of police Tom Casady, with tongue in cheek, suggested OOVOC (Our Own Version of CompStat) as an umbrella term. Various OOVOC systems are characterized by how they balance accountability with problem-solving. The New York style of CompStat features a sometimes harsh view of "accountability," with precinct commanders expected—under the threat of demotion or transfer—to know the details of crime volume, as well as individual crimes, in their areas. The precinct commanders themselves present the current crime figures and pattern information and are questioned in detail by the commissioner and chiefs.

Other models care less about who presents the data and more about facilitating a collaborative process to intercede in emerging patterns and solve long-term problems. In these models, accountability and confrontation are less important than effective results.

A properly designed CompStat-style system can make excellent use of crime analysis. Ideally, the department discusses information that the crime analysts have prepared and decides how to respond. The best systems ensure that no pattern or problem goes unaddressed, encourage creative thinking, and reward effective (rather than traditional) strategies and tactics (Bruce and Ouellette, 2008). The Fort Worth, Texas, Police Department's CIDAT process, for instance, requires a written action plan to follow any discussion of a pattern or series.

An important element of CompStat that perhaps should be adopted by every police agency with a crime analysis unit is the requirement that all units of the police department must work together. In older models in police departments, specialized units operated independently from other units and conducted police operations to achieve their own objectives. In the CompStat model, all units must be represented and held jointly responsibility for the successes and failures. The benefit is that much more creative and effective crime control measures are designed when all units develop and implement the strategy (Schick, 2004).

Process of Investigation: Pattern Crime Investigations

Quality analysis of data, information, and intelligence, when related to crime patterns, can lead to substantive results being passed along to the investigating team for consideration as viable leads to follow up on. It also serves to assist administrators who need to make strategic and tactical recommendations. So, it's safe to say that quality pattern analysis can lead to quality pattern investigative follow-up.

Critical thinking is one of the central components to tactical analysis and one of the main skills analysts must develop as they investigate the commonalities that make up pattern crimes. As previously discussed, the analyst needs to have a firm understanding of the investigative process that law enforcement follows if he or she is to form hypotheses and draw conclusions as to who is committing a series of related crimes. As Paulsen,

Bair, and Helms have written, "To identify crime patterns, analysts must be skilled in critical thinking and be able to recognize commonalities among characteristics of crime incidents" (Boba, 2009, p. 156).

Investigating a crime pattern, while working directly with the investigative team, can be a daunting task considering that the analyst is an integral part of the decision-making process and his or her analysis will form the basis of the reasoning behind investigative team decisions. At the real-time crime center located in Rochester, New York, several analysts work in specialty fields, such as homicide or robbery, and as a result work shoulder to shoulder with their law enforcement counterparts on pattern crimes. The level of input the analysts have with the investigative team is largely based on the level of confidence the investigative team has in the analysts and their investigative, analytical, and critical thinking skills.

Investigating pattern crimes, primarily violent crimes such as armed robberies, relies on quick action and decisive recommendations being made by both the investigators and the analyst as they attempt to project the next event. These recommendations are drawn from the results of exhaustive analysis of the data that pertain to the crimes.

Pattern Investigation

Unfortunately, it takes more than two events to consider a series of related crimes a pattern. During this time, the offenders can become more emboldened as they have now successfully committed their crime while eluding law enforcement in the process. This places mounting pressure for the investigating agency(s) to solve the crime.

However, once the pattern is identified, the investigative process can now directly focus on the commonalities associated with the crime pattern. Identifying factors that point to MO can be located in the data, and the data are only as good as the quality of the report that documented the crime particulars.

A well-written report should denote several critical details that an analyst uses when considering—and examining—commonalities:

- Type of crime: For example, armed robbery.
- Temporal concentration: Time(s) of occurrence(s).
- Spatial concentration: Geographical area(s) the crimes were committed in. This could incorporate space between crime locations in terms of police jurisdictions or patrol sections.

- Modus operandi: Specifics that directly relate to the crime in terms of a suspect's actions, dialogue, weapon, point of entry or exit, or any other unique aspect that differentiates the crime from others while tying the crime to those of a similar nature.
- Property taken: It is important to list, as some robberies are for specific items.

Using Analytical Results for Product Development

The results of the analysis of crime patterns should be incorporated into a workable product that can be used not only for strategic and tactical planning, but also as an investigative aid for officers in the field who need to be made aware of the emerging pattern and the details surrounding the crime (see Figure 11.1).

When creating a product intended to alert others of an emerging crime pattern (as well as an investigative aid), the format of the product should contain several key features:

Product heading:

- Type of crime
- Pattern analyst involved with the analysis and contact information
- Date of product creation

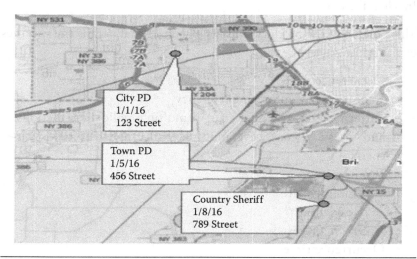

Figure 11.1 Example of an analytical pattern product.

Product body content:

- Crime summary
- Commonalities
- Incident details
- Photographs (if any)
- Map of the locations involved
- Contact information of an investigator working the case

Crime Summary

A crime summary is a brief synopsis of what the product is about. The summary should consist of a short narrative advising the reader that a specific crime pattern is emerging.

Commonalities

As indicated above, the commonality portion of the product should at least include

- Crime type
- Temporal details
- Spatial details
- MO factors

Incident Details

This portion of the product consists of a chart that details the specifics of the crime pattern:

- Occurrence date
- Reporting law enforcement agency
- Pattern crimes usually occur in multiple police jurisdictions and, as such, may have multiple police agencies reporting them.
- Location type
  - Commercial
  - Residential
- Location address
- Occurrence time
- Day of the week

- Suspect description(s)
- Suspect vehicle description(s)
- Brief narrative that highlights MO
- For example, suspect 1 held customers and employees at bay with a handgun while suspect 2 loaded a black duffel bag with phones

The above aspects of a product are not absolute, in terms of format or content, but the product should highlight most of these areas for completeness.

Photos

Photographs of suspects, suspect vehicles, and property taken may lead to an identification.

Map

A map of the crime locations can help the investigative team, analyst included, with identifying relevance in terms of entry and egress to and from the crime scene. There may be other factors that may help to identify why certain actual and geographical locations are being targeted over others.

Contact Information

The reader needs to have a way to communicate with the point of contact associated with the investigation.

Purpose of the Finished Product

The purpose of the finished product is to

- Help the reader (usually law enforcement personnel) identify the principal case and examine the distinctive characteristics of the pattern.
- Help the reader identify other key elements in the pattern from other cases that exhibit many of the same characteristics as the principal case.
- Help the reader identify additional related cases from cases that exhibit one or more of the same characteristics as the principal case.

- The following is an actual report showing an example of an analytical pattern product

Example of an Analytical Pattern Product

Robbery Pattern Crime Bulletin	PD Analysis Center
Analyst Name **Date** **Product Number** **Contact Number**	

Overview: Since 05/01/15 there have been (3) overnight gunpoint robberies of gas stations located throughout thecounty.

Commonalities:

Type: 3 Commercial Robberies

Temporal Concentration: overnight/early morning. (2100-0500 Hrs.)

Spatial Concentration: Town of Albert, Town of Baker, City of Evertt

Suspect Description: M/B, 5'10-6'0, 20's-30, wearing all dark clothing, face covered with a black bandana, armed with a black handgun

Suspect Vehicle: 2 occupants (gunman was passenger), red 2DSD, possibly older model Saturn, loud muffler, broken right tail light.

Details:

Jurisdiction	Date	Time	Dow	Location	Address	Suspect Description	Weapon Displayed	Vehicle
Albert PD	5/1/2015	2119	Friday	Fuel King	1862 Rogers Ave.	M-B/-5-10-6'/20-30's/ Dark Clothes-Black Bandana	Black Handgun	N/A
Sheriffs Dept.	5/3/2015	100	Sunday	Gas King	25 Baxter Street	M-B/-5-10-6'/20-30's/ Dark Clothes-Black Bandana	Black Handgun	Red Staurn
Evertt PD	5/10/2015	300	Sunday	Fuel King	100 East Main Street	M-B/-5-10-6'/20-30's/ Dark Clothes-Black Bandana	Handgun	Red Staurn

Map:

This pattern product reports shows an analysis of a series of gas station robberies.

Questions for Discussion

1. What can best be learned from the CompStat model?
2. What are some ways that a crime analyst can become part of an effective team within the police department?

Important Terms

CompStat: Performance management system that is used to reduce crime and achieve other police department goals. It emphasizes information sharing, responsibility and accountability, and improving effectiveness.

Crime pattern: Group of two or more crimes reported to or discovered by police that are unique because they meet certain conditions, such as sharing at least one common factor.

Crime pattern bulletin: Report issued by a crime analyst or crime analyst unit that summarizes the relevant information about crimes that have been linked together as a pattern.

Crime series: Group of similar crimes thought to be committed by the same individual or group of individuals acting in concert.

Directed patrol: Focused patrol or patrol resources concentrated at the times and in the places with the highest risks of serious crime.

Hot spot: When a crime pattern occurs in a relatively small area, it is referred to as a hot spot or a cluster.

Linkage analysis: Analysis that integrates information from three distinct, but interrelated, aspects of a crime pattern perpetrated by a single offender.

Pattern detection: Occurs when offenses are reported during a relatively short period of time and the crime analyst is able to identify common attributes among those offenses.

Target profiling: Analyst attempt to profile the subject or the suspect, that is, the target.

Study Guide Questions

For questions 1–3, indicate whether the statement is true or false.

1. _____ The profession of crime analysis lacks a common language and the terms *crime pattern, crime series, hot spot, crime trend*, and *crime problem* are often used interchangeably.

2. _____ A crime pattern is a group of two or more crimes reported to or discovered by police that are unique because they involve crime between relatives or friends.

3. _____ A crime series is a group of similar crimes thought to be committed by the same individual or group of individuals acting in concert.

4. According to Gwinn (2011), there are _____ common types of crime patterns.
   a. Three
   b. Five
   c. Seven
   d. Nine

5. A hot spot is a group of similar crimes committed by one or more individuals at
   a. Intervals of three months
   b. Locations far apart
   c. Locations within close proximity of one another
   d. Intervals of at least one year

6. A repeat incident location report is designed to provide more information about
   a. Nonrepeat incidents at various addresses
   b. Repeat incident complaints at the same location
   c. Repeat incident complaints in the same city
   d. No-repeat incidents involving no crime

7. A crime pattern bulletin is a report that summarizes the relevant information of crimes that have been
   a. Linked together as a pattern
   b. Linked together as a crime spree
   c. Linked with other crimes in other states
   d. Linked with the Mafia

8. A directed patrol use patrol resources
   a. Concentrated in the suburbs
   b. Concentrated only after midnight

c. Concentrated by using SWAT teams
d. Concentrated at the times and in the places with the highest risks of serious crime

References

Boba, R. (2009). *Crime Analysis with Crime Mapping*. Thousand Oaks, CA: Sage.

Bruce, C.W., and Ouellette, N.F. (2008). Closing the gap between analysis and response. *Police Chief* LXXV(9). Available at http://www.policechief magazine.org/magazine/index.cfm?fuseaction=display_arch&article _id=1604&issue_id=92008.

Canter, P.R. (2000). Geographic information systems and crime analysis in Baltimore County, Maryland. In Weisburd D. and J.T. McEwen (eds.), *Crime Mapping and Crime Prevention*. Monsey, NY: Criminal Justice Press pp. 157–190.

Clarke, R., and Eck, J. (2003). Classifying common police problems: A routine activities approach. *Crime Prevention Studies* 16: 7–39.

Goldsmith, V., McGuire, P.G., Mollenkopf, J.H., and Ross, T.A. (ed.). (2000). *Analyzing Crime Patterns*. Thousand Oaks, CA: Sage.

Gwinn, S. (ed.). (2011). Crime pattern definitions for tactical analysis. Overland Park, KS: International Association of Crime Analysts. Available at http:// www.iaca.net/Publications/Whitepapers/iacawp_2011_01_crime_pat-terns.pdf.

Schick, W. (2004). CompStat in the Los Angeles Police Department. *Police Chief* 71(1). Available at http://www.policechiefmagazine.org/magazine/ index.cfm?fuseaction=display_arch&article_id=190&issue_id=12004.

Sherman, L.W., and Weisburd, D. (1995). General deterrent effects of police patrol in crime "hot spots": A randomized, controlled trial. *Justice Quarterly* 12(4): 625–648.

12

TACTICAL CRIME ANALYSIS AND HOT SPOTS POLICING

Chapter Outline

1. Introduction to tactical crime analysis and hot spots policing
   a. Recap of tactical crime analysis
   b. Review of hot spots policing
   c. Definition in detail about hot spots
2. Essentials of hot spots
   a. Details
3. How analysts identify hot spots
   a. Technical
4. Tactical approaches to hot spots
   a. Approaches

Learning Objectives for Chapter 12

1. Gain a better understanding of tactical crime analysis and hot spots policing.
2. Be able to place the history of tactical crime analysis in perspective.
3. Learn the various kinds of indicators of crime and place.
4. Gain a better understanding of how analysts determine hot spots.
5. Be introduced to measures of identifying hot spots.

In recent years, crime scholars and practitioners have pointed to the potential benefits of focusing crime prevention efforts on crime places. A number of studies suggest that crime is not spread evenly across city landscapes. Rather, there is significant clustering of crime in small places, or "hot spots," that generate half of all criminal events (Pierce et al., 1988; Sherman et al., 1989; Weisburd et al., 1992). Even within the most crime-ridden neighborhoods, crime clusters at a few discrete locations and other areas are relatively crime-free (Sherman et al., 1989). A number of researchers have argued that many crime problems could be reduced more efficiently if police officers focused their attention to these deviant places (Sherman and Weisburd, 1995; Weisburd and Green, 1995). The appeal of focusing limited resources on a small number of high-activity crime places is straightforward. If we can prevent crime at these hot spots, then we might be able to reduce total crime. Hot spots policing has become a very popular way for police departments to prevent crime. A recent Police Foundation report found that 7 in 10 departments with more than 100 sworn officers reported using crime mapping to identify crime hot spots (Weisburd et al., 2003). A growing body of research evidence suggests that focused police interventions, such as directed patrols, proactive arrests, and problem-oriented policing, can produce significant crime prevention gains at high-crime hot spots (see, e.g., Braga, 2002; Eck, 1997, 2002; Skogan and Frydl, 2004; Weisburd and Eck, 2004). However, critics of place-based interventions charge that such policing strategies result in displacement—that is, criminals move to places not protected by police intervention (e.g., Reppetto, 1976). Given the growing popularity of hot spots policing, regular systematic reviews of the empirical evidence on the effects of focused police interventions on crime hot spots are necessary to assess the value of this approach to crime prevention.

Braga, 2007, p. 4

Introduction

Crime does not occur evenly in either states or cities. Some cities have very little crime and some have a great deal of crime. But, of course, no city is crime-free. And because it does not occur in even amounts throughout a city, it is generally clustered in small areas—hot spots—that account for a disproportionate amount of crime and disorder. For example,

- In Minneapolis, 3% of the city's addresses accounted for 50% of calls for service to the police in one study (National Institute of Justice, 2010).
- In Jersey City, New Jersey, about 4% of streets and intersection areas generated nearly half of the city's narcotics arrests and almost 42% of the disorder arrests (National Institute of Justice, 2010).

Criminal events, however, are not just about location. In addition to location, crime and public disorder tend to concentrate at certain times of the day or week. Assaults, for example, occur most frequently between 3:00 and 7:00 a.m., when streets are largely vacant. Residential burglaries mostly occur during daytime hours, when residents are not home. Incidents of driving under the influence occur more frequently in areas with a large number of bars or liquor stores (National Institute of Justice, 2010).

The importance of identifying hot spots is that both crime theories and practical studies support the idea that focusing police efforts at crime hot spots can effectively reduce crime (Filbert, 2008). As indicated in Chapter 11, once hot spots have been identified, the police efforts often include such approaches as directed patrols or other types of problem-solving to decrease the amount of crime in that area.

Police crime analysts work with crime incident data to find and analyze hot spots and provide information to other departments and units within the police department. Analysts often work with geographic information systems (GIS) software to create crime maps to visualize data and identify patterns and hot spots. GIS and related mapping and analysis tools have become sophisticated enough to include statistics software that allows rigorous analysis of crime hot spots.

In this chapter, more details are provided to give you a better understanding of how analysts identify crime hot spots. But first, we discuss the theory behind the hot spots approach to crime analysis.

Crime Hot Spot Theories

Crime theories are critical for useful crime mapping because they aid in the interpretation of data (Eck, 1998). Crime theories also provide guidance as to what actions are most appropriate in response to the identification of hot spots. There are several theories of crime and disorder concentration (another term for hot spots) that need to be explored. Some of these theories are somewhat contradictory. What they do, though, is explain different types of crime phenomena that occur at different geographic levels (Eck et al., 2005).

Theories of crime and place try to offer an understanding of crime in its physical or spatial environment. These theories explain crime patterns by the location of targets, offenders' choice of travel routes, use of space for various activities, and the innate ability of a place or target to defend itself. Thus, these theories of crime and place can be described as belonging together under the umbrella of what is called "environmental criminology" (Brantingham and Brantingham, 1981). Such theories trace their origins to the work of the Cartographic School in the mid-1800s. Henry Mayhew, who is considered to be the founder of the Cartographic School, pioneered the use of maps in the analysis of crime. Mayhew's maps of counties of London showed spatial relationships between crime and rates of illiteracy, teenage marriage, and number of illegitimate children (Levinson, 2002). Other statisticians, including Andre Guerry and Adolphe Quetelet, were also working with statistics and maps to represent crime patterns in France in the mid-1800s (Levinson, 2002).

In the United States, the analysis of crime and place is rooted in the work done by the members of what is known as the Chicago School early in the twentieth century. Robert Park and Ernest Burgess, founders of the Chicago School, borrowed from plant ecology to explain the development of cities. According to Park and Burgess, cities developed in a process they called "succession," whereby competition for scarce resources, primarily land, drove the development of the city outward from the city core. They proposed that cities develop in a series of successive concentric zones, with the zones at the interior being the most deteriorated.

Based on their analysis, Park and Burgess proposed a theory of crime known as concentric zone theory. They showed that the zones closest to the inner city had the highest prevalence of social ills, such as unemployment, poverty, reliance on social assistance, and rates of disease. Park and Burgess said that the prevalence of these social problems in the inner zones of the city, where social conflict was high, led to a condition they called social disorganization (Vold et al., 1998).

Other work by members of the Chicago School, notably Clifford Shaw and Henry McKay, explored the theory of social disorganization. Shaw and McKay (1969) divided the city into "natural areas." These areas shared social and demographic characteristics. Shaw and McKay went on to examine the locations of residences of juvenile delinquents and noted that areas with the highest rates of juvenile delinquents were geographic areas with weak community controls. Shaw and McKay did not attribute crime problems to the people who lived in these areas, but instead to characteristics of the areas, including physical deterioration, ethnic heterogeneity, and low rental costs (Vold et al., 1998). Shaw and McKay showed that social disorganization peaked in the central business district (CBD) (the first zone) and the zone of transition (the second concentric zone where recent immigrants first moved to and where industries were located). Social disorganization was shown to decrease in a linear fashion as one proceeds through the remaining concentric zones outward from the CBD (Vold et al., 1986). With each progressive zone away from the CBD, housing became more desirable and household income increased.

From these origins, many criminologists have sought to continue the work by these early researchers and attempt to explain or predict crime based on factors external to the individual and the individual's interaction with those factors. One strain of theories—the ecological or areal tradition of criminology—is concerned with the environmental, contextual, community, physical, or situational correlates of crime, or their interactions. Together, these ecological theories aim to explain the relationships between crime and place at three different levels of spatial aggregation: the microlevel, the mesolevel, and the macrolevel.

Often, though not always, the microlevel refers to the actual location of a crime. The mesolevel usually refers to a neighborhood or community. The macrolevel, on the other hand, may refer to a city, or an area even larger, such as a country. In what follows, we will refer to these three levels as place theories, street theories, neighborhood theories, and other large area theories.

Before we discuss these specific theories, we will take a look at what might be considered competing theories of crime causation, and the development of environmental theories following the work of Park and Burgess, and Shaw and McKay.

In a broad sense, we can say that historically—at least since the early half of the twentieth century—theories of crime can be divided into those that seek to explain the development of criminal offenders and those that seek to explain the development of criminal events. Throughout the development of criminology, theories of—and research on—offenders have been dominant (Clarke, 1980). It could even be argued that most research on crime and crime prevention has been focused on why certain types of people commit crime and what we can do about them. It is only relatively recently that serious attention has begun to be paid to explaining crimes—rather than the criminality of people involved in crime. In trying to explain crime, criminologists in the past two to three decades have been concerned with where crime occurs (Eck and Weisburd, 1995).

Although some criminologists might consider theories of crime places and theories about the criminality of offenders as competing explanations of the crime problem, Eck and Weisburd (1995) suggested it may be useful to consider that offender explanations and event explanations are more complementary than competitors.

The reasoning for this may start with this idea: while an offender may be highly motivated to commit a crime, unless he or she actually engages in a criminal event, there is nothing to explain. On the other hand, if a criminal act has occurred, a full understanding of the event must in some manner include an explanation of the offender. Offender theories should eventually tell us how people come to be criminal offenders, and the circumstances under which they either act or desist from acting as offenders. Such theories may suggest crime prevention strategies that are focused on those individuals who are likely to become high-rate offenders or even serious violent offenders. However, to date theories about the development of criminality do not provide a solid basis for making such predictions, and there is little consensus as to what such a theory in the future would look like. Consequently, a preventive strategy based on offender theories is not near at hand. But even if we were to understand more about the development of criminality than we presently do, it is not clear whether all or even most offenders could be prevented from involvement in crime (Clarke and Weisburd, 1990).

Thus, as Eck and Weisburd (1995) would conclude, even if we had a good explanation for the development of offenders, we would still need a good explanation for criminal events. Specifically, we would want a theory that could tell us why certain targets are selected by offenders—why some targets are attractive and others are less attractive, or even repellent. What are the barriers to offending that are presented to offenders, and how are they overcome? What types of routine activities of offenders, victims, and what have sometimes been termed guardians contribute to the likelihood of crime occurring in particular places? Though we may not be close to having a comprehensive crime event theory that would provide unambiguous answers to such questions, there is some agreement among some criminologists who study crime events as to what such a theory should look like. Moreover, there is growing evidence that event prevention strategies can have a dramatic and immediate impact on specific crime problems (Clarke, 1992).

But, in recent years, researchers have begun to describe how crime and place theories come together and how they can be applied to crime analysis and crime prevention.

As it turns out, three recent theoretical perspectives—rational choice, routine activities theory, and crime pattern theory—have influenced our understanding of the importance of place in crime prevention efforts. A rational choice perspective provides the basic rationale for defining place as important, since it suggests that offenders will select targets and define means to achieve their goals in a manner that can be explained (Cornish and Clarke, 1986). A rational choice perspective, according to some criminologists, can be used to develop testable propositions describing crime events and offender behavior, particularly if a rational choice perspective is used in conjunction with routine activities theory (Clarke and Felson, 1993).

Routine Activities Theory

Routine activities theory seeks to explain the occurrence of crime events as the confluence of four circumstances (Cohen and Felson, 1979; Felson, 1986, 1994). First, there must be a motivated offender. Second, there must be a desirable target. Third, the target and the offender must be at the same place at the same time. Finally, three other types of controllers—intimate handlers, guardians, or place managers—must be absent or ineffective. Intimate handlers are people who have direct personal influence over an offender (such as parents, teachers, coaches, friends, or employers). In the presence of such people, potential offenders do not commit crimes. Most adults are away from intimate handlers for many hours of the day, and many offenders, both juvenile and adult, have few or no intimate handlers (Felson, 1986). People who can protect targets are guardians. They too must be missing from the place. Guardians include friends (as when four women decide to walk together to the parking lot after a night class in order to protect each other) as well as formal authorities, such as private security guards and public police. People or objects that are separated from guardians for sustained periods have elevated risks of victimization. People who take care of the places are place managers. Place managers, such as janitors and apartment managers, regulate behavior at the locations they control. For a crime to occur, such people must be absent, ineffective, or negligent (Eck, 1994).

Crime Pattern Theory

Crime pattern theory is particularly important in developing an understanding of crime and place, as it combines rational choice and routine activities theory to help explain the distribution of crime across places. The distribution of offenders, targets, handlers, guardians, and managers over time and place will describe crime patterns. With the growth of shopping malls, strip malls, and stand-alone fitness centers, for instance, there is often an increased number of potential targets, while the people who can protect those facilities (handlers, guardians, and managers) and the people who frequent them (potential victims) may have little or no contact (e.g., in elevators, stairwells, and large parking areas). Reasonably rational offenders, while engaging in their routine activities, will note places without guardians and managers and where their handlers are unlikely to show up. Crime pattern theory explores the interactions of offenders with their physical and social environments that influence offenders' choices of targets.

According to crime pattern theory, how targets come to the attention of offenders influences the distribution of crime events over time, space, and among targets (Brantingham and Brantingham, 1993). This occurs because offenders engage in routine activities. Just like other, nonoffending individuals, offenders move among the spheres of home, school, work, shopping, and recreation. As they conduct their normal legitimate activities, they become aware of criminal opportunities. Thus, criminal opportunities that are not near the areas offenders routinely move through are unlikely to come to their attention. A given offender will be aware of only a subset of the possible targets available. Criminal opportunities found at places that come to the attention of offenders have an increased risk of becoming targets (Brantingham and Brantingham, 1993). While a few offenders may aggressively seek out uncharted areas, most will conduct their searches within the areas they become familiar with through non-criminal activities.

The concept of place is essential to crime pattern theory. Not only are places logically required (an offender must be in a place when an offense is committed), but also the characteristics of certain places influence the likelihood of a crime. Place characteristics highlighted by routine activities theory include the presence and effectiveness of managers and the presence of capable guardians. Crime pattern theory links places with desirable targets and the context within which they are found by focusing on how places come to the attention of potential offenders.

Although crime pattern theory and routine activities theory are mutually supportive in many respects, they can give rise to differing explanations of crime at specific locations. Given a set of high-crime locations, a crime pattern theorist would focus on how offenders discover and gain access to the place. A routine activities theorist would focus instead on the behaviors of the targets and the possible absence of controllers whose presence could have prevented the offenses from taking place—guardians, handlers, and place managers. In other words, for the crime pattern theorist, places are problematic because of their location and relationship to the environment. For the routine activities theorist, places are problematic because of the types of people present and absent from the location. Clearly, both explanations can be valid in different contexts and situations. It would seem that crime-specific explanations may show that for some events, crime pattern theory is a particularly useful explanation; for other events, routine activities theory offers greater insights; and for still a third group of events, some combination of the two theories is needed.

A Theory of Crime Places

Recent perspectives in criminological theory provide a basis for constructing a theory of crime places. However, such a theory must be developed in reference to a growing literature about the relationship between crime and place.

Several theories help explain why crime occurs in some places and not others. The environmental criminology approach was developed in the 1980s by Paul Brantingham and Patricia Brantingham. They focused on environmental or context factors that can influence criminal activity. These factors include space (geography), time, law, offender, and target or victim. These five components are a necessary and sufficient condition, for without one, the other four, even together, will not constitute a criminal incident (Brantingham and Brantingham, 1981).

Despite the obvious multifaceted nature of crime, scholars and practitioners often attempt to study them separately. For instance, lawyers and political scientists focus on the legal dimension; sociologists, psychologists, and civil rights groups generally look to the offenders and victims; and geographers concentrate on the location of the event. Environmental criminologists examine the place and time when the crime happened. They are interested in land usage, traffic patterns and street design, and the daily activities and movements of victims and offenders. Environmental criminologists often use maps to look for crime patterns, for example, using metric topology (Verma and Lodha, 2002). We discuss metric typology later in this chapter.

The work done on environmental criminology in the 1980s, spearheaded by Paul and Patricia Brantingham, helped to fuse the principles of geography with criminology and develop new criminological theories. Some of the new criminological theories developed since the early 1980s include

- Routine activities theory
- Situational crime prevention theory
- Broken windows theory
- Crime opportunity theory
- Social disorganization theory
- Crime pattern theory

Routine Activities Theory

While this theory has already been described in this chapter, you should recall that it suggests that crime occurs when a motivated offender, a suitable target, and the lack of a capable guardian converge in the same place at the same time. Criminals choose or find their targets within the context of their routine activities, such as traveling to and from work or shopping, and tend not to go too far out of their way to commit crimes.

Situational Crime Prevention Theory

The situational crime prevention theory suggests that crime and public disorder can be prevented by reducing opportunities for crime. For example, if crime occurs regularly in a dimly lit alley, public works could improve lighting and increase police presence in the area. Among the most important contributors to the theory is Ronald Clarke. In 1983, he defined the core of the theory and focused his new approach on the event of the crime, instead of the perpetrator. The event of the crime, to Clarke, has to do with the immediate physical and social settings, as well as wider societal arrangements. Clarke summarizes it as the science and art of decreasing the amount of opportunities for crime using "measures directed at highly specific forms of crime that involve the management, design, or manipulation of the immediate environment in a systematic and permanent way" (Clarke, 1983, 225). This approach relies on the assumptions that more opportunities lead to more crime, easier ones attract more offenders, and such an existence of easy opportunities makes a "life of crime" possible.

Broken Windows Theory

This theory, developed by George Kelling and James Q. Wilson, explains how lesser crimes, untended areas, blight, graffiti, and other signs of disorder decrease neighborhood residents' willingness to enforce social order, which in turn leads to more serious crime (Wilson and Kelling, 1982). If police target minor transgressions, they may prevent serious crime from developing in those places.

Crime Opportunity Theory

Crime opportunity theory suggests that when offenders want to commit a crime, they look for an opportunity or a practical target. For example, if a city neighborhood or busy CBD offers no guarded parking or patrolled parking facilities, it may be a prime target for vehicle thefts. These theories, because there may be several crime opportunity theories, rest on a single principle: easy or tempting opportunities entice people into criminal action (Felson and Clarke, 1998). Felson and Clarke (1998), for instance, take the position that "opportunity makes the thief." But they go further and suggest that no crimes can be understood without taking into consideration settings and opportunities.

Social Disorganization Theory

This theory suggests that crime occurs when community relationships and local institutions fail or are absent. For example, a neighborhood with high residential turnover might have more crime than a neighborhood with a stable residential community. Current versions of social disorganization theory assume that strong networks of social relationships prevent crime and delinquency (Kornhauser, 1978; Bursik and Grasmick, 1993; Sampson and Groves, 1989). When most community or neighborhood members are acquainted and on good terms with one another, a substantial portion of the adult population has the potential to influence each child. The larger the network of acquaintances, the greater the community's capacity for informal surveillance (because residents are easily distinguished from outsiders), for supervision (because acquaintances are willing to intervene when children and juveniles behave unacceptably), and for shaping children's values and interests. According to the current theory, community characteristics such as poverty and ethnic diversity lead to higher delinquency rates because they interfere with community members' abilities to work together. More recent studies continue to specify the mechanisms by which structural factors influence the ability of communities to enforce collective goals (Uchida et al., 2013). Bursik and Grasmick (1993) present a systemic model that further elaborates on the various linkages between ties and levels of social control. Other current approaches link informal controls with individual expectations and cultural processes (Uchida et al., 2013).

Crime Pattern Theory

Crime pattern theory integrates crime within a geographic context, thus demonstrating how the environments people live in and pass through influence criminality. The theory specifically focuses on places and the lack of social control or other measures of guardianship that are informally needed to control crime. For example, a suburban neighborhood can become a hot spot for burglaries because some homes have inadequate protection and nobody is home to guard the property. Crime pattern theory is a central component of environmental criminology, and it considers how people and things involved in crime move about in space and time. This theory fits well with the routine activities approach and presents three main concepts: nodes, paths, and edges.

Nodes, a term from transportation, refers to where people travel to and from. Such places can generate crime not only within, but also nearby. Each offender searches for crime targets around personal activity nodes (such as home, school, and entertainment area) and the paths among them. The paths people take in their everyday activities are closely related to where they fall victim to crime. This is why crime pattern theory pays so much attention to the geographical distribution of crime and the daily rhythm of activity. For example, it generates crime maps for different hours of the day and days of the week, linking crime to commuter flows, school children being let out, bars closing, or any other process that moves people among nodes and along paths.

The third concept of crime pattern theory—edges—refers to the boundaries of areas where people live, work, shop, or seek entertainment. Some crimes are more likely to occur at the edges—such as racial attacks, robberies, or shoplifting—because people from different neighborhoods who do not know each other come together at edges.

In an important way, crime pattern theorists and other environmental criminologists have shown that the design and management of town, city, and business areas can produce major shifts in crime rates.

How Are Hot Spots Identified?

Most experienced police officers who have spent any amount of time working in a city know exactly where the trouble spots are. They know which neighborhoods are likely to report crimes and at which bars and taverns fights and public disorders occur.

Before computers came along, police departments stuck pushpins in maps hung on the wall to better identify where crimes occurred. But today, because of advancing technology, hot spots can be identified using

- Maps and GIS
- Statistical tests

Maps and Geographic Information Systems

Analysts can create a variety of maps that visualize different aspects of a particular location. Density maps, for example, show where crimes occur without dividing a map into regions or blocks; areas with high concentrations of crime stand out.

It is very common for crime analysts to use GIS to combine street maps, data about crime and public disorder, and data about other features, such as schools, liquor stores, warehouses, and bus stops. The resulting multidimensional maps produce a visual display of the hot spots. The GIS places each crime within a grid system on a map and colors each cell based on how many incidents occurred in that area.

Crime maps that detect high-crime areas and crime are useful when they answer analytical questions based on crime theories and subsequently guide appropriate police action (Eck et al., 2005). For example, if the question has to do with which businesses in the city have been burglarized more than once in the past year, the best answer might come from using a point map that suggests potential tactics that focus on improving place management. In comparison, questions such as "Which hot streets are characterized by frequent drug deals and prostitution?" would require a street-level (line) map that suggests the possible use of high-visibility patrols on key streets. Finally, if senior police administrators were interested in which police beat had the most amount of crime in the past month, an area (polygon) map would be most appropriate.

Hot spots and high-crime areas can therefore be illustrated using varying levels of geography, such as a specific addresses or intersections, single blocks, clusters of blocks, streets, or neighborhoods (Eck et al., 2005; Paynich and Hill, 2010). Eck et al. (2005) suggest that analysts begin their exploration of hot spots by plotting points before examining larger areas of geography, since maps showing hot streets and areas may hide more minute point patterns of concentration.

Repeat addresses point maps can be useful for a variety of purposes, such as demonstrating repeat incidents at a single location. However, using single points to represent multiple incidents at the same location would be misleading, as it does not distinguish among locations that have single versus multiple incidents (Chainey and Ratcliffe, 2005; Boba, 2009). Instead, multiple incidents at a single location (repeat addresses) can be represented using graduated symbols or colors (Chainey and Ratcliffe, 2005; Eck et al., 2005; Boba, 2009; Paynich and Hill, 2010), in which differing symbol colors or sizes represent a count or range of values. Many times, these multiple locations are at apartment complexes, shopping complexes, or office buildings. For example, one would expect a large symbol might exist at an address for a large shopping mall, as all of the stores and restaurants share the same address. The analysis would be much better if the analyst could pinpoint the specific locations within these complexes, which would also provide better intelligence for further police action.

Different Kinds of Maps Generated by GIS

Up to this point, we have been discussing theories in this chapter. These theories will help you better understand why geography, place, and hot spots are important. You can see that to understand the problems of crime, each form of crime occurrence requires its own form of mapping. For instance, victim maps would be different from hot streets or place maps. Various maps are needed so that police command can make appropriate decisions as to what action to take to deal with the particular type of crime concern. The following are the different kinds of maps crime analysts can generate and the unique way each depicts hot spots.

Dot Map A dot map can show a particular place, a store or gas station, for instance, where crime problems have occurred. The specific address of the relevant place of a crime occurrence helps to distinguish between addresses that have had crime problems versus those that have not. A dot map or a dot distribution map is simply a map that uses dots or other symbols to represent the presence, quantity, or value of a phenomenon or thing in a specific area, such as a crime or crime victimization. In a dot distribution map, the size of the dots may be scaled in proportion to the intensity of the problem. For example, if two or more robberies occurred at the same convenience store, the dot may be larger than the dot depicting a convenience store experiencing only one robbery.

Line Maps Line maps are used when the hot spots are along streets. If, for example, robberies and holdups occur in the streets leading up to a stadium where sports and entertainment events are held, a dot map would be less relevant than a line map. The crimes do not occur at the stadium, but along routes leading to and from the venue. Some of the streets may not have parking, and so few people would be walking to and from the stadium on those streets. But knowing which streets have crime and which ones don't would be important for the police to know in terms of addressing the problems.

Ellipse and Choropleth Maps These maps are used when the hot spots cover broader areas and include neighborhoods. Ellipse and choropleth maps imply that the areas within the designated hot spots share the same risk level, so a specific street or a certain address within that district is less relevant (Eck et al., 2005). Ellipses are common in physics, astronomy, and engineering. For example, the orbit of each planet in the solar system is an ellipse. One of the earliest crime mapping software applications that became widely available to practitioners for crime analysis was Spatial and Temporal Analysis of Crime (STAC). STAC is not a GIS, but instead acts as an aid to persons who already have a GIS or desktop mapping capability. STAC is a spatial tool to find and examine hot spot areas within the study area. In concise terms, this means that STAC first finds the densest concentration of points on the map (hot clusters), and then fits a "standard deviational ellipse" to each one. The ellipses themselves indicate through their size and alignment the nature of the underlying crime clusters.

Examples of the use of STAC include a study of how to reduce incidents in Detroit's infamous Devil's Night period (Martin et al., 1998). An advantage of STAC is that it derives hot spots without relying on defined boundaries such as census units or police administrative boundaries. However, a limitation is that crime hot spots do not naturally form into convenient ellipses; thus, STAC hot spots do not represent the actual spatial distribution of crime and can sometimes be misleading (Eck et al., 2005).

Choropleth mapping or geographic boundary thematic mapping is a way of representing spatial distributions of crime events. The boundary areas that are used for this type of thematic mapping are usually arbitrarily defined for administrative purposes, since they can be police beats, census blocks, wards, or districts. Offenses as points on a map can be aggregated to these geographic unit areas and are then shaded in accordance with the number of crimes that fall within them. This map allows for quick determination as to which areas have a high incidence of crime, and allows further diagnosis of the problem by "zooming in" on those areas (Eck et al., 2005). Areas are shaded according to their data values, by either rate or frequency.

Isoline maps are, by definition, maps with lines that join points of equal value. Physical geography often uses isoline maps as isobars to show barometric pressure or isotherms to show temperature, but the form most likely to be used in crime analysis is the isopleth (equal crowd), in which data for areas, such as crimes per neighborhood or population density, are calculated and used as control points to determine where the isolines will be drawn.

Grid Thematic Mapping   In order to combat the problems associated with different sizes and shapes of geographical regions, uniform grids (or quadrats) can be drawn in a GIS as a layer over the study area and thematically shaded. Therefore, all areas used for thematic shading are of consistent dimensions and are comparable, assisting the quick and easy identification of hot spots. This approach does have some limitations; the usage of grids still restricts how the hot spots can be displayed. Spatial detail within and across each quadrat is correspondingly lost because the crime events have to conform to one specific quadrat, which can then lead to inaccurate interpretation by the map user. Additionally, they often have a "blocky" appearance, which is related to grid cell size (Eck et al., 2005).

Kernel Density Estimation Kernel density estimation (KDE) is regarded as the most suitable spatial analysis technique for visualizing crime data (Chainey et al., 2002; Chainey and Ratcliffe, 2005; Eck et al., 2005). It is an increasingly popular method due to its growing availability, the perceived accuracy of hot spot identification, and the aesthetic look of the resulting map in comparison with other techniques (Eck et al., 2005). Offenses are aggregated within a user-specified search radius, and a continuous surface that represents the density or volume of crime events across the desired area is calculated. A smooth surface map is produced, showing the variation of the crime density across the study area, with no need to conform to geometric shapes such as ellipses. But it is the most visually impressive and has the capability of identifying hot spots through a statistically robust methodology (Chainey et al., 2002; Chainey and Ratcliffe, 2005; Eck et al., 2005).

Polygon Map Polygon mapping is the cartographic display of regularly or irregularly shaped polygons and their attributes. Typically, this capability includes shading, symbology, and numeric labeling, as well as other map cosmetic functions for generating alphanumeric labeling of polygons. Polygons are multisided but closed figures that may indicate a large geographical area or an area as small as a building.

Hot Streets

Hot streets are slightly more challenging to demonstrate with most commonly used GIS. This is because they do not easily allow users to depict hot streets (Eck et al., 2005). Alternatively, analysts can plot crime incident locations and match them to street layouts. Another method to identify hot streets would be to join the points file to the street segments file of the map (for those unfamiliar with joins, the process essentially aggregates the count of incidents that occur within a street segment). If geocoding is based on a street file, there will be no issues. If geocoding is based on addresses, there will be an issue, as many points will not overlay the street segments and hence not join properly. One option is to set the join for an approximate distance between the point and the street segment. This may cause the points to be assigned to a street segment that is not part of the actual street address. Careful review of these results is suggested. Once the points and street segments are joined, there will be a count of points per street segment. Analysts can display the hot streets by line width or color of the street segments. This type of analysis assists in narrowing the size of a targeted neighborhood or area of your jurisdiction police district (Gwinn et al., 2008). Finally, recall that this technique is limited in that the boundaries are argued to be artificial and rarely reflect actual criminal patterns.

Hot Areas

Hot areas can be depicted using bounded areas such as polygons (e.g., see choropleth and standard deviation ellipse maps discussed in the sections below). However, analysts need to be aware that these bounded areas are artificial. Eck et al. (2005) argue that criminal activity does not necessarily conform to geographic boundaries. As such, hot area maps are not useful for showing crime patterns that cross boundaries (Eck et al., 2005). Boba (2005) also points out that these boundaries are usually artificially created administrative or political boundaries, which are constant or static (Eck et al., 2005). Analytical methods such as grid cell mapping or density analysis (discussed below) can be used to compensate for this limitation. These hot areas could develop at the block level, a set of blocks, neighborhoods, schools, and so forth. They might be affected by natural boundaries (rivers, cliffs, forests, etc.), government boundaries, man-made boundaries (highway, walls, fences, etc.), and social boundaries like gang territories.

Standard Deviation Analysis

This approach involves determining the mean center of the series and drawing rectangles or ellipses around the mean center showing the areas that represent one or two standard deviations away from the mean (Boba, 2009). They are drawn to demonstrate clusters of points that would not be expected from random chance (Paynich and Hill, 2010).

Like choropleth mapping, a limitation to depicting hot spots using ellipses is that hot spots are rarely depicted accurately with bounded polygons (Eck et al., 2005; Paynich and Hill, 2010). However they can be useful for making comparisons of hot spots across time (Paynich and Hill, 2010). For example, an analyst can be tasked with evaluating the effects of a police operation on a hot spot. As part of his or her evaluation, the analyst creates standard deviation ellipses with incident data before and after a police operation. The analyst can then determine whether there was a reduction or displacement in crime.

Grid Cell Mapping Analysis

This method is sometimes described as density analysis and compensates for the limitations noted above with choropleth mapping and standard deviation analysis. This approach uses surface estimation techniques and illustrates the surface of a geographical area (Ratcliffe, 2004) with rasters (Gorr and Kurland, 2012). This process first involves an analyst calibrating two parameters, specifically cell size and search radius, so that the results are meaningful and useful. The method involves placing a grid or fishnet on top of a map (creating a matrix of cells). Then a mathematical function visits the center of each cell and performs a calculation on that cell, as well as within a predetermined search radius or bandwidth (Harries, 1999; Eck et al., 2005; Paynich and Hill, 2010).

In simple density analysis, when the mathematical function is applied to each cell, the number of incidents within a given radius are added together and then divided by the area of the radius; this value is then assigned to the cell (Harries, 1999; Mitchell, 1999; Eck et al., 2005; Boba, 2009; Gwinn et al., 2008). Therefore "a cell's score does not represent the number of incidents in that cell but the number of incidents 'near' that cell divided by the area 'around' that cell, approximating the concentration of activity" (Boba, 2009, p. 271). In other words, the cell's density value is an estimate and is influenced by incidents found within the search radius placed on top of the grid cell (Boba, 2009).

Kernel Density Interpolation

Another approach to density analysis is kernel density interpolation or smoothing techniques. Instead of simply adding up all the points within a radius as with simple density analysis, a bell-shaped function or kernel is applied over every cell (Gorr and Kurland, 2012). In other words, greater weight is given to incidents closer to the center of the radius (Eck et al., 2005; Gwinn et al., 2008; Paynich and Hill, 2010). Dual kernel density interpolation is similar but involves producing "a risk value associated with crime density" (Paynich and Hill, 2010, p. 378) and allows for comparative density analysis. In other words, comparisons can be made between two different crime types or crimes at two different time periods (Paynich and Hill, 2010). It is apparent that density analysis does not depict physical boundaries and is consequently a "much more realistic image of the shape of the hot spot distribution" (Paynich and Hill, 2010, p. 378). It is also advantageous over point maps because overlapping points or stacked points are added together and represented with a single color (Harries, 1999). However, analysts must still consider three parameters when constructing density maps. First, the analyst must determine a threshold for what defines a hot spot. Values are assigned to the output raster cells, and it is at the discretion of the analyst to determine the numerical value at which a location is considered a hot spot. In other words, those areas of greater density above this threshold are then considered hot spots (Gorr and Kurland, 2012). Second, changes to either the search radius or grid cell size can yield different maps (Harries, 1999; Boba, 2009). A smaller search radii will reveal greater local variation or more specificity (Eck et al., 2005), while a larger selection will show long rolling hills for the surface (Gorr and Kurland, 2012). Likewise, the choice of cell size or spatial resolution (Gwinn et al., 2008) will affect the smoothness of the surface, with smaller cell sizes showing finer resolution. A third consideration is the size of the study area. Choosing different study areas can have an effect on the appearance of the computed density surface. As an example, an analyst could choose as his or her study area an artificially drawn square on a GIS map to represent a city's boundaries. Alternatively, if an analyst uses a more accurate GIS shape file containing the official boundaries of a city, kernel density calculations would then be more accurate, but they would produce a different type of map.

Currently, there are no hard rules for how analysts decide on setting these parameters in a GIS. Analysts first study crime points and visually determine the boundaries of hot spots. The analyst then calibrates parameter values in the GIS for density analysis until they resemble the analyst's expert judgment as to where the boundaries are (Gorr and Kurland, 2012). One limitation of density analysis, and another reason why density maps need to be calibrated manually, is that they do not consider "natural or manmade barriers that may affect directionality of data density" (Gwinn et al., 2008, p. 303). In other words, the radius or cell grid that is placed on top of a map does not conform to the presence of nature or man-made barriers, such as a body of water, a freeway, or a wall.

A potential solution to this problem is to incorporate raster masking in GIS. The analyst builds a mask around areas that are not appropriate for inclusion in the density analysis. For example, a large body of water is unlikely to have many crimes occurring in the center. A mask for this body of water would exclude that area in calculating the density surface. The result is a density surface based on a more realistic risk of crime. A final consideration of analysts when producing density maps is their audience. If audience members are not familiar with density analysis, it is recommended that a legend with labels such as "low density" or "medium density" be used.

Although high-crime areas can easily be identified based on the past experiences of police officers or based on the characteristics of those areas, GIS allows police departments to more accurately pinpoint hot spots to confirm trouble areas, identify the specific nature of the activity occurring within the hot spot, and then develop strategies to respond.

Statistical Testing for Hot Spots

In addition to crime mapping approaches, analysts are also able to draw upon spatial statistical testing to help crime analysts understand general patterns in the crime data. In addition, statistical tests can objectively determine the presence of high-crime areas or hot spots. These tests generally help the analyst decide whether clustering is occurring and whether the clustering is attributable to random chance.

Point Pattern Analysis

One approach to identifying a high-crime area is to use a point map. A map of points can demonstrate patterns of points that are clustered, uniform, or randomly distributed (Chainey and Ratcliffe, 2005; Boba, 2009). Point pattern analysis involves analysts developing a graduated point map and confirming clusters with spatial correlation statistics (Gorr and Kurland, 2012). Such statistical tests identify whether clustering of crimes is random (National Institute of Justice, 2010); points that cluster together more than what would be expected from random chance would then be considered a hot spot.

Tests for Clustering

Analysts searching for hot spots or high-crime areas can test for clusters of points, lines, or polygons. There are at least two methods to test for clustering: the nearest-neighbor index (NNI) and the test for spatial autocorrelation:

1. *Nearest-neighbor index*: Test that compares the actual distribution of crime data with a randomly distributed data set of the same sample size (Eck et al., 2005). For both the actual and randomly distributed data sets, distances are calculated between a point and its nearest neighbor. The process is repeated for all of the points. The average distance is then calculated for both the actual and randomly distributed sets. The NNI is the ratio between the average distance for the actual data set and the random data set. Overall, the results of the NNI test examine whether points are closer than expected under spatial randomness (Eck et al., 2005); one limitation, though, is that this test does not directly point out where clusters are, but instead answers

the question about whether they exist. Some computer programs, such as CrimeStat III (Levine, 2010), allow users to perform hierarchical clustering where analysts can search for clusters of clusters based on nearest neighbors. Analysts first identify initial clusters using ellipses (i.e., first-order clusters). After initial clusters are identified, hierarchical clustering then attempts to identify clusters of clusters (i.e., second-order clusters) (Eck et al., 2005; Paynich and Hill, 2010). This is done until "all crime points fall into a single cluster or when the grouping criteria fails" (Eck et al., 2005, p. 22).

2. *Test for spatial autocorrelation*: Spatial autocorrelation is another term for spatial dependency (Chainey and Ratcliffe, 2005). Spatial autocorrelation techniques assume that "criminal events that occur in different locations (yet in close proximity) are related" (Paynich and Hill, 2010, p. 382). Positive spatial autocorrelation suggests that areas with high crime rates are clustered together, and areas with low crime rates are clustered together (Paynich and Hill, 2010; Eck et al., 2005).

There are several tests for spatial autocorrelation. Moran's I and Geary's C are spatial autocorrelation statistics that require aggregate data (Eck et al., 2005; Paynich and Hill, 2010).

Moran's I: This is a global statistic that shows whether the pattern is clustered, dispersed, or random (ESRI, 2009). An intensity value is assigned to each aggregate point and requires some variation in the values for this statistic to be computed. Points that have similar values are reflected in high Moran's I values (positive or negative) (Eck et al., 2005). A Moran's I closer to +1 indicates clustering, while a Moran's I closer to −1 reflects dispersion. Significance can be tested by comparing it with a normal distribution.

Geary's C: This statistic is used for analyzing small neighborhoods and for describing the dispersion of hot spots (Eck et al., 2005). Computations for Geary's C are similar to those of variance in nonspatial statistics (Paynich and Hill, 2010) in that it "is a measure of the deviations in intensity values of each point with one another" (Eck et al., 2005, p. 19). Like Moran's I, the Geary's C coefficient can also be tested for significance (Eck et al., 2005). Results indicate positive or negative spatial autocorrelation (Eck et al., 2005).

Global Statistical Tests

A number of simple-to-use global statistical tests can be used to help analysts understand general patterns in the crime data. These have to do with spatial statistics. Unlike traditional statistics, spatial statistics use distance, space, and spatial relationships as part of the math for their computations. These statistics serve as spatial distribution and pattern analysis tools. They are used by analysts to answer such questions as "Where is the center?" and "How are features distributed around the center?"

Why use spatial statistics?

They help analysts assess patterns, trends, and relationships. In addition, they can lead to a better understanding of geographic phenomena while assisting in pinpointing causes of specific geographic patterns.

These statistical tests include the following:

- *Mean center*: The mean center is a point constructed from the average *x* and *y* values for the input feature centroids. The mean center point can be used as a relative measure to compare spatial distributions between different crime types or against the same crime type for different periods of time (Eck et al., 2005). A crime analyst might want to see if the mean center for burglaries shifts when evaluating daytime versus nighttime incidents. This information could be used to make recommendations for reallocating resources.

- *Standard deviation distance*: Standard deviation measures the distance of features around the mean. Measures of standard deviation distance help explain the level and alignment of dispersion in the crime data. By comparing crimes within one standard deviation, the analyst can determine which crimes are least dispersed and which are most dispersed.

- *Standard deviation ellipse*: The standard deviation ellipse is a way of presenting the information found by using the measures of standard deviation. The size and shape of the ellipse help to explain and illustrate the degree of dispersion of different crimes.

Another group of spatial association statistics is the local indicators of spatial association (LISA) statistics. Two statistics from this group are Gi and Gi*, which perform computations on a grid cell output, such as those of a density map or at least aggregate data. You may recall that the output of a density map is a grid of raster cells (a set of cells arranged in rows and columns, and a commonly used data set in GIS). These tests examine each cell in the grid and assume initially that the values within that cell and its surrounding neighbors are similar to the values anywhere else on the grid; that is, they are not unusually different than would be expected from random chance (Chainey and Ratcliffe, 2005). On the other hand, if local spatial autocorrelation exists as well as clustering, we would see spatial clustering of high values with high values and low values with low values (Chainey and Ratcliffe, 2005).

One parameter that analysts need to calibrate when using LISA statistics is determining the distance from the target cell and its neighbors (Eck et al., 2005); in other words, how far is and what is considered a "neighbor"? In sum, LISA statistics reflect the idea that a single block may have a high crime count, but it is not considered a hot spot unless there are other nearby blocks that also have high crime counts (i.e., there is a significant positive spatial correlation) (Gorr and Kurland, 2012).

Analysts can use statistical software to determine whether an area with a high number of crimes is a hot spot or whether the clustering of those crimes is a random occurrence. CrimeStat III and GeoDa are two computer software programs for hot spot analysis.

CrimeStat III: CrimeStat is a spatial statistical program used to analyze the locations of crime incidents and identify hot spots.

GeoDa: The GeoDa Center for Geospatial Analysis and Computation at Arizona State University develops state-of-the-art methods for geospatial analysis, geovisualization, geosimulation, and spatial process modeling, and implements them through software tools.

What Is Hot Spots Policing?

Over the past two decades, a series of rigorous evaluations have suggested that police can be effective in addressing crime and disorder when they focus on small units of geography with high rates of crime. These areas are typically referred to as hot spots, and policing strategies and tactics focused on these areas are usually referred to as hot spots policing or place-based policing.

This place-based focus stands in contrast to traditional notions of policing and crime prevention more generally, which have often focused primarily on people. Police, of course, have never ignored geography entirely. Police beats, precincts, and districts determine the allocation of police resources and dictate how police respond to calls and patrol the city. With place-based policing, however, the concern is with much smaller units of geography than the police have typically focused on. Places here refer to specific locations within the larger social environments of communities and neighborhoods, such as addresses, street blocks, or small clusters of addresses or street blocks. Crime prevention effectiveness is maximized when police focus their resources on these microunits of geography.

Hot spots policing covers a range of police responses that all share in common a focus of resources on the locations where crime is highly concentrated. Just as the definition of hot spots varies across studies and contexts (from addresses to street segments to clusters of street segments), so do the specific tactics police use to address high-crime places. There is not one way to implement hot spots policing. The approaches can range rather dramatically across interventions (Braga et al., 2012).

Crime Prevention through Environmental Design

According to this perspective, areas within a city emit "cues" about their characteristics that offenders use to select suitable targets. Urban settings can discourage crime and limit the number of targets that are perceived as "suitable" by motivated offenders through physical design that incorporates cues that show how the living space is well maintained, well cared for, and hence well controlled. Under such conditions, the potential offenders realize that they will be (1) easily recognized and (2) not tolerated (Newman, 1972).

In this chapter, we covered hot spots policing from history to identification to implications of locating where hot spots exist. At this point, you should have an increased understanding of what hot spots are, how crime analysts locate and identify hot spots, and the role of tactical crime analysts in hot spots policing. In Chapter 13, you will learn more about strategic crime analysis.

Questions for Discussion

1. Could you make a case for the use of place in crime analysis and the use of hot spots policing as a factor in the reduction of crime in this country?
2. What is the difference between individual theories of crime causation and geographic theories of crime causation?

Important Terms

Broken windows theory: Theory proposed by Wilson and Kelling that links disorder and incivility within a community to subsequent occurrences of serious crime. Serious crime, in this theory, is the final result of a lengthy chain of events emanating from disorder.

Crime opportunity theory: Theory that suggests that when offenders want to commit a crime, they look for an opportunity or a practical target.

Crime pattern: Group of two or more crimes reported to or discovered by police that are unique because they meet certain conditions, such as sharing at least one common factor.

Crime pattern theory: Theory that integrates crime within a geographic context, thus demonstrating how the environments people live in and pass through influence criminality.

Dot map: Show a particular place, a residence or store, for instance, where crime problems have occurred.

Ellipse and choropleth maps: Used when the hot spots cover broader areas and include neighborhoods.

Environmental criminology: Various theories of crime and place.

Geographical information system (GIS): System designed to capture, store, manipulate, analyze, manage, and present all types of spatial or geographical data. In criminal justice, geographical information systems help to create crime maps to visualize data and identify patterns and hot spots.

Grid thematic mapping: Used to cope with the problems associated with different sizes and shapes of geographical regions. Uniform grids (or quadrats) can be drawn in a GIS as a layer over the study area and thematically shaded.

Hot spot: When a crime pattern occurs in a relatively small area, it is referred to as a hot spot or a cluster.

Hot spots policing: Policing that covers a range of police responses that all share in common a focus of resources on the locations where crime is highly concentrated.

Kernel density estimation: Spatial analysis technique that is seen by many as the most popular and suitable for visualizing crime data.

Line maps: Used when hot spots are along streets.

Nearest–neighbor index (NNI): Test that compares the actual distribution of crime data with a randomly distributed data set of the same sample size.

Point pattern analysis: One approach to identifying a high-crime area is using a point map; a map of points can demonstrate patterns of points that are clustered, uniform, or randomly distributed.

Polygon map: Cartographic display of regularly or irregularly shaped polygons and their attributes.

Routine activities theory: Developed by Cohen and Felson, a theory that seeks to explain the occurrence of crime events as the confluence of four circumstances: a motivated offender; a desirable target; the target and offender being in the same place at the same time; and intimate handlers, guardians, or place managers being absent or ineffective.

Situational crime prevention theory: Theory that suggests that crime and public disorder can be prevented by reducing opportunities for crime.

Social disorganization theory: Theory that suggests that crime occurs when community relationships and local institutions fail or are absent. Contemporary versions of social disorganization theory assume that strong networks of social relationships prevent crime and delinquency.

Spatial autocorrelation: Has to do with statistical techniques that assume that criminal events that occur in different locations (yet in close proximity) are related.

Theories of crime and place: Theories that provide an understanding of crime in its physical or spatial environment.

Study Guide Questions

For questions 1–4, indicate whether the statement is true or false.

1. _____ The importance of identifying hot spots is that both crime theories and practical studies support the idea that focusing police efforts on crime hot spots can effectively reduce crime.

2. _____ Theories of crime and place suggest that the personality of the offender is the most important factor in understanding crime.

3. _____ There are many theories of crime and place, but they all tend to fall under the umbrella of what is called "environmental criminology."

4. _____ The analysis of crime and place is rooted in the work done by the Chicago School.

5. Three theoretical perspectives are important in the development of current crime prevention efforts. They are
    a. Crime, time, and place
    b. Geographical information systems, computer graphics theory, and gaming theory
    c. Routine activities theory, rational choice theory, and crime pattern theory
    d. Crime analysis theory, hot spots policing theory, and Blue Bloods theory

6. The environmental criminology approach was developed in the 1980s by Paul Brantingham and Patricia Brantingham, who focused on environmental factors that can influence criminal activity. These factors include space (geography),

   a. Time, law, offender, and target
   b. Time, hot spots, convenience stores, and court decisions
   c. Time, body, and mind
   d. Time, civil rights, and victim restitution
7. In the theory developed by George Kelling and James Q. Wilson, it is explained that minor transgressions may lead to more serious crime. This theory is known as
   a. Repeated addresses theory
   b. Hot spots policing theory
   c. Crime pattern theory
   d. Broken windows theory
8. Hot spots policing is based on the theory that the police can be more effective in preventing crime if they
   a. Concentrate their resources in the suburbs
   b. Focus on small geographical units with high crime rates
   c. Cover wider areas and scatter their resources in all neighborhoods
   d. Employ paramilitary tactics even in low-crime areas

References

Boba, R. (2005). *Crime Analysis and Crime Mapping.* Thousand Oaks, CA: Sage.

Boba, R. (2009). *Crime Analysis with Crime Mapping.* Thousand Oaks, CA: Sage.

Braga, A. (2002). *Problem-Oriented Policing and Crime Prevention.* Monsey, NY: Criminal Justice Press.

Braga, A. (2007). The effects of hot spots policing on crime. *Campbell Systematic Reviews.* DOI: 10.4073/csr.2007.1.

Braga, A., Papachristos, A., and Hureau, D. (2012). Hot spots policing effects on crime. *Campbell Systematic Reviews* 8. DOI: 10.4073/csr.2012.8.

Braga, A.A. (2006). The crime prevention value of hot spots policing. *Psicothema* 18(3): 630–637.

Brantingham, P.J., and Brantingham, P.L. (1981). *Environmental Criminology.* Thousand Oaks, CA: Sage.

Brantingham, P.L., and Brantingham, P.J. (1993). Environment, routine and situation: Toward a pattern theory of crime. *Advances in Criminological Theory* 5: 259–294.

Bursik, R.J., Jr., and Grasmick, H.G. (1993). *Neighborhoods and Crime: The Dimensions of Effective Community Control.* New York: Lexington Books.

Chainey, S.P., and Ratcliffe, J.H. (2005). *GIS and Crime Mapping.* London: Wiley.

Chainey, S.P., Reid, S., and Stuart, N. (2002). When is a hotspot a hotspot? A procedure for creating statistically robust hotspot maps of crime. In G. Higgs (ed.), *Innovations in GIS 9 Socio-Economic Applications of Geographic Information Science*, London: Taylor and Francis, pp. 22–36.

Clarke, R.V. (1983). Situational crime prevention: Its theoretical basis and practical scope. *Crime and Justice: An Annual Review of Research* 4: 225–256.

Clarke, R.V., (1992). *Situational Crime Prevention: Successful Case Studies*. Albany, NY: Harrow and Heston.

Clarke, R.V., and Felson, M. (eds.). (1993). *Routine Activity and Rational Choice. Advances in Criminological Theory*. Vol. 5. New Brunswick, NJ: Transaction Press.

Clarke, R.V., and Weisburd, D. (1990). On the distribution of deviance. In: D.M. Gottfredson and R.V. Clarke (eds.), *Policy and Theory in Criminal Justice*. Aldershot, UK: Avebury.

Cohen, L.E., and Felson, M. (1979). Social change and crime rate trends: A routine activity approach. *American Sociological Review* 44: 588–605.

Cornish, D.B., and Clarke, R.V. (eds.). (1986). *The Reasoning Criminal: Rational Choice Perspectives on Offending*. New York: Springer-Verlag.

Eck, J.E. (1994). Drug markets and drug places: A case-control study of the spatial structure of illicit drug dealing. Unpublished Doctoral dissertation, University of Maryland, College Park.

Eck, J.E. (1997). Learning from experience in problem-oriented policing and situational prevention: The positive functions of weak evaluations and the negative functions of strong ones. *Crime Prevention Studies* 14: 93–117.

Eck, J.E. (1998). Preventing crime by controlling drug dealing on private rental property. *Security Journal* 11(4): 37–43.

Eck, J.E. (2002). Preventing crime at places. In L.W. Sherman, D. Farrington, B. Welsh, and D. Layton MacKenzie (eds.), *Evidence-Based Crime Prevention*, New York: Routledge, pp. 241–294.

Eck, J.E., Chainey, S.P., Cameron, J.G., Leitner, M., and Wilson, R.E. (2005). *Mapping Crime: Understanding Hot Spots*. Washington, DC: National Institute of Justice. Available at http://www.ojp.usdoj.gov/nij.

Eck, J.E., and Weisburd, D. (1995). Crime places in crime theory. Available at http://www.popcenter.org/library/crimeprevention/volume_04/01-eckweisburd.pdf

ESRI. (2009). Spatial autocorrelation (Morans I) (spatial statistics). Available at http://webhelp.esri.com/arcgisdesktop/9.2/index.cfm?id=1692&pid=1689&topicname=Spatial%20Autocorrelation%20(Morans%20I)%20(Spatial%20Statistics).

Felson, M. (1986). Routine activities, social controls, rational decisions, and criminal outcomes. In D. Cornish and R.V.G. Clarke (eds.), *The Reasoning Criminal*. New York: Springer-Verlag.

Felson, M. (1994). *Crime and Everyday Life: Insights and Implications for Society*. Thousand Oaks, CA: Pine Forge Press.

Felson, M., and Clarke, R.V. (1998). Opportunity makes the thief: Practical theory for crime prevention. Police Research Series. Paper 98. Available at http://www.popcenter.org/library/reading/pdfs/thief.pdf.

Filbert, K. (2008). Targeting crime in hot spots and hot places. *Geography and Public Safety* 1(1): 4–7.

Gorr, W.L., and Kurland, K.S. (2012). *GIS Tutorial for Crime Analysis*. Redlands, CA: ESRI Press.

Gwinn, S.L., Bruce, C., Cooper, J.P., and Hick, S. (2008). *Exploring Crime Analysis: Readings on Essential Skills*. (2nd ed) Overland Park, KS: International Association of Crime Analysts.

Harries, K. (1999). *Mapping Crime: Principle and Practice*. NCJ 178919. Washington, DC: National Institute of Justice.

Levine, N. (2010). *CrimeStat: A Spatial Statistics Program for the Analysis of Crime Incident Locations*. Vol. 3.3. Houston, TX: Ned Levine and Associates; Washington, DC: National Institute of Justice.

Levinson, D. (ed.). (2002). *The Encyclopedia of Crime and Punishment*. Thousand Oaks, CA: Sage.

Martin, D., Barnes, E., and Britt, D. (1998). The multiple impacts of mapping it out: Police, geographic information systems (GIS) and community mobilization during Devil's Night in Detroit, Michigan. In N. LaVigne and J. Wartell (eds.), *Crime Mapping Case Studies: Successes in the Field*. Washington, DC: Police Executive Research Forum, pp. 3–14.

Mitchell, A. (1999). *The ESRI Guide to GIS Analysis*. Redlands, CA: Environmental Systems Research Institute.

National Institute of Justice. (2010). How to identify hot spots. Washington, DC: National Institute of Justice, Office of Justice Programs. Available at http://www.nij.gov/topics/law-enforcement/strategies/hot-spot-policing/pages/identifying.aspx.

Newman, O. (1972). *Defensible Space*. New York: Macmillan.

Paynich, R., and Hill, B. (2010). *Fundamentals of Crime Mapping*. Sudbury, MA: Jones and Barlett.

Ratcliffe, J. (2004). Crime mapping and the training needs of law enforcement. *European Journal on Criminal Policy and Research* 10: 65–83.

Reppetto, T. (1976). Crime prevention and the displacement phenomenon. *Crime and Delinquency* 22: 166–177.

Sampson, R.J., and Groves, W.B. (1989). Community structure and crime: Testing social disorganization theory. *American Journal of Sociology* 94(4): 774–802.

Shaw, C.R., and McKay, H.D. (1969). *Juvenile Delinquency and Urban Areas*. Rev, ed. Chicago: University of Chicago Press.

Sherman, L., Gartin, P., and Buerger, M. (1989). Hot spots of predatory crime: Routine activities and the criminology of place. *Criminology* 27: 27–56.

Sherman, L.W., and Weisburd, D. (1995). General deterrent effects of police patrol in crime "hot spots": A randomized, controlled trial. *Justice Quarterly* 12(4): 625–648.

Skogan, W., and Frydl, K. (eds.). (2004). *Fairness and Effectiveness in Policing: The Evidence*. Committee to Review Research on Police Policy and Practices. Committee on Law and Justice, Division of Behavioral and Social Sciences and Education. Washington, DC: The National Academies Press.

Uchida, C.D., Swatt, M.L., Solomon, S.E., and Verano, S. (2013). Neighborhoods and crime: Collective efficacy and social cohesion in Miami-Dade County. Silver Spring, MD: Justice and Security Strategies, Inc. Available at https://www.ncjrs.gov/pdffiles1/nij/grants/245406.pdf.

Verma, A., and Lodha, S.K. (2002). A typological representation of the criminal event. *Western Criminology Review* 3(2). Available at http://www.westerncriminology.org/documents/WCR/v03n2/verma/verma.html.

Vold, G.B., and Bernard, T. (1986). *Theoretical Criminology*. New York: Oxford University Press.

Vold, G.B., Bernard, T.J., and Snipes, J.B. (1998). *Theoretical Criminology*. 4th ed. New York: Oxford University Press.

Weisburd, D., and Eck, J. (2004). What can police do to reduce crime, disorder, and fear? *Annals of the American Academy of Political and Social Science* 593: 42–65.

Weisburd, D., and Green, L. (1994). Defining the street-level drug market. In D. MacKenzie and C. Uchida (eds.), *Drugs and Crime: Evaluating Public Policy Initiatives*. Thousand Oaks, CA: Sage, pp. 61–76.

Weisburd, D., and Green, L. (1995). Measuring immediate spatial displacement: Methodological issues and problems. In J. Eck and D. Weisburd (eds.), *Crime and Place*. Monsey, NY: Criminal Justice Press, pp. 349–361.

Weisburd, D., Maher, L., and Sherman, L. (1992). Contrasting crime general and crime-specific theory: The case of hot spots of crime. In F. Adler and W.S. Laufer, *Advances in Criminological Theory*. Vol. 4. New Brunswick, NJ: Transaction Press, pp. 45–69.

Weisburd, D., Mastrofski, S., McNally, A.M., Greenspan, R., and Willis, J. (2003). Reforming to preserve: Compstat and strategic problem solving in American policing. *Criminology and Public Policy* 2, 421–456.

Wilson, J.Q., and Kelling, G.L. (1982). The police and neighborhood safety: Broken windows. *Atlantic Monthly*, March: 29–38.

13

STRATEGIC CRIME ANALYSIS

Chapter Outline

1. What is strategic crime analysis?
   a. Definition of strategic crime analysis
   b. Focus of strategic crime analysis
   c. Long-range perspective of strategic crime analysis
   d. How is it similar to tactical crime analysis?
   e. How is it different from tactical crime analysis?
2. What crime trends are analyzed?
   a. Data analyzed
3. Strategic crime analysis and its methods
   a. Qualitative versus quantitative methods
   b. Qualitative methods
   c. Field research
4. Strategic crime analysis process
   a. Analyzing research
      i. Environmental assessment
      ii. Scanning, analysis, response, and assessment (SARA) model
      iii. Formulating hypotheses
5. Strategic crime analysis and its reports
   a. Types of reports
   b. How reports are disseminated
6. Conclusion
   a. End result of strategic crime analysis
   b. Looking ahead to the next chapter

Learning Objectives for Chapter 13

1. Understand strategic crime analysis
2. Be able to differentiate strategic crime analysis from tactical crime analysis

3. Learn the various qualitative research methods of strategic crime analysis
4. Understand the historic significance of the SARA model
5. Be able to apply the SARA model to a practical crime problem or crime trend

Because so much effort has been concentrated on crude groupings of crime types, such as burglary, robbery or auto theft, it has been virtually impossible to find truly common facts about the conditions which lead to each of these groups of crimes. This implies that we have to be very patient and try to solve the problems of crime gradually and progressively, piece by piece.

Barry Poyner (1986)

Introduction

In contrast to tactical crime analysis, strategic crime analysis is the analysis of data in order to develop long-term strategies, policies, and prevention techniques. The subjects most often associated with strategic crime analysis include long-term statistical trends, hot spots, and chronic problems.

Although strategic crime analysis often starts with data from police records systems, strategic analysis usually includes the collection of primary data from a variety of other sources through both quantitative and qualitative methods.

The notable processes and techniques of strategic crime analysis include trend analysis, hot spot analysis, and problem analysis. While there is overlap between tactical crime analysis and strategic crime analysis, it is helpful to think of strategic crime analysis as trying to understand and solve long-standing crime problems (International Association of Crime Analysts, 2014).

Focus in Strategic Crime Analysis

As indicated, strategic crime analysis focuses on long-term crime trends and involves projecting or forecasting increases or decreases in crime. In addition, it looks at geographical changes by crime type, identified hot spots, or other areas of concern. Strategic crime analysis takes into account factors such as population, demographics, and geographic changes and is an important part of planning for the future.

Again, the contrast between tactical crime analysis and strategic crime analysis is that the former focuses on short-term and immediate problems, such as crime patterns, series, and sprees. Tactical crime analysts assist officers and investigators with developing potential leads and suspects following a crime, identifying the relationship between a suspect and one or more crimes, attempting to predict the date, time, and location of the next hit of a crime series.

Tactical crime analysis will typically concentrate on information from recent crimes reported to the police. The term *recent* can refer to the last few months or longer periods of time for specific ongoing problems. Similarly, tactical crime analysis will also focus on specific information about each crime, such as method of entry, point of entry, suspect's actions, type of victim, and type of weapon used, as well as the date, time, location, and type of location. Field information, such as suspicious activity calls for service, criminal trespass warnings, and persons with scars, marks, or tattoos, collected by officers is also considered in the analysis.

Tactical crime analysis attempts to link cases together and identify the notable characteristics of patterns and trends, identify potential suspects of a crime or crime pattern, and, ultimately, assist in clearing cases. By examining data daily in order to identify patterns, trends, and investigative leads for recent criminal and potential criminal activity, the tactical crime analyst compiles information and disseminates it to patrol units or investigators to try to effect an arrest.

On the other hand, strategic crime analysis consists primarily of quantitative analysis of aggregate data. That is, the strategic crime analyst will examine monthly, quarterly, or yearly compilations of criminal and noncriminal information such as crime, calls for service, and traffic information. General categories such as date, time, location, and type of incident are analyzed, as are variables such as race, class, sex, income, population, and location of crimes. But strategic crime analysts also use qualitative research to gather other information that will help them accomplish their primary goals. The two major goals or purposes of strategic crime analysis are (1) to assist in the identification and analysis of long-term problems, such as drug activity or auto theft, and (2) to conduct studies to investigate or evaluate relevant responses and procedures as part of a problem-solving process.

Long-Range Perspective of Strategic Crime Analysis

The collection and analysis of data spanning a long period of time is the essence of strategic crime analysis. This type of analysis is *research focused* because it includes the use of statistics to make conclusions (Canter, 2000). This form of analysis can be useful to police departments in terms of crime trend forecasting, or using data to estimate future crime based on past trends (Canter, 2000). With crime trend forecasting, important decisions can be made as to the deployment of patrol as a reflection of the changing volume of criminal activity. Another important benefit of strategic crime analysis is the analysis of changing community dynamics and risk factors that might be contributing to the particular crime trends of a specific area (Canter, 2000). Once again, this type of analysis over time can result in more informed decision-making that can lead to police partnerships with other city and community agencies that can help create more long-term, sustainable reductions in criminal activity.

Crime Trends Analyzed by Strategic Crime Analysis

Strategic crime analysis and tactical crime analysis differ in that tactical crime analysis looks at current crime patterns, whereas strategic crime analysis examines long-term trends or chronic problems in crime and disorder. Examining those long-term trends generally takes longer and requires the analyst to collect his or her own data instead of relying exclusively on police reports.

In Chapter 12, you learned about crime patterns, but now it is time to learn about trends. A crime pattern is not a crime trend. In general, crime trends are long-term increases and decreases in crime, or simply changes in the characteristics of a crime over a period of time. Crime trends can occur over months, years, decades, or even centuries, but are rarely discussed in terms shorter than a month or longer than a decade. Sometimes, they can be traced to a single cause (e.g., a new shopping mall or a shortage of heroin), but at other times they have numerous obscure and indirect social, environmental, economic, or political causes.

Positive crime trends represent increases in crime, while negative crime trends represent decreases in crime. Neutral crime trends have to do with a consistent volume of crime, although there may be shifts in the characteristics of crime from time to time.

Another term that is important to define is *problems*, which is to be distinguished from *trends*. A crime problem usually refers to multiple crime or disorder incidents with common causal factors. Some experts have suggested that trends can be viewed as the symptoms, while problems should be perceived as the underlying causes. Problems occur over the long term and keep returning each year or are committed by multiple offenders.

Crime trend information can be useful in alerting the police to increases and decreases in levels of activity. However, since crime trend analysis does not examine shared similarities between specific crime incidents, a crime trend is not a crime pattern. A crime pattern is not a chronic problem. The most all-encompassing definition of a crime problem comes from Ron Clarke and John Eck, who define a problem as "a recurring set of related harmful events in a community that members of the public expect the police to address" (Clarke and Eck, 2005, p. 40).

By analyzing trends and chronic problems, strategic crime analysts hope to contribute to new ways of dealing with ongoing crime problems.

Data That Strategic Crime Analysts Examine

The primary purpose of tactical analysis is to effect an arrest and gather adequate evidence for a conviction. Strategic crime analysis looks at more long-term goals, such as crime reduction plans that might be implemented by an agency or in cooperation with municipal officials.

Many police agencies are trying to implement problem-solving approaches to understand crime and address trends and patterns of criminal activity. But problem-solving works best with an infusion of both crime analysis and intelligence gathering (Peed et al., 2008).

As with tactical crime analysis, strategic crime analysis may start with police data. However, too often police data are inadequate in trying to explain the root causes and underlying opportunity factors associated with problems. Analysts must collect qualitative data using qualitative methods, such as interviews, surveys, focus groups, environmental assessments, and external research. Initially, analysts use police data to form hypotheses and then test these hypotheses with further field research.

Qualitative versus Quantitative Research

Two predominant types of methods are available for crime analysts, as well as other criminologists. Those are quantitative and qualitative methods. Quantitative research is typically considered to be the more scientific approach to doing social science (Tewksbury, 2009). The focus in quantitative research is on using specific definitions and carefully operationalizing what particular concepts and variables mean. Quantitative research usually involves statistics and data that can be scored and presented easily on graphs or in tables. Qualitative research methods, on the other hand, provide more emphasis on interpretation and providing consumers with complete views, looking at contexts, environmental immersions, and a depth of understanding of concepts (Tewskbury, 2009).

Tewskbury (2009) argued that because of the differences in data, how data are collected and analyzed, and what the data and analyses are able to tell us about our subjects of study, the knowledge gained through qualitative investigations is more informative, richer, and offers enhanced understanding compared with that which can be obtained via quantitative research.

At its most basic, qualitative research focuses on the meanings, traits, and defining characteristics of events, people, interactions, settings and cultures, and experience.

Strategic crime analysts must use qualitative methods in order to gain a true understanding of the social aspects of how crime occurs and how the agents, structures, and processes of responding to crime operate in culturally grounded contexts. Thus, qualitative methods provide a depth of understanding of issues that is not possible through the use of quantitative, statistically based investigations. Therefore, if trends are to be understood and lead to problem solutions, then qualitative methods must be utilized.

Qualitative Methods

Strategic crime analysis is, then, the systematic study of crime and disorder trends and problems in order to assist the police in crime and disorder reduction, crime prevention, and evaluation. Crime analysis is not haphazard or anecdotal; rather, it involves the application of social science data collection procedures, analytical methods, and statistical techniques.

While crime analysts employ both qualitative and quantitative data and methods, strategic crime analysts use qualitative data and methods when they examine nonnumerical data for the purpose of discovering underlying meanings and patterns of relationships. The qualitative methods specific to crime analysis include

- Field research
- Content analysis
- Interviews
- Surveys
- Focus groups
- Environmental assessment

Field Research

If a crime analyst is going to help deal with a crime trend, he or she is most likely going to have to get off the computer and get out and do research. While police data have always been available, and while various units or command personnel have discussed the particular trend or problem, no solution has been found. Continuing to go over the same data is not going to be productive for the strategic crime analyst. He or she has to do something different. That something different is likely to involve field research.

Field research can mean observing the characteristics of various crime locations or immersion in a setting where crime occurs so as to better understand the what, how, when, and where of the social structure or the action and interaction of a neighborhood, a group, or victims.

Observation, the actual looking at and breaking down of actions and interactions of people, is an approach to data collection that looks quite simple and straightforward (after all, we all do this as we go through our daily lives), but is actually a very challenging method for gathering systematic information about people, places, and things. Researchers who draw on observational data do so in one of two general ways: overtly, in which they openly acknowledge to those being observed that this is what the researcher is doing, and covertly, when the researcher "spies" on the people, places, and things that she is studying. The approach that is used varies by the setting in which observations are conducted and, most importantly, by the research questions being addressed (which will necessitate different things to be observed, some of which may not be accessible to an "outsider" who appears and proclaims that he or she wants to see what is going on). The challenge of observational data collection methods is to be able to simultaneously see the obvious (e.g., large and surface-level) actions involved and look beyond the obvious and see those things that might always be present, but are so "normal" and taken for granted that the observer typically fails to note their presence. These challenges are most difficult in settings and with people and things for which the researcher is most familiar. That which is known to us on a regular basis is often seen with little attention to detail, or a failure to realize that details are important to the larger scheme of actions and interactions.

The actual data that a crime analyst observes are generally notes that the researcher takes while doing observation. To be able to take notes on everything one sees, and to be sure to get beyond the obvious, surface level of structures and events can be very challenging. Especially for researchers observing things covertly, identifying a means to simultaneously watch, think about what one sees, make notes that capture the details of actions and structures, and manage their own presence so as not to be detected presents a serious challenge that requires significant degrees of both intellectual abilities and expenditures of energy.

Immersion in a setting, for purposes of gaining an understanding of how that setting operates, is the data collection method that drives the production of ethnography. Originally advanced by anthropologists, ethnographic methods combine observational skills with interpersonal skills of navigating a new environment so as to find one's way through a new world while learning how to be a nondisruptive presence in that new world. If a crime analyst was taking on the task of analyzing gang violence or crack addiction, she would likely end up living in the world of a gang or spending time in rundown crack houses. While the analyst may have a new appreciation for the problems of adolescent gang members or crack addicts, the observations are likely to be indelibly etched in the mind of the analyst, or the inherent dangers of the environment may cause chills—if not nightmares.

Content Analysis

Content analysis is the examination of some kind of document or report for identifying and analyzing patterns or series. Crime analysts who engage in content analysis take as their data police reports, magazine articles, newspaper articles, blogs, suicide notes, or criminal confessions. Analysts may do this to develop knowledge about a certain problem or trend.

Content analysis is said by some experts (e.g., Fritz et al., 2008) to be the primary method of qualitative analysis. But the data utilized in content analysis are almost always text or narrative, and the analyst is always searching for a specific subject, such as a person's name, a location, or a common pattern. The emphasis remains on the information sought or the meaning of text; this distinguishes it from quantitative methods, which usually concern statistics.

The effective crime analyst must read reports and documents carefully, looking for details and patterns. By doing this with rapt attention to detail, the analyst may be able to not only identify trends but also propose solutions.

Interviews

Interviews are typically structured conversations that researchers have with individuals. Just as in everyday life, one of the most productive ways to learn about a person, place, or set of activities is to actually ask questions of people who have knowledge about that topic. Interviews are used to solicit information from people, just as quantitative researchers ask questions with surveys. However, the difference is that when a qualitative researcher asks questions of a person, he or she is interested in understanding how the person being interviewed understands, experiences, or views some topic (Tewksbury, 2009).

Strategic crime analysts may interview police officers, criminal offenders, witnesses, and citizens, which will add information for analysis, but can lead to valuable insights. Essentially, interviews can provide a richer, more in-depth picture of the phenomenon under study (Fritz et al., 2008). For instance, by asking additional questions, the analyst may learn more about a crime or series of crimes than an officer may have written in a report. Similarly, although a witness may have made a statement to a detective right after a crime, a follow-up interview may elicit observations that were not stated at the time of the original interview.

Intensive interviewing consists of open-ended, relatively unstructured questioning in which the interviewer seeks in-depth information on the interviewee's feelings, experiences, or perceptions (Schutt, 1999). Unlike the participant observation strategy, intensive interviewing does not require systematic observation of respondents in their natural setting.

Surveys

Surveys are the most frequently used mode of observation within the social sciences, including criminology (Maxfield and Babbie, 1995). Basically, survey research involves the collection of information from a sample of individuals through their responses to questions (Schutt, 1999). Survey research can be carried out through mail or email, by telephone, or in person.

Typically, surveys contain a combination of open- and close-ended questions. Open-ended questions ask the respondent to provide an answer to a particular question. For example, the respondent may be asked, "What do you think is the most important problem facing residents in your neighborhood today?" Then, in his or her own words, the respondent would provide his or her answer. On the other hand, close-ended questions ask the respondents to select an answer from a list of choices provided. For example, the question asked above would read exactly the same, only now respondents are provided with a list of options to choose from: "What do you think is the most important problem facing residents in your neighborhood today? (a) Crime, (b) drugs, (c) education, or (d) employment."

Surveys offer a number of attractive features that make them a popular method of doing research. They are versatile, efficient, inexpensive, and generalizable. At the same time, survey methods may be limited due to problems in sampling, measurement, and overall survey design. When creating a survey, researchers should take care in making sure that the items in the survey are clear and to the point.

A crime analyst might survey residents in an apartment building where there have been a number of burglaries in order to determine the rate of victimization and what methods residents have used to protect themselves from becoming victims.

Focus Groups

Focus groups, sometimes referred to as group interviews, are guided conversations in which an analyst meets with a collection of similarly situated, but usually unrelated persons for purposes of uncovering information about a topic.

The advantage of a focus group over a series of one-on-one interviews is that in the group setting, the comments and statements of each participant are available to all other participants. Thus, the statements of participants can serve to stimulate memories, alternative interpretations, and more depth of information than is likely to come from individual interviews. The focus group therefore provides not only the data that likely would be generated in a series of individual interviews, but also, when it works well, more in-depth information from the participants interacting among themselves and engaging with one another.

Typically, the researcher asks specific questions and guides the discussion to ensure that group members address these questions, but the resulting information is qualitative and relatively unstructured (Schutt, 1999).

For example, an analyst might conduct a focus group with a number of liquor store managers to learn more about armed robberies and the perpetrators of those robberies. Often, a focus group, in situations like this, can provide a context for a more complete understanding of the robberies than might be provided in just reading police reports of those incidents.

Environmental Assessment

Environmental surveys are used to systematically observe the physical features of a location. This direct observation could include observing the lighting, the parking, and the physical conditions of the buildings. The analyst would want to know from direct observation how the space is used, what types of people are generally present, how they congregate, and the potential for criminal activity (Santos, 2013).

In other words, environmental assessments or surveys seek to assess, as systematically and objectively as possible, the overall physical environment of an area. A physical environment may include the buildings, parks, streets, transportation facilities, and overall landscaping of an area, as well as the functions and conditions of each of these. The crime analyst is concerned with figuring out how the physical environment affects the social environment—how do the features of the physical environment contribute to crime and disorder?

Therefore, environmental surveys are a component of a larger problem-solving process. In analyzing the environment where crime problems occur, analysts can use the information they gather from the environmental survey, along with other intelligence they've collected, to gain an understanding of conditions contributing to a problem. By analyzing an area, the analyst may conclude that poor lighting contributes to nighttime holdups, or that graffiti on several buildings, along with a litter-strewn environment, might encourage drug dealers and prostitutes to congregate in the area (Taylor and Harrell, 1996).

The data that are collected in qualitative research come from a range of collection methods. These methods usually require the strategic crime analyst to get out from behind his or her computer screen and interview people, hold focus groups, observe citizens and places, examine the contents of documents, and assess the location of crime problems. All of this is done to further the ultimate goal of the strategic crime analyst—pulling together information to help in identifying and solving crime problems and crime trends.

After Identifying Crime Trends, Then What?

Data analysis and field research will lead to some hypotheses or conclusions about a crime problem or a crime trend. The hypotheses or conclusions will be contained in a report, along with recommendations, to the command of the police department.

It is not enough for the strategic crime analyst to identify a crime trend. He or she must go beyond this and make recommendations for amelioration of the problem or trend. Usually, unlike the reports or recommendations of the tactical crime analyst, the report of the strategic crime analyst will not result in the capture or arrest of crime suspects or perpetrators. Instead, the report that emanates from the strategic crime analyst will lead to recommendations for action. That action might involve the police administration, community leaders, business associations, the city council or mayor, and even other legislative bodies.

Recommendations for Crime Trend Solutions

In order to make recommendations for the amelioration of crime trends, the analyst must analyze the trend and come up with a strategic plan. Fortunately, a process for analyzing and determining a strategy has been proposed and evaluated. First, Professor Herman Goldstein described the problem-oriented approach to policing in a 1979 article, which he expanded upon in his 1990 book, *Problem-Oriented Policing*. Others—especially John Eck and Ronald Clarke—would be inspired to implement and advance problem-oriented policing in police agencies around the world. It would be John Eck who took problem-oriented policing to a new level.

John Eck, a professor of criminal justice at the University of Cincinnati, began contributing to problem-oriented policing in the 1980s, when he studied the first full-scale attempt to implement the concept in the United States at Newport News, Virginia. Since then, he has helped to develop a number of now-standard techniques in problem-solving, including the SARA model and the crime analysis triangle. Eck, along with Ronald Clarke, has, through SARA, provided an agenda for the crime analyst. Clarke and Eck (2005) have basically outlined a role in which the crime analyst invests heavily in seeking new responses to the problems that are diagnosed and participates directly in efforts to test and implement them. The primary program is called problem-oriented policing, and the process used is the SARA model.

In the SARA model, the strategic crime analyst will collect the data, define the scope of the problem-solving effort, find an effective response, and set up the project so that it can be evaluated and the police can learn from the results. This necessarily means that the crime analyst is not waiting patiently by his computer for a unit in the police department to ask for his or her help. Instead, the analyst is an integral member of a team that will investigate and propose solutions to crime trends.

In the following pages, we will describe the four stages of SARA, a problem-oriented program to provide viable solutions to trends. But first, we will provide further background on problem-oriented policing.

It has become clear since the 1970s that effective police work requires both focused attention and diverse approaches. The least effective policing uses neither element (Clarke and Eck, 2005). The explanation for this is also clear. If diverse approaches are used without focus, it is difficult to apply the appropriate approach to the places and people who most require it. If police are focused on hot spots, but only enforce the law, they limit their effectiveness. A fully effective police agency must diversify its approaches to crime and disorder (Clarke and Eck, 2005). That is, policing must address crime and disorder using a greater range of tools than simply enforcing the law.

The second element necessary to highly effective policing is focus. There is generally solid evidence that geographically concentrated enforcement at crime or disorder hot spots can be effective, at least in the short run (Clarke and Eck, 2005). That is, focused patrolling of very small high-crime places (e.g., street corners and block faces) has a modest effect on crime and a large effect on disorder. Also, if a few individuals are responsible for most crime or disorder, then removing them should reduce crime. Though sound in principle, the research testing this idea is very poor, so we do not know whether repeat offender programs work in actual practice, or if they are a seemingly promising notion that cannot effectively be carried out. Certainly, we know that mass incarceration has not worked to reduce crime and produced many adverse side effects (Petersilia, 2011).

While mass incarceration has proven to be ineffective, so has much of traditional policing. What this really means is that much police work is carried out to meet public expectations, and this is of limited value in controlling crime (Clarke and Eck, 2005). Today, the police need to find new and better ways to control crime, while continuing aspects of their traditional work that is still effective. The innovations that have come along since the 1990s have been trying to do just that. For instance, police leadership across the country has been experimenting with CompStat, zero tolerance, community policing, and, more recently, problem-oriented policing to get smarter about controlling and preventing crime.

While crime analysts have a role in all these innovations, problem-oriented policing thrusts them into the limelight and gives them an important team function. Herman Goldstein originated the concept of problem-oriented policing in a paper published in 1979. His idea in "Improving Policing: A Problem-Oriented Approach" (Goldstein, 1979) was simple. That simple idea was this: policing should fundamentally be about changing the conditions that give rise to recurring crime problems and should not simply be about responding to incidents as they occur or trying to forestall them through preventive patrols.

Goldstein stated that police officers find it demoralizing to return repeatedly to the same place or to deal repeatedly with problems caused by the same small group of offenders. They feel overwhelmed by the volume of calls and rush around in a futile effort to deal with them all. To escape from this trap, Goldstein said the police must adopt a problem-solving approach in which they work through the following four stages:

1. Scan data to identify patterns in the incidents they routinely handle.
2. Subject these patterns (or problems) to in-depth analysis of causes.
3. Find new ways of intervening earlier in the causal chain so that these problems are less likely to occur in the future. These new strategies are not limited to efforts to identify, arrest, and prosecute offenders. Rather, without abandoning the use of the criminal law when it is likely to be the most effective response, problem-oriented policing seeks to find other potentially effective responses (that might require partnership with others), with a high priority on prevention.

4. Assess the impact of the interventions and, if they have not worked, start the process all over again (Clarke and Eck, 2005).

SARA is the acronym used to refer to these four stages of problem-solving: scanning, analysis, response, and assessment. The SARA acronym was not created by Goldstein, but by Eck and Spelman (1987). Eck and Spelman defined SARA as a strategy consisting of four parts:

1. Scanning. Instead of relying on broad, law-related concepts—robbery and burglary, for example—officers are encouraged to group individual related incidents that come to their attention as "problems" and define these problems in more precise and therefore useful terms. For example, an incident that typically would be classified simply as a "robbery" might be seen as part of a pattern of prostitution-related robberies committed by transvestites in center-city hotels.
2. Analysis. Officers working on a well-defined problem then collect information from a variety of private and public sources—not just police data. They use the information to illuminate the underlying nature of the problem, suggesting its causes and a variety of options for its resolution.
3. Response. Working with citizens, businesses, and public and private agencies, officers tailor a program of action suitable to the characteristics of the problem. Solutions may go beyond traditional criminal justice system remedies to include other community agencies or organizations.
4. Assessment. Finally, the officers evaluate the impact of these efforts to see if the problems were actually solved or alleviated (Eck and Spelman, 1987, p. 2).

Although using the stages of SARA can be difficult, the greatest challenges will almost always be found at analysis and assessment. But, as Eck and Clarke (2005) suggest, it is precisely at these stages where the strategic analyst can make the greatest contribution. From the very first, Goldstein has argued that problem-oriented policing depends crucially on the availability of high-level analytic capacity in the department (Goldstein, 1979).

Indeed, the role of the strategic crime analyst is crucial. Using problem-oriented policing, the analyst must (1) carefully define specific problems, (2) conduct in-depth analyses to understand their causes, (3) undertake broad searches for solutions to remove these causes and bring about lasting reductions in problems, and (4) evaluate how successful these activities have been (Eck and Clarke, 2005). This is a form of action research in which analysts work alongside practitioners, helping to formulate and refine interventions until success is achieved. This is not the usual role of the researcher, in which he or she often works apart from practitioners, collects background information about problems, and conducts independent evaluations. In action research, however, the researcher is an integral member of the problem-solving team. This is the role of the crime analyst, who must inform and guide action at every stage.

Here is a brief overview showing what is essential to each stage of SARA:

Scanning

- Identifying recurring problems of concern to the public and the police
- Identifying the consequences of the problems for the community and the police
- Prioritizing those problems
- Developing broad goals
- Confirming that the problems exist
- Determining how frequently the problems occur and how long they have been taking place
- Selecting problems for closer examination

Analysis

- Identifying and understanding the events and conditions that precede and accompany the problem
- Identifying relevant data to be collected
- Researching what is known about the problem type
- Taking inventory of how the problem is currently addressed and the strengths and limitations of the current response
- Narrowing the scope of the problem as specifically as possible

- Identifying a variety of resources that may be of assistance in developing a deeper understanding of the problem
- Developing a working hypothesis about why the problem is occurring

Response

- Brainstorming for new interventions
- Searching for what other communities with similar problems have done
- Choosing among the alternative interventions
- Outlining a response plan and identifying responsible parties
- Stating the specific objectives for the response plan
- Carrying out the planned activities

Assessment

- Determining whether the plan was implemented (a process evaluation)
- Collecting pre- and postresponse qualitative and quantitative data
- Determining whether broad goals and specific objectives were attained
- Identifying any new strategies needed to augment the original plan
- Conducting ongoing assessment to ensure continued effectiveness (Eck and Clarke, 2005)

Using the Problem Analysis Triangle

Many, if not most, of the criminological theories focus on what makes people criminals. Some of these theories find causes of criminality in such factors as child-rearing practices, genetic makeup, and psychological or social processes. These theories are very difficult to test, are of varying and unknown scientific validity, and yield ambiguous policy implications that are mostly beyond the reach of police practice (Eck and Clarke, 2005). But crime analysts have found that the theories and concepts of environmental criminology are very helpful in understanding crime patterns and crime trends and formulating strategies for solutions. This is because the theories and concepts of environmental criminology deal with the immediate situational causes of crime events, including temptations, opportunities, and inadequate protection of targets. Crime analysts will typically be stronger members of the problem-oriented team if they are familiar with these concepts.

The problem analysis triangle (also known as the crime triangle) comes from one of the main theories of environmental criminology—routine activities theory. This theory, originally formulated by Lawrence Cohen and Marcus Felson (and previously discussed in this book), states that predatory crime occurs when a likely offender and suitable target come together in time and place, without a capable guardian present. It takes the existence of a likely offender for granted since normal human greed and selfishness are sufficient explanations of most criminal motivation. It makes no distinction between a human victim and an inanimate target since both can meet the offender's purpose. And it defines a capable guardian in terms of both human actors and security devices. This formulation led to the original problem analysis triangle, with the three sides representing the offender, the target, and the location or place (see inner triangle of the figure).

By directing attention to the three major components of any problem, the inner triangle helps to ensure that an analysis covers all three. Police are used to thinking about a problem in terms of the offenders involved; the usual focus is almost exclusively on how to identify and arrest them. But problem-oriented policing requires exploring a broader range of factors, and this requires information about the victims and the places involved.

The latest formulation of the problem analysis triangle adds an outer triangle of "controllers" for each of the three original elements (see figure):

- For the target/victim, this is the capable guardian of the original formulation of routine activities theory—usually people protecting themselves, their own belongings, or those of family members, friends, and coworkers. Guardians also include public police and private security.
- For the offender, this is the handler, someone who knows the offender well and who is in a position to exert some control over his or her actions. Handlers include parents, siblings, teachers, friends, and spouses. Probation officers and parole officers may augment or substitute for normal handlers.
- For the place, the controller is the manager, owner, or designee who has some responsibility for controlling behavior in the specific location, such as a bus driver or teacher in a school, bar owners or bartenders in drinking establishments, landlords in rental housing, or flight attendants on commercial airliners.

Formulating Hypotheses

Whenever an analyst confronts some new and perplexing crime trend or crime problem, that analyst should form hypotheses about its causes. Unfortunately, newly formed hypotheses will often be based on incomplete information. But the experiences, training, and background of an analyst will be relevant in the initial formulation of hypotheses.

However, the initial hypothesis should be clear, although you should not be wedded to it, and you should use data to objectively test it. It is important to expect all hypotheses to be altered or discarded once relevant data have been examined because no hypothesis is completely right. For this reason, it is often best to test multiple conflicting hypotheses. A set of hypotheses is a road map for analysis. Hypotheses suggest types of data to collect, how these data should be analyzed, and how to interpret analysis results (Eck and Clarke, 2005).

For example, if you were investigating carjacking episodes at particular service stations, you might begin with the question, "How many service stations are in problem locations?" Based on common sense and the 80/20 rule (Center for Problem-Oriented Policing, 2015), you would state the hypothesis that some service stations will have many carjackings, but most will have few or none. You would then test this hypothesis by listing the service stations in the city and counting the number of carjacking reports at each over the last 12 months.

If your hypothesis was supported, you might ask, "What is different about the service stations with many carjackings compared with the service stations with few or no carjackings?" The concept of risky facilities (Center for Problem-Oriented Policing, 2015) would help you form a set of three hypotheses:

1. Risky service stations have more customers.
2. Risky service stations have features that carjackers find attractive.
3. The management or staff in risky service stations either fail to control behaviors, allow loitering, or provoke carjacking.

These hypotheses can be tested by gathering data on the number of customers at high- and low-risk service stations, analyzing the number and rate of carjackings per customer or per automobile, observing the interactions of people at troublesome and trouble-free service stations, and interviewing management, staff, and customers. If your first hypothesis was contradicted by the data, and you found that there was no great difference in the number of carjackings across all service stations, then you might ask, "Why are so many service stations troublesome?" But, this suggests another hypothesis: it's a perception problem; the city has about as many carjackings as other comparable cities. This hypothesis suggests that you will need data from comparable cities. If, after you collected the relevant data, you found that your city has an abnormally high number of problem service stations, you might ask, "What is common to most service stations in the city that produces a large number of carjackings?"

One hypothesis is that it is the way service stations are run in the city and the way customer behavior is regulated at service stations. Another hypothesis is that there is something about the nature of service station customers in this city. Testing each would require you to collect relevant data and assess the validity of the hypothesis.

You will note how the questions and hypotheses structure the analysis. As you test each hypothesis, no matter what the results of the testing, new, more specific questions will come to you. The objective is to start with broad questions and hypotheses and, through a pruning process, come to a set of highly focused questions that point to possible answers.

Hypotheses suggest the type of data to collect. In the carjackings at service stations example, the test of each hypothesis requires specific data. Sometimes, the same data can test multiple questions. In the end, when enough data are collected and all of the questions are answered, a strategy should present itself. Following our carjacking problem to a conclusion, the analyst may decide, based on the data gathered, that carjackings are most likely to occur at a small number of service stations, but only at certain hours of the night, and only when a small number of staff are on duty. Furthermore, observation may tell the analyst that carjackings occur at these service stations only near gas pumps where the lighting is very poor and when young people are allowed to loiter both inside and outside of the service station. The analyst's recommended plan would include meeting with the city and the management of the problem service stations and strongly recommending stricter regulation of young customers, improvement of the lighting at all pumps, and that security staff be stationed outside the service stations.

Although this kind of problem-solving project may sound easy, it is usually more complex and difficult. But in action research, the analyst and others who constitute a team should persist until success is achieved. That typically means refining and improving proposed interventions in the light of what is learned from earlier experiences. The process is not necessarily completed once the assessment has been made. If the problem persists, or has changed its form, the analyst and the team may have to start over. This is indicated by "Assessment" in the SARA problem-solving process. Assessment may read to starting over with "Scanning" (see Figure 13.1).

Final Report

In-house research, field research, and data analysis will generally lead to a final report and recommendations to the police department command. When the hypotheses have been proposed and tested, and a

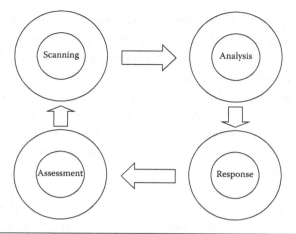

Figure 13.1   SARA problem-solving process.

plan for amelioration of the crime trend or crime problem has been decided, there must be a report to the police department's command so that action can be considered.

But, what kind of report should be written, and how should both the data and the recommended solution be presented?

According to Christopher W. Bruce, an International Association of Crime Analyst certified crime analyst, there are basically two kinds of reports that come from strategic crime analysts. One is publications that track and describe trends; the other is publications that analyze crime problems (Bruce, 2008).

The publications that track and describe trends include periodic statistical reports that might be issued on a weekly, monthly, quarterly, or annual basis. These periodic reports typically show increases and decreases in crime, and ideally analyze the most important changes (Bruce, 2008). On the other hand, reports that analyze problems usually combine police data with primary data collected by the analyst to explore the underlying causes and recommended solutions of long-term crime problems or crime trends. These, in fact, might be called "strategic analysis reports" or "problem analyses" (Bruce, 2008). In general, these strategic analysis reports aim to assist long-term planning and direct problem-solving efforts. Thus, they are written not for the general public, but with the higher-level police administrators in mind.

The following is a sampling of the kinds of reports strategic crime analysts might write:

- *Identifying problems report*: This report details information related to the systematic identification of long-term problems, such as the locations of problem areas, specific offenders known to be suspects in crime problems or crime trends, victims of crime problems, and property involved in crime trends or problems. It could be a list of the top addresses, streets, areas, offenders, victims, or products by either the number of calls or percent of calls for service or crime over at least a one-year period.

- *Identifying problems or 80/20 analysis report*: This report is an extended analysis that might be a follow-up to an identifying problems report. In addition to frequency and percent of crime at certain locations or on certain streets, an 80/20 analysis could include computation of the cumulative percentage of crime, as well as the unit of analysis (e.g., addresses and areas) to determine the cumulative percentage of repeat offenses, as well as the cumulative percentage of repeat targets.

- *Problem location analysis guidelines*: This report contains guidelines for different types of analysis products that are relevant in an in-depth analysis of a problem location. Using citizen-generated calls for service data for at least a 12-month period, the crime analyst can report on the frequency and percent of types of calls at the location, the frequency of calls by month, the time of day and day of week analysis for all calls, the time of day and day of week for selected calls, and the frequency and percent of dispositions of the calls. These statistics can be displayed in various kinds of charts or graphs for easy interpretation. In addition, this kind of report could also analyze police officer–generated calls for service for at least a 12-month period. The report could display the frequency and percent of types of calls at the location, the frequency of calls by month, the time of day and day of week analysis for all calls, and the frequency and percent of disposition of the calls. Finally, this report can provide crime report and arrest data at the location for at least a 12-month period. The report might well include the frequency and percent of crime types; the frequency of crime by month; the frequency and percent of arrest types; the frequency of arrests by month; the arrests by age, sex, and race; and the report of any crime patterns at specific locations.

- *Compound problem report*: This report gives information and recommendations about the highest-level problems that strategic crime analysts face. These are crime problems or crime trends that encompass various locations, offenders, and victims and, in many instances, exist throughout an entire jurisdiction. The analyst may end with a recommendation for a tailored crime prevention response for the agency in order to achieve a reduction in the problem.

- *Three-year crime or disorder trend chart*: This report evaluates the success of crime reduction strategies overall, as well as helps to identify emerging long-term problems. A three-year crime trend chart may include a line chart that depicts the frequency of a specific type of crime or disorder by month for three years, as well as a trend line for the entire time period.

- *Three-year seasonal crime or disorder trend chart*: This report identifies trends of seasonally reoccurring problems. It could be a line chart that displays the frequency of a specific type of crime or disorder by month, comparing each month with the same month in the previous two years.

- *Comparison crime trend chart*: This report shows the success of crime reduction strategies overall, as well as helps to identify emerging long-term problems by comparing the jurisdiction's crime rate with that of other entities. The other entities could be other jurisdictions, cities, or states. Often a line chart, this report compares monthly or yearly rates (by population) of specific crime types or disorders of the analyst's jurisdiction with those in other similar jurisdictions, the state, or the nation.

- *Change in crime or disorder density map*: This report is a density map that compares two periods of time (baseline time period and target time period) and displays areas where the selected crime or disorder has increased or decreased. This report could also use other kinds of maps, such as a graduated area map (a map that consists of aggregated data displayed in groupings with visual variables used to denote specific data). These groupings can be graduated by size or by color, and graduated maps could be created separately for each type of crime or disorder addressed in the agency's goals or by geographic area.

Writing and Distributing Reports

The reports generated by strategic crime analysts may be distributed to personnel in a variety of ways. In some police agencies, reports may be disseminated as emails or even memos that are sent to various units or administrators. In some police departments, reports are simply placed in officers' mailboxes. In some instances, reports can be passed out by roll call supervisors or read during the shift-change staffing by briefing officers.

In some instances, the crime analyst may attend briefing sessions and verbally describe the report and strategic recommendations. This would be particularly important to do if requested by police command or if the recommendations are vital for patrol officers to know.

Although most reports may be distributed in printed form in the mailboxes of the police staff, it can be particularly useful for crime analysts to deliver their reports in person. This not only enables the analyst to discuss the report, but also can be useful for soliciting feedback while at the same time building personal relationships that may be crucial to future collaborations and networking.

Final Goal of Crime Analysis

The final goal of crime analysis is to help with the evaluation of police efforts by determining the level of success of programs and initiatives implemented to control and prevent crime and disorder, and measuring how effectively police organizations are run. In recent years, local police agencies have become increasingly interested in determining the effectiveness of their crime control and prevention programs.

Furthermore, strategic crime analysts also assist police departments in evaluating internal organizational procedures, such as resource allocation (i.e., how officers are assigned to patrol areas), realignment of geographic boundaries, the forecasting of staffing needs, and the development of performance measures. Police agencies keep such procedures under constant scrutiny in order to ensure that the agencies are running effectively.

When all is said and done, however, the primary objective of crime analysis is to assist the police in reducing and preventing crime and disorder. Present cutting-edge policing strategies, such as hot spot policing, problem-oriented policing, disorder policing, intelligence-led policing, and CompStat management strategies, are centered on directing crime prevention and crime reduction responses based on crime analysis results. In Chapter 14, we move on to discuss administrative crime analysis.

Questions for Discussion

1. Think of a crime problem or crime trend in your community. How could you apply the SARA model to that trend or problem?
2. Why does routine activities theory make sense as an operating system for strategic crime analysts?

Important Terms

Compound problem report: Gives information and recommendations about the highest-level problems that strategic crime analysts face, crime problems or crime trends that usually encompass various locations, offenders, and victims.

Crime problems: Usually refers to multiple crime or disorder incidents with common causal factors.

Crime trends: Long-term increases and decreases in crime, or simply changes in the characteristics of a crime over a period of time. Crime trends can occur over months, years, decades, or even centuries. Often, crime trends have numerous obscure and indirect social, environmental, economic, or political causes.

Field research: Observing the characteristics of various crime locations or immersion in a setting where crime occurs so as to better understand the what, how, when, and where of the social structure or action and interaction of a neighborhood, a group, or victims.

Focus groups: Sometimes referred to as group interviews, focus groups are guided conversations in which an analyst meets with a collection of similarly situated, but usually unrelated persons for purposes of uncovering information about a topic.

Identifying problems report: Report that details information related to the systematic identification of long-term problems, such as the locations of problem areas, specific offenders known to be suspects in crime problems or crime trends, victims of crime problems, and property involved in crime trends or problems.

Interviews: Typically structured conversations that researchers have with individuals to learn more about crime problems or crime trends.

Problem analysis triangle: Also known as the crime triangle, the problem analysis triangle comes from one of the main theories of environmental criminology—routine activities theory. This theory states that predatory crime occurs when a likely offender and suitable target come together in time and place, without a capable guardian present. The problem analysis triangle is a graphic description of routine activities theory.

Problem-oriented policing: Professor Herman Goldstein first described the problem-oriented approach to policing in a 1979 article, which he expanded upon later in his 1990 book, *Problem-Oriented Policing*.

Qualitative research: Qualitative research methods, as opposed to quantitative research, provide more emphasis on interpretation and usually look at contexts, the environment, and the people involved in a crime problem.

Quantitative research: Usually involves statistics and data that can be scored and presented easily on graphs or in tables.

Routine activities theory: Developed by Cohen and Felson, a theory that seeks to explain the occurrence of crime events as the confluence of four circumstances: a motivated offender; a desirable target; the target and the offender being in the same place at the same time; and intimate handlers, guardians, or place managers being absent or ineffective.

SARA model: In the SARA model, the strategic crime analyst will collect the data, define the scope of the problem-solving effort, find an effective response, and set up the project so that it can be evaluated and the police can learn from the results.

Strategic crime analysis: Analysis of data in order to develop long-term strategies, policies, and prevention techniques. In contrast, tactical crime analysis deals more often with short-term and current crime problems.

Surveys: Survey research involves the collection of information from a sample of individuals through their responses to questions, which may be submitted through the mail or email, by telephone, or in person.

Study Guide Questions

For questions 1–4, indicate whether the statement is true or false.

1. _____ One of the major goals of strategic crime analysis is to assist in the identification and analysis of long-term problems, such as drug activity or auto theft.

2. _____ Crime trends are long-term increases or decreases in crime.

3. _____ Ron Clarke and John Eck define a crime problem as a recurring set of related harmful events in a community that members of the public expect the police to address.

4. _____ Initially, strategic crime analysts use information from the public library as their data.

5. One of the two major goals of strategic crime analysis is to conduct studies to investigate or evaluate relevant responses and procedures as part of a problem-solving process
   a. To find short-term solutions to short-term crime problems
   b. To investigate corruption within the police department
   c. To conduct studies to investigate or evaluate relevant responses and procedures as part of a problem-solving process
   d. To conduct studies to determine why there are so many poor drivers on the highways

6. The qualitative research methods specific to crime analysis include field research, content analysis, interviews, surveys, and

    a. Statistical analysis of data
    b. Talking to Supreme Court justices
    c. Meditation
    d. Focus groups

7. Although the SARA model is based on the problem-oriented policing work of Herman Goldstein, the acronym SARA actually was developed by _____ and _____ in _____.
    a. Eck and Spelman in 1987
    b. Clarke and Eck in 1998
    c. James Q. Wilson and George Kelling in 1982
    d. Elliot and Spitzer in 1995

8. There are basically two kinds of reports that come from strategic crime analysts. One is publications that track and describe trends; the other is publications that
    a. Describe geopolitical crime mapping
    b. Analyze crime problems
    c. Are distributed to convenience stores
    d. Focus on the data provided in the Uniform Crime Reports

References

Bruce, C.W. (2008). Crime analysis publications. In S.L. Gwenn, C. Bruce, J.P. Cooper, and S.R. Hick (eds.), *Exploring Crime Analysis: Reading on Essential Skills*. Overland Park, KS: International Association of Crime Analysts, pp. 342–363.

Canter, P.R. (2000). Geographic information systems and crime analysis in Baltimore County, Maryland. In Weisburd, D. and McEwen, J.T. (eds.), *Crime Mapping and Crime Prevention*. Monsey, NY: Criminal Justice Press, pp. 157–190.

Center for Problem-Oriented Policing. (2015). Learn if the 80-20 rule applies. Albany, NY: Center for Problem-Oriented Policing. Available at http://www.popcenter.org/learning/60steps/index.cfm?stepNum=18.

Clarke, R., and Eck, J. (2005). *Crime Analysis for Problem Solvers: In 60 Small Steps*. Washington, DC: U.S. Department of Justice, Office of Community Oriented Policing.

Eck, J.E., and Spelman, W. (1987). Problem-oriented policing. Research in Brief. Washington, DC: National Institute of Justice. Available at https://www.ncjrs.gov/pdffiles1/Digitization/102371NCJRS.pdf.

Fritz, N.J., Baer, S., Helms, D., and Hick, S.R. (2008). Qualitative analysis. In S.L. Gwenn, C. Bruce, J.P. Cooper, and S.R. Hick (eds.), *Exploring Crime Analysis: Reading on Essential Skills*. Overland Park, KS: International Association of Crime Analysts, pp. 128–157.

Goldstein, H. (1979). Improving policing: A problem-oriented approach. *Crime & Delinquency* 25(20): 236–243.

International Association of Crime Analysts. (2014). Definition and types of crime analysis. Standards, methods & technology methods. White Paper 2014-02. Overland Park, KS: International Association of Crime Analysts.

Maxfield, M.G., and Babbie, E. (1995). *Research Methods for Criminal Justice and Criminology.* Belmont, CA: Wadsworth.

Peed, C., Wilson, R.E., and Scalisi, N.J. (2008). Making smarter decisions: Connecting crime analysis with city officials. *Police Chief* LXXV(9). Available at http://www.policechiefmagazine.org/magazine/index. cfm?fuseaction=display_arch&article_id=1603&issue_id=92008).

Petersilia, J. (2011). Beyond the prison bubble. *NIJ Journal* 268, October.

Poyner, B. (1986). A model for action. In G. Laycock and K. Heal (eds.), *Situational Crime Prevention.* London: Her Majesty's Stationery Office.

Santos, R.B. (2013). *Crime Analysis with Crime Mapping.* Thousand Oaks, CA: Sage Publications.

Schutt, R.K. (1999). *Investigating the Social World: The Process and Practice of Research.* 2nd ed. Thousand Oaks, CA: Pine Forge Press.

Taylor, R.B., and Harrell, A.V. (1996). Physical environment and crime. National Institute of Justice. Research Report. Available at https://www. ncjrs.gov/pdffiles/physenv.pdf.

Tewksbury, R. (2009). Qualitative versus quantitative methods: Understanding why qualitative methods are superior for criminology and criminal justice. *Journal of Theoretical and Philosophical Criminology* 1(1): 38–58.

14

ADMINISTRATIVE
CRIME ANALYSIS

Chapter Outline

1. What is administrative crime analysis?
   a. Definition of administrative crime analysis
   b. Focus of administrative crime analysis
   c. Differences from strategic crime analysis and tactical crime analysis
2. What administrative crime analysts do
   a. Data analyzed
   b. Reports produced
3. Administrative crime analysis and its methods
   a. Quantitative methods
   b. Qualitative methods
4. Administrative crime analysis process
   a. Data and analyzing research
5. Administrative crime analysis and its reports
   a. Types of reports
   b. How reports are disseminated
6. Conclusion
   a. End result of administrative crime analysis
   b. Looking ahead to the next chapter

Learning Objectives for Chapter 14

1. Understand administrative crime analysis
2. Be able to differentiate administrative crime analysis from strategic crime analysis from tactical crime analysis
3. Learn the various ways data are analyzed in administrative crime analysis
4. Know the audience for administrative crime analysis reports

The largest difference between administrative crime analysis and the other types of crime analysis is that administrative crime analysis focuses on the presentation of information rather than pattern identification, statistical analysis, or evaluation. The creation of a crime bulletin for departmental use only is an example of administrative crime analysis. This crime bulletin would likely identify a problematic offender the agency is trying to capture, and would provide incident information as well as contact information for the lead investigator or analyst working the case.

Providing information to citizens about a crime spree in a local neighborhood is another example of a task an administrative crime analyst would partake in. (Stevenson, 2013, pp. 34–35)

Introduction

Administrative crime analysis is different from the previous types of crime analysis—tactical crime analysis and strategic crime analysis—that we have discussed so far. By definition, administrative crime analysis is the presentation of interesting findings of crime research and analysis based on legal, political, and practical concerns to inform audiences within the police administration, the city government or the city council, and citizens.

Therefore, the major difference from those previously discussed crime analysis types is that administrative crime analysis refers to presentations of findings rather than to statistical analysis or research. Administrative crime analysis is not about solving crimes or determining crime trends. Instead, it is more about the decision of what information to present and how to do so. Often, the type of information that is presented represents the "tip of the iceberg" of all the work and analysis that has previously been done (Santos, 2013). For example, in administrative crime analysis an executive summary of a report might be presented, rather than a full report.

Why Is It Called Administrative Crime Analysis?

There is a simple explanation as to why administrative crime analysis is so named. And that is because administrative crime analysis is analysis directed toward the administrative needs of the police department, its government, and its community (International Association of Crime Analysts, 2014). As a type of crime analysis, it can include a wide variety of techniques and products, performed both regularly and on request. These techniques and products include statistics, data print-outs, maps, and charts. They also include workload calculations by area and shift, officer activity reports, responses to media requests, statistics provided for grant applications, reports to community groups, and cost–benefit analyses of police programs. However, as you will learn in Chapter 15, some of the later reports may fall into a fourth category of crime analysis, often called operations crime analysis or police operations analysis (International Association of Crime Analysts, 2014).

Are There Areas of Administrative Crime Analysis That Have Little to Do with Analysis?

The brief answer to this question is yes. Administrative crime analysis, while a valid and valuable category of crime analysis, exists to support a police agency's efforts in planning, community relations, and funding, among many other areas (International Association of Crime Analysts, 2014). The reality of the profession of crime analyst is that analysts often do many things unrelated to analysis. Processes and techniques of administrative crime analysis include

- Districting and redistricting analysis
- Patrol staffing analysis
- Cost–benefit analysis
- Resource deployment for special events (International Association of Crime Analysts, 2014)

What Reports Do Administrative Crime Analysts Present?

Although the administrative crime analyst will prepare reports and products based on the requests and needs of the police administration, the type of report is basically determined by the audience for which the report or presentation is intended.

The primary purpose of administrative crime analysis might be said to be to inform audiences. These audiences may vary from one situation to the next, which is why the type and quantity of information will vary as well. The audiences that administrative crime analysts may be preparing a presentation for can be police executives, city council, media, citizens, and neighborhood groups, or a combination of these audiences. The type of information prepared and presented should be appropriate for the intended audience. However, in all instances, the information should be simple, clear, and concise and should not disclose sensitive information (Boba, 2001).

Since there is an eclectic selection of administrative and statistical reports, research, and other projects not focused on the immediate or long-term reduction or elimination of a pattern or trend, reports and presentations can be diverse. Here are more examples of the type of product the administrative crime analyst might expect to be asked to produce, along with the audience for which the product is intended:

PRODUCT	AUDIENCE
Report on demographic changes in the jurisdiction	Police administration/city council
Historical research project on crime during the Prohibition period	College lecture/city council
Miscellaneous crime statistics to support grant applications	Police agency/city grant writers
Preparation of Uniform Crime Reports or Incident-Based Reporting System (IBRS) reports	Police administration/FBI
Creation of charts and graphs to support the chief's year-end summary of police activities presentation to the city council	Chief of police/city council
Creation of patrol deployment maps for a special event	Police administration/mayor/city council
List of individuals with warrants by police beat and seriousness of offense	Police command
Charts and maps showing trends in business robberies during past six months	Police command/business association/ mayor/city council
Statistics on a series of residential break-ins and rapes	Police command/city council/neighborhood association
Homicides and burglaries during the past two years in the city	Police administration/mayor/city council/ citizen groups
Presentation on police–community relations	City council/citizen groups

As can be seen in the above table, often administrative crime analysis is conducted to educate and assist law enforcement administration and city government officials about the extent of crime and the effect crime and disorder have on the city and the citizens. At times, the police administration and city council will request long-range comparisons (quarterly, semiannually, or annually) of various categories of crime in the city.

Administrative Crime Analysis: Low-Priority Analysis?

Administrative crime analysis has, according to some experts in the field (Bruce, 2008), received a bad rap over the years. It has been suggested that it is a low-priority category (Bruce, 2008). On the other hand, this is a type of crime analysis that may, in fact, keep many analysts employed. As Christopher Bruce (2008) points out, having an individual in the police department who can answer virtually any question, provide information on demand, and arrange data in an appealing format is of tremendous value. Also, when the products of an administrative crime analyst might substantially affect public safety or lower crime, both the product and the analyst become valuable assets.

How Administrative Crime Analysts Gather Data

While a great deal of the data that administrative crime analysts may use in preparing reports and presentations may come from the data contained in police files, because of the nature of many of the products of the administrative crime analyst, qualitative information is often useful.

For example, if the analyst was asked to put together a presentation on police–community relationships over the past three years, there may be just a few traditional police reports related to this assignment. If there were reports about incidents in which the police were the target of violent protests, or if there were formal complaints to the department about police brutality, the analyst may be able to find those reports and use them as data. However, in order to put together a more comprehensive report, the analyst may need to use qualitative methods, such as interviews, focus groups, researching archived newspaper stories, or reading public email forums or blogs by local residents.

The analyst may interview patrol officers or officers who might work in the community policing unit. Asking them questions and getting their candid views of the state of police–community relations and how it has changed over the past three years may yield valuable insights. Similarly, putting together focus groups of police officers or community leaders may also produce important observations and recommendations. However, newspapers usually have their fingers on the pulse of the community, and exploring newspaper stories and editorials over the past three years may give the analyst a broad perspective of how the police are viewed by the community.

Newspapers and news broadcasts, as well as Internet forums and blogs, are likely to show with much more insight what is important to the citizens in the local community. Then, after gathering information about what has been printed or said in Internet forums or blogs, the analyst can compare this with the messages, mission statements, and stated goals of the police administration to provide an accurate picture of what the true state of police–community relations is at present, what it's been over the past three years, and what still needs to be done to improve it.

In regard to the qualitative research method to gather the kinds of data we have used in this example, the analyst should have access to LexisNexis as a comprehensive database. If there are certain Internet blogs that would provide a steady stream of possible useful information, the analyst might best follow them. To find those blogs in the first place, there are Google directions for doing so at https://support.google.com/blogger/answer/104226?hl=en. In addition, an analyst can figure out what topics are trending using Twitter or other tools: http://blog.hootsuite.com/5-ways-find-trending-topics/. Finally, there is a database called iPoll that can be searched by topic to find opinion polls on all kinds of subjects from many different sources (https://ropercenter.cornell.edu/CFIDE/cf/action/ipoll/index.cfm).

Crime Mapping and Administrative Crime Analysis

As Santos (2013) points out, crime mapping (which was discussed in Chapter 12) is useful in all forms of crime analysis. It does, in fact, play an important role in administrative crime analysis, as it often helps to convey essential information to the media and the public. A police department could—as many police agencies these days do—post maps on their website to show areas of crime.

Using geographic information system technology, the crime analyst can not only transform information into actionable intelligence, but also educate the public with visual information to clarify crime concerns and enlist community action.

Using the Internet

Like the rest of society, police departments must make use of the Internet and social media these days to communicate with the community. While there may be some disadvantages to using the Internet to communicate with the public (it is impersonal and requires resources to keep updated), the benefits, many police departments have decided, outweigh any potential drawbacks.

Police departments, with presentations developed by crime analysts, can do much to communicate important information to citizens. This kind of information dissemination can include lists or maps of criminal activities in particular neighborhoods, recommendations for public safety, current or ongoing dangerous situations, or emergency alerts.

Below is an example of an administrative crime analysis report. This report was prepared for the administration of a police department that wanted more information about the use of tasers by the officers in the department in order to properly respond to questions from the city council about taser usage.

Administrative Analysis report Taser usage

Example of an administrative crime analysis report:

Taser Usage Study	PD Analysis Center

The center studied data regarding Taser Usage, To Include;
- The ratio of Taser deployments to Tasers in service
- Level of resistance by the subject,
- Areas of the body hit
- Hospitalization of subjects

Data and Methods:

To accomplish the analysis, data was drawn from two sources.

- Internal Affairs reports related to subject resistance reports
- The original Subject Resistance Reports logged into the RMS system

Also included is the number of Tasers that were in service, and their issued dates.

Tasers in service, and Taser deployments per year:

Table 1: Tasers in Service by Year

Year	TASER model	Number in service
2015	X2	218
2014	X2	235
2013	X2	82
2012	X26	90
2011	X26	80
2010	X26	68
2009	M26 - X26	60
2008	M26	48
2007	M26	59
2006	M26	58
2005	M26	48
2004	M26	35
2003	M26	35

Type of subject action:

Table 2: Subject Resistance Actions

	No	Yes
Verbal	13.1%	86.9%
Passive	81.5%	18.5%
Active	5.6%	94.4%
Armed	81.1%	18.9%

Area of the body in which subjects were hit:

The front torso was the most common area of the body hit by Taser deployments.
Table 3: Location of Taser strikes on subjects, if any

	No	Yes
Upper limb	90.0%	2.2%
Lower limb	69.0%	18.6%
Back torso	47.3%	38.2%
Front torso	44.3%	35.2%
Missed subject	89.0%	4.5%
Taser use was threatened	89.0%	1.6%

Hospitalization:

Table 4: Hospitalization, compared to injuries suffered during the SRR. Note, all persons injured were either admitted to the hospital, treated and released, or refused treatment (with one unknown and one deceased).

	Not injured	Injured
Admitted to hospital	39	45
Deceased	0	2
N/A	0	0
Not Treated	22	0
Refused	15	8
Treated & released by hospital	168	128
Unknown	6	5
Totals	250	188

This administrative crime analysis reports provides information about taser usage by police officers which may help lead to administrative policy decisions.

Next Chapter

In Chapter 15, you will learn about a final type of crime analysis: operations crime analysis.

Questions for Discussion

1. Why do you think administrative crime analysis has been considered low-priority crime analysis? Should it be considered low priority? Why or why not?
2. How would you go about gathering and analyzing research if you, as a crime analyst, were assigned to do a presentation on whether your police agency should request military equipment from the Department of Defense?

Important Terms

Administrative crime analysis: Presentation of interesting findings of crime research and analysis based on legal, political, and practical concerns to inform audiences within the police administration, the city government or the city council, and citizens.

Focus groups: Sometimes referred to as group interviews, focus groups are guided conversations in which an analyst meets with a collection of similarly situated, but usually unrelated persons for purposes of uncovering information about a topic.

Interviews: Typically structured conversations that researchers have with individuals to learn more about crime problems or crime trends.

Qualitative research: Qualitative research methods, as opposed to quantitative research, provide more emphasis on interpretation and usually look at contexts, the environment, and the people involved in a crime problem.

Study Guide Questions

For questions 1–4, indicate whether the statement is true or false.

1. _____ The reality of the profession of crime analyst is that analysts often do many things unrelated to analysis.
2. _____ The type of report the administrative crime analyst will produce is often determined by the audience for which the report or presentation is intended.
3. _____ Administrative crime analysis is all about solving crimes or determining crime trends.
4. _____ Like other crime analysts, administrative crime analysts may start a project by reviewing police data.
5. Often, the type of information that is presented by administrative crime analysts represents just the tip of the iceberg of all the work and analysis that has previously been done. This is because their presentations are
   a. Short
   b. Just for citizens
   c. Quickly done
   d. Summaries and intended to give the highlights of research and analysis
6. Qualitative research methods are _____ used in administrative crime analysis.
   a. Never
   b. Seldom
   c. Often
   d. Always
7. The primary purpose of administrative crime analysis might be said to be to
   a. Inform audiences
   b. Detect crime patterns
   c. Solve violent crimes
   d. Locate hot spots

References

Boba, R. (2001). *Introductory Guide to Crime Analysis and Mapping.* Washington, DC: Community Oriented Policing Office, U.S. Department of Justice. Available at http://ric-zai-inc.com/Publications/cops-w0273-pub.pdf.

Bruce, C.W. (2008). Crime analysis publications. In S.L. Gwenn, C. Bruce, J.P. Cooper, and S.R. Hick (eds.), *Exploring Crime Analysis: Reading on Essential Skills*. Overland Park, KS: International Association of Crime Analysts, pp. 342–363.

International Association of Crime Analysts. (2014). Definition and types of crime analysis. Standards, methods & technology methods. White Paper 2014-02. Overland Park, KS: International Association of Crime Analysts.

Santos, R.B. (2013). *Crime Analysis with Crime Mapping*. Thousand Oaks, CA: Sage.

Stevenson, M.R. (2013). *Crime analysis: The history and development of a discipline*. Western Oregon University. Digital commons@WOU. Available at http://digitalcommons.wou.edu/cgi/viewcontent.cgi?article=1076&context=honors_theses.

15

POLICE OPERATIONS
CRIME ANALYSIS

Chapter Outline

1. What is police operations crime analysis?
   a. Definition of police operations crime analysis
   b. Focus of operations analysis
   c. Differences from other types of crime analysis
2. What police operations analysts do
   a. Data analyzed
   b. Audience for police operations analysts' reports
   c. Reports produced
3. Police operations analysis and its methods
   a. Analyzing police data
   b. Qualitative methods
4. Police operations analysis reporting
   a. Types of reports
   b. Examples of reports and recommendations
5. Conclusion
   a. End result of police operations analysis
   b. Looking ahead to the next chapter

Learning Objectives for Chapter 15

1. Understand police operations analysis
2. Be able to differentiate police operations analysis from other types of crime analysis
3. Learn about the various data analyzed in operations analysis
4. Know the audience for police operations analysis reports

The Ontario Police Department does not currently maintain any dedicated detective personnel or criminal investigations unit. Additionally, there is no single supervisor designated to supervise and coordinate the efforts of all patrol officers conducting extended investigations or follow-ups. Officers will coordinate, to whatever degree possible, investigative efforts bearing similar offender characteristics or modus operandi. All investigations maintained in-house by the OPD are investigated by patrol officers.... This organizational structure is contrary to best practices, marginalizes patrol effectiveness and agility, and facilitates recidivism as investigative resources are necessarily limited by the ongoing demands placed upon patrol. It is not reasonable to assume that patrol officers are either equipped or available to conduct criminal investigations in a manner that would increase clearance rates and thus appreciably reduce crime. OPD staffing should be increased to provide at least three full-time detectives to investigate crimes within Ontario city limits. These detectives should not be affiliated with any task force. Additionally, a revised Table of Organization, described elsewhere in this document, would provide defined supervision for these detectives and better coordination of effort between patrol, detectives, and any OPD personnel assigned to a task force or specialized unit external to the OPD.

The three detectives should receive advanced training in investigative techniques including general principles of investigation, interview and interrogation, crime scene processing, and the collection and preservation of evidence. OPD should then provide the necessary equipment for these detectives to carry out their duties.

Under current practice, OPD assigns a patrol officer to respond to a reported crime. Typically, that officer will remain as the primary investigating officer. The department does have one patrol officer with expertise in computer-related crime, but the officer does not have any formal certifications. There is also one officer certified as a drug recognition expert, or DRE. Reporting thresholds, such as the value of a stolen item, are not used in determining whether an incident will receive additional investigation.

ICMA (2014, p. 41)

Introduction

Police operations analysis describes the study of a police department's policies and practices—including its allocation of personnel, money, equipment, and other resources, geographically, organizationally, and temporally—and whether these operations and policies have the most effective influence on crime and disorder in the jurisdiction. Operations analysis is often defined as the analysis of police operations, including workload distribution by area and shift (IACA, 2014).

By defining operations analysis as concerning itself with a police department's policies and practices, it is relatively easy to see how this type of crime analysis differs from the other types of crime analysis that have been discussed in this book: tactical crime analysis, strategic crime analysis, and administrative crime analysis. However, operations analysis goes hand in hand with strategic crime analysis, as many operations decisions (including geographic and temporal allocation of officers) are based on long-term crime trends.

Because many operations analysis tasks require good evaluative research, analysts who engage in it should have a solid understanding of social science research methods (Bruce, 2008). Some questions that operations analysis might seek to answer are

- What is the best way for the police agency to divide the city into beats?
- What is the optimal allocation of officers per shift?
- What effect has the department's mandatory arrest policy for misdemeanor domestic assault had on domestic violence recidivism?
- Can the agency justify a request for more police officers?
- How much time and money would the department save if it enacted a policy that limited its response to unverified burglar alarms (Bruce, 2008)?

What Techniques and Methods Are Used by Operations Analysis?

The techniques associated with these processes are varied, but basically involve police records, Federal Bureau of Investigation (FBI) data, and several qualitative research methods.

Analysts who perform operations analysis tasks may begin by looking at the calls for service and raw data from the department's dispatch system. By sorting and analyzing service calls, the data can be compared with that of other cities the same size. But there are a number of areas that are usually critical to an analysis of operations—response times, workload of patrol officers, and peak times of the most critical calls.

Following a look at dispatch data, the analyst might collect and review a number of key operational documents. These operational documents often include the police department's policies and procedures manual, a list of the department's assets, and personnel lists.

The qualitative methods will include interviews, often with the police department's management and supervisors, as well as rank-and-file officers. In some instances, there may be interviews with the mayor, the city council, and other city staff. Other qualitative approaches will include observations, surveys, and focus groups.

Depending on the exact nature of a particular operations assignment, the analyst will be looking for strengths, weaknesses, deficiencies, and under- or overutilized staff, related to each unit and the department as a whole. What the analyst will want to determine based on the analysis of data is whether the department's operations are comparable to those of departments in other similarly sized cities, and whether the department is effectively and adequately meeting the needs of the community.

Often, the data provided by the police agency will be compared with information obtained from the FBI's Uniform Crime Reports, where the amount of crime in various categories can be compared with the city being analyzed.

Many times, operations analysis will rely on intensive interviews with the police department's personnel to determine the effectiveness of operations, morale, and even such things as the labor management climate in this particular department.

As you learned in Chapter 13, focus groups are unstructured group interviews in which the analyst actively encourages discussion among participants. A focus group can be helpful to explore issues that are difficult to define. Group discussion permits greater exploration of topics, and various police department staff might be asked to sit in and contribute to a focus group.

Analysts might solicit and collect documents from the police agency related to strategic plans, personnel staffing and deployment, evaluations, training records, and performance statistics. These kinds of documents will be helpful for the analyst to determine whether there is adequate staff (particularly at critical times of the day or night), whether officers are deployed to hot spots, whether officers are being adequately trained for the duties they are expected to carry out, and whether the performance evaluations are utilized to make personnel decisions.

Finally, observations can be carried out by the analyst to see how patrol officers carry out their assignments, whether special enforcement duties are done, how officers handle special event assignments, how detectives work investigations, and how trainings are conducted.

What Kinds of Recommendations Do Operations Analysts Make?

Police operations analysts may make any kind of recommendation that they see as important or necessary to improve the functioning and efficiency of the police department. Operations analysis may also include pointing out deficiencies in police–community relations, problems in living up to the department's own mission statement, and changes in the community that may require concomitant changes within the police department. That could mean adding or changing the focus of some units within the department or reassigning command staff or officers to other tasks or units. But, the recommendations that are made are also related to the assignment given to the operations analyst.

Examples of Recommendations

In an analysis of one Midwestern city's police department, it was found that there were no specific crime prevention activities conducted by this particular police department. Having experienced a reduction in staff because the city was forced to lay off police officers, as well as other city employees, the police department was struggling to keep up with calls for service. While the analyst conceded that the department was doing a good job of responding to citizen calls for service, there were no resources directed at crime prevention. The analyst, responding to a city council request for an overall appraisal of the police department's functioning, in the final report stated that crime prevention could be a valuable approach to community safety and community relations. Arising from this was a recommendation for a full-time position to be dedicated to crime prevention, with the ultimate goal of crime reduction in the city (ICMA, 2012).

The same report concerning the same Midwestern city also pointed out problems in terms of where calls for service in the downtown business district occurred and the deployment of officers. The analysis of police operations determined that of the more than 800 calls for service in the downtown business district during one 120-month period, 55% of those calls for service occurred at just 5 of the 58 establishments serving alcohol. So, just 10% of the establishments generated 50% of the workload for the police department in that district (ICMA, 2012). Furthermore, it was determined by analysis data available within that state that only two of the five establishments received sanctions from the state, and that there was no incentive to make changes to reduce calls for service.

The recommendation from the analyst was that there would be appointed a supervisor within the department to be dedicated to following up on enforcement of sanctions after calls for service and when it was found that the establishment was responsible in some way (e.g., serving alcohol to already intoxicated patrons or allowing intoxicated patrons to engage in assaults on the premises). The supervisor, it was suggested, would supervise officers at the scene and then do aggressive follow-up with both the state and the owners of the establishment (ICMA, 2012).

For another Midwestern city, the operations report addressed the identification and property unit of the police department. The report pointed out that the identification and property unit is staffed by one police officer and one community service officer. However, these two individuals were responsible for maintaining a 1500-square-foot facility to label and track property stored for safekeeping. This property consists of the physical, photographic, digital, and forensic property and evidence that comes into the custody of the police department. In any one year, that could mean that the unit would handle more than 6600 items related to almost 2900 new cases. In addition to property management, the unit is also responsible for processing subpoenas, expunging documents processed by the records unit, providing fingerprinting services to the public, processing licenses for cab drivers, and processing video and digital evidence required by officers for presentation in court (ICMA, 2014). In one recent year, that amounted to photo or video evidence for 1100 cases (ICMA, 2014).

The report went on to indicate that although regular unannounced inspections of the property are carried out, the property room has not been subject to a rigorous inventory in recent years. This led to a recommendation that a complete and thorough inventory of the property room needs to be conducted. Furthermore, it was recommended that more community service officers (civilian employees) be hired to replace the one police officer and beef up the staff to handle the workload (ICMA, 2014). Specifically, the recommendation was to fully staff the identification and property unit with nonsworn personnel and provide appropriate training in criminalistics and information technology.

In an operations report for a West Coast city, an analysis recommended that the police department establish a credible intelligence function within the department. The report stated that the police agency needs to develop an intelligence function to sift through the enormous amounts of information processed daily to identify crime patterns and trends, help locate offenders, and support proactive missions with intelligence information (ICMA, 2012). It was further recommended that a new intelligence unit work hand in hand with the patrol and investigative units of the department.

For one of the Midwestern cities mentioned above, the operations analysis report made statements regarding patrol staffing. The report stated that, in general, a "rule of 60" can be applied to evaluate patrol staffing. The report explained that this rule has two parts. The first part states that 60% of the sworn officers in a department should be dedicated to the patrol function (patrol staffing), and the second part states that no more than 60% of their time should be committed to calls for service. This commitment of 60% of their time, the report stated, is referred to as the patrol saturation index (ICMA, 2014). The report explained that the rule of 60 for patrol deployment does not mean the remaining 40% of time is downtime or break time. It is a reflection of the extent to which patrol officer time is saturated by calls for service. The time when police personnel are not responding to calls should be committed to management-directed operations (ICMA, 2014). This is a more focused use of time and can include supervised allocation of patrol officer activities toward proactive enforcement, crime prevention, community policing, and citizen safety initiatives.

This report recommended that fewer sworn officers be assigned to patrol. A specific number of officers for patrol duty was suggested, along with a specific number for traffic duty.

Operations analysis can extend to the maintenance of facilities and the acquisition and maintenance of equipment. If there is too great a reliance on military equipment, or if the resources, such as police automobiles, are not properly maintained, that could lead to recommendations, too.

In Chapter 16, the final chapter of this book, we will discuss the education and training needed to become a skilled crime analyst.

Questions for Discussion

1. How is police operations analysis different from other types of crime analysis? And how could you argue that in some ways it is the most critical of all types of crime analysis?
2. If you were assigned the task of assessing how the police department you worked for handled training officers about use of force, where would you start? And what methods would you use to gather the data you would need for a final report and recommendations?

Important Terms

Administrative crime analysis: Presentation of interesting findings of crime research and analysis based on legal, political, and practical concerns to inform audiences within the police administration, the city government or city council, and citizens.

Patrol saturation index: Related to the rule of 60, the patrol saturation index means that 60% of the time, officers in a police department should be dedicated to responding to service calls.

Police operations analysis: Analysis of police operations, including workload distribution of officers, the efficiency of units, and various other aspects of police department functioning.

Qualitative research: Qualitative research methods, as opposed to quantitative research, provide more emphasis on interpretation and usually look at contexts, the environment, and the people involved in a crime problem.

Rule of 60: Rule related to patrol staffing. The rule states that 60% of the sworn officers in a department should be dedicated to the patrol function (patrol staffing), and that no more than 60% of their time should be committed to calls for service.

Study Guide Questions

For questions 1–4, indicate whether the statement is true or false:

1. _____ Operations analysis concerns itself with a police department's policies and practices.
2. _____ It can be said that operations analysis goes hand in hand with strategic crime analysis, as many operations decisions are based on long-term crime trends.
3. _____ Police operations analysis is all about solving crimes or determining crime trends.
4. _____ Operations analysis may include examining FBI data.
5. Which question is appropriate for assignment to an operations analyst?
   a. Should the city hire more fire department staff?
   b. Should citizens be allowed to apply for concealed carry permits?
   c. Should more officers be hired for the police department?
   d. Should bars and taverns sell alcohol to minors?
6. Qualitative research methods are _____ used in police operations analysis.
   a. Never
   b. Seldom
   c. Often
   d. Always

7. An operations analyst's final report would almost never include recommendations for
   a. Higher pay for police officers
   b. Improving police–community relations
   c. Methods to be used to solve a series of arsons
   d. Hiring more detectives

References

Bruce, C.W. (2008). Crime analysis publications. In S.L. Gwenn, C. Bruce, J.P. Cooper, and S.R. Hick (eds.), *Exploring Crime Analysis: Reading on Essential Skills.* Overland Park, KS: International Association of Crime Analysts, pp. 342–363.

ICMA (International City/County Management Association). (2012). Police operations analysis and data analysis. Washington, DC: ICMA. Available at http://www.ci.royal-ak.mi.us/sites/default/files/meetings/City%20Commission/2012/RO%20Police%20Final%20Report.pdf.

ICMA (International City/County Management Association). (2014). Operations analysis report for the Skokie Police Department. Washington, DC: ICMA. Available at http://www.egovlink.com/public_documents300/skokie/published_documents/Police%20Department/Police_Operations_Analysis_Report.pdf.

IACA (International Association of Crime Analysts). (2014). Definition and types of crime analysis. Standards, methods and technology methods. White Paper 2014-02. Overland Park, KS: International Association of Crime Analysts.

PART V
CRIME ANALYSIS AND THE FUTURE

16

CRIME ANALYSIS AND THE FUTURE OF POLICING

Chapter Outline

1. Brief recap of book
   a. Areas we have covered
   b. Importance of crime analysis
2. Becoming a crime analyst
   a. Education
   b. Training
   c. Employment opportunities
3. Crime analysis in the future
   a. Need for trained analysts
   b. Integration of crime analysis into policing
   c. Future of technology
   d. Real-time crime centers
   e. Future of policing
4. Concluding remarks about crime analysis

Learning Objectives for Chapter 16

1. Understand the requirements for crime analysts
2. Gain a better understanding of the future of crime analysis
3. Be knowledgeable about the future of policing

Police departments have increased their investments in technology and the results are beginning to show. Robert Davis, director of research at the Police Executive Research Forum, said officers are becoming more professional in how they operate and that includes how they apply technology. "They are getting better at procuring technology that can deliver capabilities they didn't have before," he said.

Newcombe (2014, p. 1)

So what does the 2008 mapping of the entire human genome have to do with law enforcement? Well, for one, the technology is now available to code the DNA from a cigarette butt and use the profile to compose a computerized three-dimensional image of the donor's face. Couple that with the steadily advancing facial recognition programs, and you could have a suspect identified with very little effort. Gone are the days of combing a file drawer full of photo mug shots (Clark, 2013, p. 1).

Predictive technologies are being used to support police operations ... Although some of the methods are promising and describe the current state of field, they are still more academic than practical (Perry et al., 2013).

Introduction

This book has been about the past—and the future—of American policing. In many ways, the future of policing is here today. In other ways, we can only imagine at this point what we will have the capacity to do in the future. But what we do know is that crime fighting and policing are rapidly changing and discovering new and innovative ways to make communities safer while being better able to predict crime, respond to emergency situations, and make the lives of criminal offenders more perilous.

We have written at various times in this book that routine activities theory and environmental approaches to crime prevention pay off dividends in terms of preventing crime—rather than investing time and resources in crime detection and apprehension of offenders.

As you will recall, routine activities theory holds that crime takes place when a motivated offender and a suitable target coincide in time and space with the absence of a committed guardian. Traditional policing pays attention to the offender and apprehending and trying to make sure the offender gets his comeuppance. And the traditional thinking is that if you put away enough criminals, then the supply of motivated offenders will be reduced and crime will go down.

A great theory—however, there are two problems with this traditional policing approach. One is that the police, in general, have a pretty dismal rate of solving crimes; it ranges from about 14% for motor vehicle thefts to 48% for violent crimes (FBI, 2013). The second problem is that locking up more people than any other country, we haven't seemed to run out of motivated offenders. Therefore, we need another approach.

Routine activities theory and other environmental approaches hold out greater promise for the future. And that's where crime analysis can play a role in our society. Crime analysts can detect crime problems, crime patterns, and hot spots of crime, and make recommendations that lead toward solutions of problems—instead of trying to view every crime as an isolated event that requires the detection, solution, and (if things go extremely well) arrest and (hopefully, eventually) conviction of one criminal offender.

Crime analysts with their technology have a much better chance for reducing crime and crime rates than do patrol officers and detectives. And that's what this book has tried to emphasize. By introducing you to the technology, methods, and goals of different types of crime analysis, we hope that we can influence students to become acquainted with crime analysis, find it fascinating, and go on to greater training, with the end goal of becoming a crime analyst in a police department. There, we believe, you can become an integral member of both a unit and the department in order to serve as a beacon for what the future of policing is all about.

The Need for Crime Analysts

The police departments of the future, as is becoming clearer each year, will be about integrating technology with policing. But, as technology becomes more sophisticated and increasingly critical to police department operations, departments will need to hire more trained and professional crime analysts. In fact, crime analysts are an increasingly necessary resource in today's policing agencies (Bond, 2015). As we discussed the different types of crime analysis in this book, it is clear that crime analysts may bring needed skills and insights into the various tasks of today's police agency. Although each police department has specific requirements, responsibilities, and needs, at a minimum most departments require skilled crime analysts who can optimize crime mapping software, discover crime trends, pinpoint crime hotspots, and produce informative reports for the agency and the public (Bond, 2015).

More police departments are developing crime analysis units and real-time crime centers (RTCCs, or fusion centers, as they are sometimes called), which must be staffed by qualified and skilled crime analysts. Many departments choose to hire civilian (nonsworn) crime analysts to manage crime mapping efforts, gather and analyze data, and present information in a visual-friendly display for department supervisors to use for tactical, operational, and strategic planning (Bond, 2015).

However, as more crime analysis courses are taught in criminal justice and criminology departments around the United States, more students will be trained to play roles in either crime analysis units or RTCCs. But, to be sure, the role of the crime analyst will continue to evolve as technology advances. Educated and well-trained crime analysts who want to make a career supporting the needs of law enforcement agencies and the community should find many opportunities (Bond, 2015).

What Makes for a Good Crime Analyst?

Are you thinking about becoming a crime analyst after you leave college? Do you have what it takes to be a competent crime analyst?

Opinions differ somewhat concerning what makes a "good" crime analyst. And what some people believe makes for a good crime analyst may differ depending on their experience and background. Some crime analysts who were formerly police officers may hold the notion that a good analyst should be a police officer first. A civilian analyst may, on the other hand, believe that an analyst needs to be free of traditional "cop" thinking. Certainly, there are some people who believe that no matter what, a good crime analyst needs a strong background in computers and technology.

While we subscribe to none of these positions in a firm and rigid way, we are of the opinion that a good crime analyst must bring three things to the job: (1) an educational background in criminology or criminal justice, (2) a working knowledge of policing and investigation, and (3) training and skills in computers and statistical analysis.

Yet, one of the drawbacks of this nascent field of crime analysis is that many crime analysts are civilians who are viewed as entry-level employees lacking professionalism (Santos, 2013). This tends to mean that for the most part, and in most police departments, there is little room for advancement, especially for the crime analyst who is not a police officer. So, in order for many crime analysts to get a promotion, they must move to a larger police agency, particularly one with a fusion center or real-time crime center (RTCC).

With these limitations stated, there are important skills that are needed in order to be a successful crime analyst. Certainly the three elements of a good crime analyst listed above are essential, but also to be successful in the job, a crime analyst must be able to communicate complex ideas in a clear and down-to-earth manner. Furthermore, the crime analyst must be able to relate to police officers, work within the police culture, think clearly under pressure, defend his or her views on important issues, and keep a sense of humor (Santos, 2013).

Crime Analyst Qualifications and Job Descriptions

Here are two announcements for crime analyst jobs we found recently. The first comes from the website Monster.com and concerns a crime analyst position opening in West Allis, Wisconsin:

Crime Analyst I

Duties: A Crime Analyst prepares, analyzes, and disseminates information and recommendations relevant to actual and anticipated criminal activity for the purpose of increasing the effectiveness the effectiveness of patrol deployment, crime prevention, criminal investigations, and the apprehension of suspects. An employee in this classification must be adaptable to address changing trends in both technology and crime.

Typical duties include: assists in researching, analyzing, and collecting data from a variety of sources to identify and evaluate crime series, patterns, and trends; reviews police officers' crime and arrest reports, field interviews, and pawn slips for content; provides statistical information to supervisory and management staff as necessary; performs tactical analysis, strategic crime analysis, and administrative analysis dependent on situational demands; conducts and evaluates searches of databases and other information systems to assist in locating suspects and victims and to identify stolen property; provides timely and valuable investigative assistance to sworn law enforcement personnel for the purpose of identifying victims and offenders; assists sworn law enforcement personnel in developing target profiles; uses profiles to track criminals; utilizes a variety of databases and computer programs to generate maps, hotspots, reports, and statistical and tactical information; assists in reviewing and responding to requests for information related to crime analysis from other divisions, departments, outside agencies, and the public; attends community meetings, department in-service/training programs, and patrol briefings to discuss crime patterns and review current events; reviews crime data to ensure proper reporting to state, regional, and federal agencies; communicates with other jurisdictions regarding mutual crime problems; notifies detectives of possible multi-jurisdictional links between crimes and criminals; assists in preparing and developing crime summaries, statistical reports, spreadsheets, charts, maps, diagrams, graphs, and related materials in order to track and present findings related to criminal activity, patterns, and trends; prepares predictions based upon previous reported activity and an analysis of typical behavior patterns; communicates/coordinates with the City of West Allis (COWA) GIS Coordinator regarding the tracking and mapping of information on COWA Internet and Intranet; maintains records and develops reports concerning crime analysis; maintains records for in-house statistics; maintains and files crime analysis and management reports; prepares statistical reports as required; provides staff assistance to Shift Commanders, Crime Prevention Commander and COWA Neighborhood Services staff; attends meetings to maintain awareness of new developments in the field of crime analysis and to share information with others; prepares and assists in the administration of grants and accreditation process, including the preparation of quarterly and annual reports, and other special administrative projects; maintains prompt, predictable, and regular physical attendance; provides truthful and accurate written and verbal communications; maintains the ability to competently and credibly testify in court; performs other related duties as required.

Desirable knowledge, skills, and abilities: Knowledge of the principles and practices of management, research methodology, organizational planning, and statistical analysis; law enforcement and criminal justice systems; laws applicable to record keeping and dissemination of restricted information; microcomputer systems, applications, and software; and training techniques. Ability to communicate clearly both orally and in writing; apply principles, practices, methods, and techniques of public administration, management analysis, and statistics to the gathering, organization, and analysis of data; prepare technical reports with a high degree of skill and clarity; use mainframe and PC based computer systems, including creating, maintaining, and accessing database files; prepare statistical charts, graphs, and exhibits; and establish and maintain effective work relationships with supervisors, other employees, the public, and other government officials; maintain physical condition appropriate to the performance of assigned duties and responsibilities which may include sitting for extended periods of time and operating assigned office equipment; maintain effective audiovisual discrimination and perception needed for making observations, communicating with others, reading and writing, and operating assigned office equipment; maintain mental capacity which allows for effective interaction and communication with others.

Minimum requirements: Associates Degree in Criminal Justice, Crime Analysis or related field or at least 60 college credits from an accredited college or university and/or attendance at an approved crime analyst certification program; or an equivalent combination of education and experience that would likely provide the required knowledge and abilities; or three to five years of recent responsible paid work experience in criminal justice crime analysis, research, or a combination thereof.

Competent in the use of office computers and applicable software, including but not limited to, Microsoft Office Suite, GIS, SQL, report management systems, graphing programs, and statistical programs.

Pass a police background check due to access to confidential Police Department information.

Possess the physical capacity to perform the duties of the position including, but not limited to, continuous sitting, walking, and standing; occasional lifting/carrying up to 20 lbs.; continuous stretching/reaching of arms; continuous arching of neck; the ability to occasionally bend, kneel, twist, stoop, squat, pull, push, etc.; and the ability to continuously focus for long periods of time on projects or while working on computers.

Salary: The 2015 West Allis resident hourly rate range is $20.86 to $23.47. The non-West Allis resident hourly rate range is $20.43 to $23.00.

Benefits: Benefits include vacation accrual upon date of hire based on the vacation schedule; a sickness disability benefit plan; twelve (12) paid holidays; a comprehensive health insurance plan (which is contributory) covering the employee and his/her family, with eligibility the first of the month following thirty (30) days of service; fully paid dental insurance covering the employee and his/her family, with eligibility the first of the month following six (6) months of service; a dual pension system comprised of the Wisconsin Retirement Fund* and federal Social Security (both of which are contributory); after six (6) months of service, a fully paid life insurance program* with coverage in the amount of the employee's annual salary adjusted to the next highest one thousand dollars, with the option for additional coverage; an educational reimbursement plan for the pursuit of job related courses; and voluntary benefit programs consisting of Section 125: Flexible Benefits for Dependent Care and Medical Reimbursement, Section 457: Deferred Compensation, TreasuryDirect Payroll Savings Plan for Savings Bonds, Employee Assistance Program (EAP), and Employee Wellness Program.

---

* The Wisconsin Retirement Fund and Life Insurance program benefits are provided according to plan guidelines of the State of Wisconsin Department of Employee Trust Funds.

Here is one from the San Jose, California, Police Department:

Job title: Program Manager—Crime Analysis (Full Time)

Salary Min:	$87838.40
Salary Max:	$108160
Full/Part Time:	Full Time
Regular/Temporary:	Regular

About the department: The City of San Jose, the Capital of Silicon Valley, is one of the nation's best managed cities and one of the top ten cities in which to live, work, and do business. Moreover, San Jose is the center of cultural, government and economic activity for the region. The employees of the City of San Jose have embraced the following values: Integrity, Innovation, Excellence, Collaboration, Respect and Celebration. The San Jose Police Department is seeking an individual whose values align with the values of the City's employees. The mission of the San Jose Police Department is to create safe places to live, work and learn through community partnerships.

Position and duties: The San Jose Police Department (SJPD) is recruiting to fill a Crime Analysis Program Manager in the Research and Development Unit (R&D). R&D is in the Office of the Chief of Police and is responsible for research and preparation of complex reports and specialized projects involving inter-Departmental issues and intergovernmental topics. The Crime Analysis team analyzes crime data, produces crime-related reports, and ensures accurate and timely reporting of crime data to the Department of Justice, the Federal Bureau of Investigation, other City departments and police management.

Under the direction of a Lieutenant, the Crime Analysis Program Manager is responsible for managing all functions of the Crime Analysis Unit by performing work of considerable difficulty in planning, coordinating, and directing the utilization of complex computerized systems for crime analysis functions; insures the accuracy and integrity of the various databases; provides management support and specialized expertise to users of crime data, systems analysts, and operations personnel.

The essential functions of this position are as follows:

Plan, implement, and manage the Crime Analysis Program; establish objectives; maintain project timelines for various projects; ensure efficient utilization of resources; and administer program budget. Establish and/or direct the development of detailed procedures to retrieve, integrate, and analyze crime data, including data sharing and data transfer. Perform complex statistical analyses to monitor crime levels throughout the City and to support strategic deployment of police resources. Summarize statistics into concise reports for review by the Mayor and Council, City Manager's Office and Police Command personnel. Supervise subordinates and professional staff in a manner which they are able to prioritize assigned work; conduct performance evaluations, and ensure that staff member(s) are properly trained. Anticipate, plan and implement actions to solve problems effectively. Performs related work as required.

This recruitment may be used to fill multiple positions in this, or other divisions or departments. If you are interested in employment in this classification, you should apply to ensure you are considered for additional opportunities that may utilize the applicants from this recruitment.

Minimum qualifications:

1. Education: Bachelor's Degree from an accredited college or university in public or business administration, information management, criminal justice, statistics, computer science or other related field.
2. Experience: Five (5) years of paid, increasingly responsible experience in crime analysis, including two (2) years of supervisory experience.
3. Background: Submit to and successfully pass a comprehensive background investigation as required by the SJPD.
4. Employment Eligibility: Federal law requires all employees to provide verification of their eligibility to work in this country. Please be informed that the City of San Jose will not prepare or file a labor condition application with the Department of Labor.

Desirable qualifications: Possession of certification in Crime and Intelligence Analysis from the California Department of Justice with the designation of Certified Crime and Intelligence Analyst for the State of California or its equivalent.

Competencies: The ideal candidate will possess the following competencies, as demonstrated in past and current employment history. Desirable competencies for this position include:

- Job Expertise—demonstrates knowledge of and experience with applicable professional/technical principles and practices, Citywide and departmental procedures/policies and federal and state rules and regulations including but not limited to: law enforcement systems and software; theory, principles, practices, and methods of crime analysis; geographic information systems (GIS) and intelligence applications.
- Supervision—sets effective long and short-term goals based on sound leadership and management practices; establishes realistic priorities within available resources.
- Analytical Thinking—approaches a situation or problem by defining the problem or issue; identifies a set of features, parameters, or considerations to take into account, collects and analyzes data, uses logic and intuition to arrive at conclusions and recommendations.
- Communication Skills—Communicates and listens effectively and responds in a timely, effective, positive, and respectful manner; written reports and correspondences are accurate, complete, current, well-organized, legible, concise, neat, and in proper grammatical form.
- Team Work and Interpersonal Skills—Demonstrates a positive attitude and flexibility along with the ability to develop effective relationships with staff, colleagues, and the City's departments by helping others accomplish tasks and using collaboration and conflict resolution skills.
- Collaboration—develops networks and builds alliances; engages in cross-functional activities.
- Change Management—demonstrates support for innovation and for organizational changes needed to improve the organization's effectiveness; facilitates the implementation and acceptance of change within the workplace.

- Planning—acts to align own unit's goals with the strategic direction of the organization.

Selection process: The selection process will consist of an evaluation of the applicant's training and experience based on the application and responses to the Job-Specific Questions. Only the candidates whose backgrounds best match the position will be invited to proceed in the selection process. Additional phases of the selection process will consist of one or more interviews, one of which may include a practical/writing exercise.

You will be prompted to answer the following job-specific questions during the online application process:

- Do you have a Bachelor's Degree from an accredited college or university in public or business administration, information management, criminal justice, statistics, computer science or other related field? If yes, please indicate the name of the college or university and degree.
- Do you have at least five (5) years of paid, increasingly responsible experience in crime analysis? If yes, describe your duties and list where you obtained your experience (your answer must correspond to the detailed information provided in your application).
- Do you have two (2) years of experience supervising staff? If yes, please describe the number of staff you have supervised and where you obtained this experience (your answer must correspond to the detailed information provided in your application).
- Do you possess a Crime and Intelligence Analysis Certification from the California Department of Justice or equivalent? If so, please list any and all relevant certification(s) you possess.
- Do you have experience using computer applications for crime and intelligence analysis? If so, describe your experience including the applications you have used for crime and intelligence analysis, your level of expertise with the application(s), and examples of the work performed.
- Do you have experience managing a program? If yes, please describe the program you managed, the number of personnel

you managed for the program, and include the level and scope of all other related responsibilities.

- Do you have experience in summarizing statistics into accurate, well-organized, written reports or correspondence? If so, please describe the nature of the reports and to whom they were presented or ultimately utilized.

You may answer these questions directly in the on-line application system or on a separate document and then cut and paste your answers into the appropriate spaces when prompted.

You must answer all job-specific questions in order to be considered for this vacancy or your application will be deemed incomplete and withheld from further consideration.

Application instructions: Submission of a resume is optional. The Education History and Work History sections of the application must be completed or the application will be considered to be incomplete and may be withheld from further consideration.

Application must be completed or the application will be considered to be incomplete and may be withheld from further consideration.

E-mail is the default method of communication with applicants. To ensure that you receive timely notification regarding your application status, please provide a current e-mail address when submitting your application. It is also recommended that you adjust any spam filters to ensure that you can receive e-mails from @sanjoseca.gov.

The application deadline is 11:59 PM on the final filing date. Please allow adequate time to complete the application and submit before the deadline or the system may not save your application.

If your online application was successfully submitted, you will receive an automatic confirmation email to the email address you provided (San Jose Police Department, 2015).

As is evident from these two crime analyst job postings, the job market is varied in terms of different types of positions available and with divergent salary ranges. However, as is also readily apparent from these job descriptions, the skills and qualifications for a crime analyst can be analyst are extensive and broad.

Education for Crime Analysts

It has been emphasized at places in this book that crime analysts should possess an overview of the investigative process from the law enforcement perspective. With that in mind, what follows is an ideal curriculum, based on the classes Glenn Grana teaches to crime analysts in New York. He refers to it as a basic criminal investigations course for crime and intelligence analysts, and the intent is to introduce the analyst to the investigative mindset that a police officer/ investigator uses when conducting a real-time criminal investigation, interview, or follow-up investigation. The goal, upon completion of the curriculum, is to help the analyst better understand the investigative process that their law enforcement counterparts follow while developing an investigative skill set that can help enhance their own investigative process at the same time.

Course curriculum:

- Introduction to criminal investigations
  - Historical
  - The analyst's role
- Basic investigative techniques/locating suspects
  - Creating actionable intelligence from information
  - Understanding solvability factors
  - Working and creating leads
- Interview techniques
  - Active listening
  - Command of Q and A process when extracting information from LE
- Pattern investigations: beyond traditional analysis
  - Understanding commonalities and their relevance to MO
- Case management
  - Follow-up
  - Closing the case out
- Courtroom testimony
  - Demeanor
  - Understanding Brady and Rosario
- Case study: homicide investigation
  - Understanding the analyst's role in a large-scale, multiple homicide investigation

The follow-up to this course would be courses to provide essential knowledge, similar to what has been featured throughout this book, about analysis criminal intelligence.

Where to Go for More Information about Crime Analyst Jobs

The first place to go for information is the International Association of Crime Analysts (IACA). This is probably the most well-known professional association for the crime analyst field. It maintains a Current Job Opportunities page on its website that lists crime analyst jobs (http://www.iaca.net/resources.asp?Cat=Job). You may want to note the types of requirements listed. Many require at least a bachelor's degree or some other combination of college and experience. Usually, the degrees required are in criminal justice, sociology, public administration, or computer sciences. IACA also offers a variety of training courses and professional conferences.

Technology and the Future of Policing

Getting a job and working in criminal justice today means having the opportunity to utilize robots, global positioning systems (GPS), advanced cameras, and high-powered computer systems. These important technologies have improved investigation, surveillance, and analysis procedures. But, as with all technology in all fields, technology works great so long as it is being utilized by workers with the requisite skill set and intelligence to properly use it.

Every aspect of law enforcement has a computer program associated with the job, from DNA testing to robotic cameras to automatic license plate recognition systems—just to name a few. The number of electronics now available to make criminal justice jobs more effective is rapidly growing. Of course, criminals also utilize these technologies, so professionals in the industry have to remain one step ahead in technology to combat illicit usage.

As we hope has been made clear in this book, one of the most important technological tools in the field today is the computer database. There are now database systems for DNA testing and profiling, fingerprints, and hot spot crime mapping programs. For each type of database that exists, there have been corresponding technological advancements in that niche.

Everyone is familiar with computers, but the criminal justice field also gets to see more unique forms of technological advancements, such as the following:

- Robots, robotic cameras, and flying drones. Instead of sending in an officer to check out a dangerous situation or diffuse a bomb, it's now possible to send in a robot. There are even flying robotic drones that give officers a bird's-eye view of a crime scene without a person having to go up in the air.
- Gunshot detection system (GDS). This system of electronic sensors installed in high-crime areas helps police quickly detect where any gunshots come from. They allow for an improved response time that helps reduce crime.
- GPS and GIS. Police departments can use GPS and geographic information systems (GIS) in so many ways these days. They can help officers get to a crime scene using the most effective route, and they can pinpoint where a suspect is located. One great way GPS is used is to track fleeing criminals without having to engage in a dangerous high-speed chase. GIS can be used to track police vehicles so departments always know where they are located.
- Automatic license plate recognition (ALPR). There are now cameras inside police cars that can automatically run every single license plate the camera sees. An officer immediately sees if the car is stolen or if the driver has warrants out for his or her arrest.

But, as you have learned, police departments, through the skills and expertise of crime analysts, can use data mining and predictive analytics to identify crime trends and highlight "hidden" connections between disparate events. This helps the police gain a more complete picture of crime, predict patterns of future criminal behavior, and identify the key causal factors of crime in their area.

Just over the horizon of coming law enforcement technologies is biometrics, including facial recognition. The same software that has been used to identify high rollers and cheats in casinos, for example, can now be used to single out people banned from football stadiums or terrorists on a watch list at key border control points. Biometrics, including iris recognition, is ready to be used to match passengers to their digital images on e-passports at border crossings all over the world. This wasn't even imagined as possible in the twentieth century.

The most exciting news is that the potential for technology to reduce crime is real and proven. However, all law enforcement agencies must prepare their officers to embrace new technologies as they become available. It is apparent that our future safety and security depends on this.

One important tool in the present—and future—arsenal of police departments is predictive policing. As the ability to collect, store, and analyze data becomes cheaper and easier, law enforcement agencies are adopting techniques that harness the potential of technology to provide more and better information. But while these new tools have been welcomed by law enforcement agencies, they're raising concerns about privacy, surveillance, and how much power should be given over to computer algorithms.

Jeffrey Brantingham, a professor of anthropology at the University of California, Los Angeles (UCLA), helped develop the predictive policing system that is now licensed to dozens of police departments under the brand name PredPol (Hoff, 2013). PredPol's technique and proprietary algorithm is all about predicting where and when crime is most likely to occur, although not necessarily who will commit it.

PredPol is now being used in a third of the Los Angeles Police Department's 21 geographic policing divisions, and officers on patrol are equipped with maps sprinkled with a dozen or more red boxes indicating high probabilities of criminal activity (Hoff, 2013). Dozens of other cities across the United States are using the PredPol software to predict crime, including gang activity, drug crimes, and shootings.

Challenges to Integrating Crime Analysis into Policing

Even though there are numerous advantages to using technology in police work, there are still barriers and challenges to implementation. One of the most significant barriers is an incomplete understanding on the part of police department leadership of how to use both intelligence analysis and crime analysis more effectively (Peed et al., 2008). In one study, Taylor et al. (2013) found that while most police agencies have at least one staff member conducting crime analysis, and while most police departments consider crime analysis a priority and critical to achieving the agency mission, there still is much work to be done to bring about an integrated approach within police organizations to make crime analysis an important part of how patrol operates. Taylor et al. discovered that few patrol officers make use of crime analysis or have contact with crime analysis personnel, many police agencies have no feedback mechanism for the impact of crime analysis, and analysts only infrequently make use of opportunities (e.g., roll call briefings or ride-alongs) to better understand the operations and culture of patrol (Taylor et al., 2013).

Other research suggests that training for both intelligence analysts and crime analysts is often inadequate and limited (Peed et al., 2008). However, development of what Peed et al. describe as an integrated crime analysis model is not out of reach, given the right leadership direction and proper resources and training. They recommend that police management should tailor crime analysis training to support the specific missions and products most needed by command staff members and line officers.

Although many law enforcement administrators and managers have not yet fully grasped the full potential of what skilled crime analysts can do, and they have not quite figured out how to apply crime analyst skills effectively and efficiently, ultimately we believe that police departments will come to appreciate the extraordinary benefits of crime analysis. By making greater use of crime analysts working in RTCCs or fusion centers, the services of crime analysts will enhance the safety and efficiency of the police to better serve and protect their communities.

Questions for Discussion

1. Would you like to be a crime analyst? Why or why not?
2. Based on what you have learned throughout this book and based on what you know about the steady advances in technology, how would you envision technology will revolutionize policing in the next 25 years?

Important Terms

Biometrics: Measuring and analysis of such physical attributes as facial features and voice or retinal scans, often used for identification.

Crime analysis unit: Police department unit responsible for crime analysis.

Fusion centers: Information sharing centers, which were first developed by the U.S. Department of Justice. Now the term *fusion center* is often used as another name for real-time crime center.

Predictive policing: Any policing strategy or tactic that develops and uses information and advanced analysis to lead to forward-thinking crime prevention.

PredPol: Jeffrey Brantingham, a professor of anthropology at UCLA, helped develop the predictive policing system that is now licensed to dozens of police departments under the brand name PredPol.

Real-time crime center (RTCC): Centralized technology center that gives field officers and detectives instant information to help identify patterns and stop emerging crime.

Routine activities theory: Theory that holds that crime takes place when a motivated offender and a suitable target coincide in time and space with the absence of a committed guardian.

Study Guide Questions

For questions 1–4, indicate whether the statement is true or false.

1. _____ Routine activities theory and other environmental approaches hold great promise for the future of policing and crime prevention.
2. _____ The authors of this book take the position that crime analysts with their technology have a much better chance for reducing crime and crime rates than do patrol officers and detectives.
3. _____ The police departments of the future, as is becoming clearer each year, will be about integrating technology with policing.

4. _____ Although more police departments are developing crime analysis units and RTCCs, these units do not have to be staffed by qualified and skilled crime analysts.

5. As technology becomes more sophisticated and increasingly critical to police department operations, police agencies will need to
   a. Be led by traditional police administrators
   b. Hire more trained and professional crime analysts
   c. Hire more detectives
   d. Become more militarized

6. A good crime analyst must bring three things to the job: (1) an educational background in criminology or criminal justice, (2) a working knowledge of policing and investigation, and (3) _____.
   a. An ability to put a positive spin on crime
   b. Skills in fighting the war on drugs
   c. Training and skills in computer analysis
   d. Skills in accounting and business practices

7. To be successful in the job, a crime analyst must be able to communicate complex ideas in
   a. A clear and down-to-earth manner
   b. A way that sounds impressive
   c. A way so that no one really understands what the police are doing
   d. Double-talk

References

Bond, M. (2015). Crime mapping technology and its impact on law enforcement intelligence. *In Public Safety*. Available at http://inpublicsafety.com/2015/01/crime-mapping-technology-and-its-impact-on-law-enforcement-intelligence/.

Clark, M. (2013). Are you ready for the future of policing? *Police: The Law Enforcement Magazine*. Available at http://www.policemag.com/blog/technology/story/2013/12/future-trends-in-accelerating-technology-conference.aspx.

FBI. (2014). Crime in the United States, 2013. Uniform Crime Report. FBI. Available at https://ucr.fbi.gov/crime-in-the-u.s/2013/crime-in-the-u.s.-2013/offenses-known-to-law-enforcement/clearances/clearancetopic_final.pdf.

Hoff, S. (2013). Professor helps develop predictive policing by using trends to predict, prevent crimes. *Daily Brun.* Available at http://dailybruin. com/2013/04/26/professor-helps-develop-predictive-policing-by-using-trends-to-predict-prevent-crimes/.

Moraff, C. (2015). Eight ways American policing could change this year. *Next City.* Available at https://nextcity.org/daily/entry/police-technology-changes-2015.

Newcombe, T. (2014). Forecasting the future for technology and policing. *Government Technology.* Available at http://www.govtech.com/public-safety/Forecasting-the-Future-for-Technology-and-Policing.html.

Peed, C., Wilson, R.E., and Scalisi, N.J. (2008). Making smarter decisions: Connecting crime analysis with city officials. *Police Chief.* Available at http://www.policechiefmagazine.org/magazine/index. cfm?fuseaction=display_arch&article_id=1603&issue_id=92008.

San Jose Police Department. (2015). Join SJDB Blue. Available at http://www. sjpd.org/JoinSJPDBlue/JobPostings/20151102-Program_Manager-Crime_Analysis.html.

Perry, W.L., McInnes, B., Price, C.C., Hollywood, J. S., and Smith, S.C. (2013). Predictive policing: The role of crime forecasting in law enforcement operations. RAND Corp. Available at http://www.rand.org/content/dam/rand/pubs/research_reports/RR200/RR233/RAND_RR233.pdf.

Santos, R.B. (2013). *Crime Analysis with Crime Mapping.* Thousand Oaks, CA: Sage.

Taylor, B., Boba, R., and Egge, J. (2013). The integration of crime analysis into patrol work: A guidebook. Washington, DC: U.S. Department of Justice, Community Oriented Policing Services. Available at http://ric-zai-inc. com/Publications/cops-p209-pub.pdf.

Index